Moments of Modernity

Moments of Modernity

RECONSTRUCTING BRITAIN 1945–1964

Becky Conekin, Frank Mort, Chris Waters

Rivers Oram Press
London and New York

First published in 1999 by
Rivers Oram Press, an imprint of Rivers Oram Publishers Ltd
144 Hemingford Road, London N1 1DE

Distributed in the USA by
New York University Press
Elmer Holmes Bobst Library
70 Washington Square South
New York
NY10012–1091

Set in Baskerville by NJ Design Associates, Romsey, Hants
and printed in Great Britain by T.J. International Ltd, Padstow, Cornwall

A catalogue record for this book is available from the British Library

ISBN 1 85489 104 9 (cloth)
ISBN 1 85489 105 7 (paperback)

Contents

List of Illustrations

Notes on the Contributors

Peter Bailey is Professor of History at the University of Manitoba. He is the author of *Leisure and Class in Victorian England*, Routledge and Kegan Paul, 1978, Methuen, 1987 and the editor of *Music Hall: The Business of Pleasure*, Open University Press, 1986. He has written extensively on popular culture in Britain and a collection of his essays and articles, *Popular Culture and Performance in the Victorian City*, is published by Cambridge University Press.

Becky Conekin recently completed her Ph.D. at the University of Michigan, Ann Arbor, '"The Autobiography of a Nation": The 1951 Festival of Britain, Representing Britain in the Post-War Era'. She is a Research Fellow in Cultural and Historical Studies at the London College of Fashion, the London Institute.

Martin Francis is Lecturer in History at Royal Holloway and Bedford New College, University of London. He is the author of *Ideas and Policies Under Labour, 1945–1951*, Manchester University Press, 1997, and co-editor, with Ina Zweiniger-Bargielowska, of *The Conservatives and British Society, 1880–1990*, University of Wales Press, 1996. In 1996–7 he was the Fulbright-Robertson Visiting Professor in British History at Westminster College, Fulton, Missouri.

Harriet Jones is Senior Lecturer in Contemporary British and European History at the University of Luton. A specialist on post-war Conservative Party history, her publications include *The Myth of Consensus*, edited with

Michael Kandiah, Macmillan, 1997. She is working on a study of Conservative politics and the welfare state to be published by Oxford University Press.

Peter Mandler is Professor of Modern History at London Guildhall University. His most recent books are *After the Victorians: Private Conscience and Public Duty in Modern Britain*, co-edited with Susan Pedersen, Routledge, 1994, and *The Fall and Rise of the Stately Home*, Yale University Press, 1997.

Frank Mort is Professor of Cultural History and Director of the Raphael Samuel Centre for Metropolitan Cultural History at the University of East London. He is the author of *Dangerous Sexualities: Medico-Moral Politics in England Since 1830*, Routledge, 1987, and *Cultures of Consumption: Masculinities and Social Space in Late Twentieth-Century Britain*, Routledge, 1996. He is working on a cultural history of London in the 1950s and 1960s.

Bill Schwarz is reader in Communications and Cultural Studies at Goldsmiths' College, University of London. He is an editor of *History Workshop Journal*, *New Formations* and *Cultural Studies*.

Carolyn Steedman is Professor in History and Director of the Centre for Social History at the University of Warwick. She is the author of numerous books, including *Landscape for a Good Woman*, Virago, 1986, *Childhood, Culture and Class in Britain: Margaret McMillan, 1860–1931*, Virago and Rutgers University Press, 1990, *Past Tenses: Essays on Writing, Autobiography and History*, Rivers Oram Press, 1992, and *Strange Dislocations: Childhood and the Idea of Human Interiority, 1780–1930*, Virago and Harvard University Press, 1995. She is working on eighteenth-century servants, service and servitude in the making of modern identity.

Pat Thane has been Professor of Contemporary History at the University of Sussex since 1994. Her publications include *The Foundations of the Welfare State*, Longman, second edition, 1996, and *Maternity and Gender Policies: Women and the Rise of the European Welfare States*, with Gisela

Bock, Routledge, 1991. She is working on a study of the history of old age in England to be published by Oxford University Press.

Nick Tiratsoo is Senior Research Fellow at the University of Luton and Visiting Research Fellow at the Business History Unit, London School of Economics. His works include *Reconstruction, Affluence and Labour Politics: Coventry, 1945–1960*, Routledge, 1990, and with Steven Fielding and Peter Thompson, *'England Arise!' The Labour Party and Popular Politics in the 1940s*, Manchester University Press, 1995. He is writing a history of British management in the post-1945 period.

Chris Waters is Associate Professor of History at Williams College, Massachusetts. He is the author of *British Socialists and the Politics of Popular Culture, 1884–1914*, Stanford and Manchester University Presses, 1990. In 1996–7 he was a fellow at the National Humanities Center, North Carolina, where he worked on two books, one on collective memory and the working-class past in twentieth-century Britain and the other provisionally entitled *Queer Treatments: The Rise and Fall of the Therapeutic Ideal in Britain*.

Noel Whiteside is Reader in Public Policy in the School of Policy Studies at the University of Bristol. She is co-author with Gordon Phillips of *Casual Labour*, Oxford University Press, 1986, author of *Bad Times: Unemployment in British Social and Political History*, Faber & Faber, 1991, and of a number of articles on employment and policy issues. She has recently co-edited *Aux Sources du Chômage, 1880-1914*, Editions Belin, 1994, and *Governance, Industry and Labour Markets in Britain and France*, Routledge, 1998, both with Robert Salais. She is working on changing political apprehensions of labour market flexibility in Europe.

Acknowledgments

'I think the British have the distinction above other nations
of being able to put new wine into old bottles without bursting
them.' This was Clement Attlee's assessment of Britain's distinctive
contribution to post-war modernisation in 1950. British pragmatism and
an Anglo-Saxon ability to orchestrate change under the guise of continuity and tradition have long been celebrated as national virtues. Studies of
Britain's engagement with the explicitly modern, however, have fared less
well, especially in twentieth-century studies. It was our sense of frustration
with existing work on the immediate post-1945 period which led us to
conceive of this book. The collection is an attempt to reconceptualise this
moment of British history through the prism of modernity. Most of the
essays were first presented at a conference held at the University of
Portsmouth in July 1996 and it was the enthusiasm generated by the event
which led to the publication of this volume. We are grateful to the
University of Portsmouth, particularly to the Research Committee of the
Faculty of Humanities and Social Sciences, for support and funding. Chris
Waters acknowledges the travel grant he received from the American
Council of Learned Societies, together with support from the National
Endowment for the Humanities, which awarded him a fellowship at the
National Humanities Center where he worked on this volume. Becky
Conekin would like to thank the Social Science Research Council (New
York), the Program in British Studies at the University of Michigan and
the London College of Fashion for funding her project, and Tamsyn Hill
for photographic help.

Several scholars commented at various stages on the essays and contributed to our discussions: their astute criticism raised important issues which otherwise might not have been addressed. We therefore wish to thank Graham Dawson, Fred Leventhal, Michael Roper, Sonya Rose and Ina Zweiniger-Bargielowska. We also benefited from the insights of Rohan McWilliam and James Vernon, both of whom engaged with our intellectual project: Rohan McWilliam in *History Workshop Journal* (no. 43, Spring 1997, pp. 284–6) and James Vernon in *Social History* ('The Mirage of Modernity', vol. 22, no. 2, May 1997, pp. 208–15). Finally, we would like to thank our editors at Rivers Oram Press, Liz Fidlon and Katherine Bright-Holmes, for their support and patience.

If we have achieved our aim, of presenting a volume which opens a debate about the history of post-war Britain, it is in part due to the collective endeavours of all our contributors.

Becky Conekin, Frank Mort and Chris Waters
London and Williamstown

Introduction

Becky Conekin, Frank Mort and Chris Waters

The Queen's Coronation in June 1953 was the occasion for the most extended display of official spectacle in Britain since the end of the Second World War. It was also a Janus-faced event. Orchestrated against a background of elaborate tradition, it simultaneously strove to project a vision of the future. The mood of 1953, as Ben Pimlott has characterised it, combined a sense of the 'restoration of the *status quo ante bellum* together with an anxious optimism'.[1] These contradictory images were evident at every level of the Coronation drama: in the activities of the major social actors, in the political significance awarded to the event, and in the ways it was communicated to national and international audiences. Souvenir literature, as well as the writings of more serious commentators, strove to place the ceremony as part of an historic tradition of British monarchy, which had its origins in the medieval bond between Crown and people.[2] Yet, as one of the principal players in the drama reflected: 'The Coronation was a phoenix-time. Everything was being raised from the ashes. There was ... nothing to stop anything getting better and better.'[3] This amalgamation of the traditional and the self-consciously modern — of the past with what was to come — was captured in the idea of the Coronation as making a *return to the future* — a fresh start which recalled earlier moments of Britain's national greatness. The sense of the new reign ushering in a second Elizabethan age — with a tableau of modern celebrities to rank with Drake, Raleigh and the rest — was a recurrent motif.[4] Such double consciousness was powerfully carried in the international symbolism of the event. At one level the Coronation celebrated the continuity of Britain as a great power. In that sense it was backward-looking; the last great imperial display.[5] But set against the background of the Cold War and renewed foreign competition, it also evoked a reinvented and explicitly modern idea of the Commonwealth. This post-war reworking of empire — with the monarchy as the cord uniting a unique group of nations and peoples — was proclaimed as a progressive political entity. As the former Commonwealth Secretary, Patrick Gordon Walker put it at the time: 'in the Commonwealth we have made the revolutionary adaptation of a medieval concept to the purposes of ... democracy'.[6]

It was the medium in which the Coronation was communicated which revealed most about its hybrid status. Elizabeth II was the first British monarch to be crowned — as protocol required — 'in the sight of all her people'.[7] In Britain, over twenty million people (almost half the nation) watched a two-and-a-half-hour television broadcast of the ceremony. The power and prestige of the monarch as a resplendent hierophant was conveyed in what was to become the quintessentially post-war medium. Television came of age with the Coronation. Through television, the crowning of the Queen became both a world event and a peculiarly intimate drama, for this public spectacle could now be consumed by audiences in the domestic setting of the home. Moreover, for many contemporary commentators the televised Coronation crystallised a sea-change in popular attitudes to the monarchy. It was not simply that the Queen and her family now enjoyed mass popularity. As Sebastian Haffner observed, 'the Britain of the early 'fifties is not simply loyally monarchist; it is *monarchy conscious* to a degree which calls for some special consideration'.[8] This cult of monarchy was most evident in the flurry of speculation about the character, personalities and psychology of the royal family that now appeared daily in women's magazines and in the popular press. These discussions appeared to signify not only a popularisation of royalty, but a qualitatively different understanding of its importance, grounded in a contemporary understanding of human character and its motivations.

With its confusing messages about tradition and innovation, the Coronation is a particularly appropriate way of introducing a study of the modernity of post-war Britain. Many of the concerns developed in this collection are dramatised in microcosm in the Coronation story. *Moments of Modernity* is centrally concerned with the extraordinarily contradictory impulses towards the modern as they were expressed within British society in the period from the end of the war through to the early 1960s. Like the Coronation itself, the modern in this period was a hybrid affair, assembled out of tales about the past as well as narratives of the future. Tracking these stories involves an engagement with many of the multi-layered themes which were present in the events of June 1953, moving across and between different sites — of national and international politics, culture, and economic affairs, to the level of popular experience and to the interiority of human psychology. This volume is, then, necessarily concerned with the story of 'modern Britain' at widely different levels of society. The contributors range across the terrain of formal politics and government, through the commercial world and the corridors of the newly established welfare state, to design, the built environment and the comparative intimacy of the family, sexuality and personal life. They explore the different languages in which the impulse towards modernisation was expressed — the how of its articulation as well as its content. As such the book is self-consciously and avowedly interdisciplinary, working to integrate established historical methods with more experimental forms of enquiry pioneered in adjacent disciplines. Although all of the contributors are historians, their different understandings of the methods of writing contemporary history reflect a series of ongoing and unresolved debates within the discipline. There are now signs that these discussions are beginning to reshape dominant conceptions of post-war British history. Situating this volume therefore requires some engagement with the historiography of the post-war years. It demands an explanation of our own dissatisfactions with existing accounts and suggested alternative readings. It also involves an explanation of the paradigm framing the writing of this book — the concept of modernity.

It has become respectable for historians in the 1990s to write the history of post-war Britain. This has not always been the case. In 1963, Michael Sissons and Philip French lamented that little had been written about the decade after the end of the Second World War, 'beyond the inevitably partisan memoirs of the political protagonists'.[9] More than thirty years later, a growing number of historical studies, attempting to understand half a century of profound change, appears to have addressed their complaint. Institutionally, the Economic History Society has done much to chart Britain's economic fortunes during these years, while the work of the

Institute of Contemporary British History has conferred a degree of legitimacy on the academic study of post-war Britain. Despite these undertakings, the historiography of this period is marked by peculiarities which appear eccentric when compared with current research on the nineteenth and early twentieth centuries. Our reading of the difficulties here is twofold. The first centres on the persistence of a set of particular interpretative frameworks which continue to determine historical understandings of the post-war period. The parameters marked out by much of the research are restricted. A narrow conception of what constitutes a legitimate field of historical enquiry (accompanied by 'approved' methodologies) predominates, together with a compartmentalised notion of specialisms and sub-domains. The present volume grew out of our discontent with these types of history writing. Our intention is to interrogate the dominant narratives of post-war history and to review new avenues of enquiry and points of departure. We do not wish to erect some new meta-narrative through which the history of this period can be explained; rather, our aim is to analyse some of the deficiencies of established accounts. In so doing, we wish to suggest how different approaches might lead to a broadening of the scope of the historical enterprise and a re-evaluation of the methods by which post-war history might be written.

Risking a massive generalisation, the historiography of the years 1945 to 1964 has projected a series of comfortable and familiar images of the period which are instantly recognisable, both to practising historians and to a wider general audience. Stories of economic growth and modernisation, the decline of empire, political consensus, affluence, the rise of the welfare state and concomitant patterns of social stability, have set the terms of enquiry. Histories written in this vein deal in a familiar range of social actors and *mise en scène*: the monarchy, political élites, the civil service, collectivities massed as class, party and the electorate. As James Vernon has pointed out, this version of history is a self-referential affair, a relatively closed circuit of characters and plots in which the heroes and villains occasionally swap roles.[10] The origins of the genre are to be found in those nineteenth and early twentieth-century accounts of industrialisation and government growth and their terms of reference would be perfectly recognisable to the conservative and whig/liberal commentators of a century ago.

The advent of the idea of political consensus after the Second World War witnessed the revitalisation of this tradition in the writings of a generation of historians — scholars who both celebrated Britain's post-war political achievements and attempted to ground them historically. In 1966, Samuel Beer isolated the main stages in what he referred to as the 'modernization of British politics' and heralded the coming of the collectivist present: 'Happy', he wrote, 'is the country in which consensus and conflict are ordered in a dialectic that makes of the political arena at once a market of interests and a forum for debate of fundamental moral concerns.'[11] Historians and social scientists like Beer looked self-consciously to the past in order to contextualise the achievements of the post-war moment. Nowhere was this more true than in the work of those historians who traced the antecedents of Britain's post-war welfare state. As early as 1960, David Roberts argued that post-war society was in part rooted in the ideas that had inspired the social policies of the Victorians. More recently, Derek Fraser offered his own celebratory and somewhat whiggish study of the emergence of welfarism. In a different context Paul Addison traced the post-war order to the collective sense of national purpose which he saw emerging during the Second World War.[12]

These types of optimistic accounts have enjoyed extensive circulation, and not simply among academic historians. They have shaped the autobiographies of many of those doyens of early post-war collectivism, men and women who continue to advocate its virtues.[13] Such narratives have also exercised a powerful hold on the collective memories and the political unconscious of a generation who came to adulthood at the end of the war, together with their children — the first beneficiaries of the welfare state. Amidst the recent commemorations of wartime and immediate post-war solidarities, these experiences have been given a new lease of life, most notably in Peter Hennessy's award-winning and televised study, *Never Again* (1992). While Hennessy admitted that the years 1945 to 1951 certainly had their failures, his book was an unabashed celebration of the policies implemented by Clement Attlee's Labour government. Despite Britain's 'reluctance to modernise the state', he believed that 'those brave, semi-collectivist years' witnessed the emergence of a new 'combination of hope and public purpose'.[14] It was, of course, the erosion of that 'hope' and 'purpose' in the 1970s and 1980s, decades in which the post-war consensus was undermined, that has led a number of writers to share Hennessy's evocation of the years after 1945. Writing in 1988, during Margaret Thatcher's final term of office, Norman Dennis and A.H. Halsey called for a restoration of those values which existed before 'casino capitalism' undermined 'the hope of a society united by the service of its members to the common weal'.[15]

While such accounts have tended to dominate the historical record, they have not been without their critics. The myth of post-war affluence was being challenged as early as the mid-1950s, especially by those sociologists who rediscovered 'poverty' in Britain.[16] Equally, economic historians in the 1960s and 1970s began to point to the nation's comparatively weak economic performance in the 1950s, particularly when compared with Germany and Japan.[17] More recently, Labour historians have re-examined the nature of the collectivist discourse which had been assumed to underpin the party's post-war agenda. In doing so they have raised the question of whether the achievements of 1945 were in fact as consensual as they frequently have been portrayed.[18] Moreover, in the wake of the evident failure of so much post-war planning, particularly of the built environment, the intellectual assumptions which informed post-war policies have come under attack, largely for disregarding the needs and aspirations of the very people who were supposed to benefit from them.[19] Commenting on this trend, Peter Jenkins has suggested that, while expert knowledge was central to the post-war consensus, one of the greatest casualties of the 1980s was the widespread faith in mandarins to plan the good society.[20]

If left-of-centre critics forced historians to adopt a more nuanced picture of the society that emerged between the 1940s and the 1970s, the intellectual right challenged the whole consensus project. Margaret Thatcher, for example, attacked the historical view of the later 1940s as a period of collective aspiration and instead portrayed those years as a time of hardship, selfishness and petty bickering.[21] Andrew Roberts has expressed similar views. Finding fault with the Conservatives for attempting to emulate Labour's policies, considering Churchill to be 'wet' on immigration and the trade unions, Roberts concluded that the Conservative Party in the 1950s presided over a culture of decline which reduced Britain to her present status of 'Italy with rockets'.[22] More recently, Correlli Barnett has offered the most sustained critique of the aspirations and policies of 1945. Britain after the war, he argued, was led by a technically ill-trained public school élite unable to face the tasks of reconstruction which confronted it. Unwilling to admit the truth about national decline, it set about erecting a costly and utopian welfare state that the nation could not afford, the consequences of which we are still suffering today.[23]

Scholars like Roberts and Barnett have formulated a different story: of a nation that took a wrong turn in 1945 and, in consequence, almost ended up in the dustbin of history. These two antithetical sets of accounts — the one consensual and developmental, the other critical and deliberately divisive — are on the surface hardly reconcilable. Yet between them they share many underlying assumptions about how a history of this period should look. Despite their internal disagreements, policy and policy-making dominate most of this work, accompanied by the voices of the political and establishment élites. Concepts such as 'politics', 'welfare' and 'education' are taken as given and the reader is not encouraged to analyse their social meanings or their frames of reference. Finally, there are also notable areas of absence or understatement in these studies. One of the most significant of these are cultural processes and forms, which are either read as an effect of political structures or relegated to a minor status.

One consequence of the obsession with formal politics and policy-formation has been a lack of engagement with the pioneering work undertaken in the fields of women's history and cultural studies. In the 1980s a number of important works on women in post-war British society began to appear.[24] Taken together, they neither celebrated nor attacked collectivism; rather they carved out a new intellectual space in which a different kind of history writing could take place. Such texts placed on the agenda a set of issues about language, memory and the ways in which the post-war years had been represented publicly and autobiographically. Because this body of work did not appear to engage with the debates that pre-occupied consensus and Thatcherite intellectuals, it tended to be ignored by many practising historians. Likewise, there has been little dialogue between historians of post-war Britain and scholars working in adjacent disciplines. The proliferation of important work in the fields of cultural and media studies, literary theory, sociology and social geography has not been widely registered in mainstream historical circles. The questions raised and methodologies these approaches have advanced are often criticised as ahistorical and hence easily dismissable.[25]

In addition to remaining suspicious about the value of research that orig-
inates outside their own discipline, many historians have reproduced overly
discrete accounts of British history during these years. In part this has been
justified as a reaction against grand explanatory sociological narratives.
However, such approaches can appear to vacate the terrain of explanation
altogether. While rightly insisting that post-war British society is incapable
of being summed up in any simple formula, Peter Catterall and James
Obelkevich offer the readers of their recent collection of essays no tools
with which to fit the disparate pieces together.[26] Likewise, Jim Fyrth's two
edited books on post-war Labour Britain retain the division between
'government and the economy' on the one hand and 'culture and society'
on the other, each presented in its own separate volume.[27] In short, the writings of political historians like David Childs and social historians like
Arthur Marwick remain locked in wholly distinct realms, as if 'politics' and
'society' had very little to do with each other.[28]

It would be misguided, and inappropriate, to suggest that this work has
not produced an impressive body of scholarship, setting standards for ongoing research. All of the contributors to this book rely in part on the ideas
developed by established historians. Moreover, there are encouraging signs
that some of the difficulties with existing post-war historiography are beginning to be addressed. Recent studies of the political culture of the 1940s and
1950s have moved beyond an exclusive focus on political élites and the
machinery of government. There has, for example, been innovative and
exciting research on the dynamics of mass politics in the late 1940s, work
that avoids narrow compartmentalisation and demonstrates how culture and
politics are intimately related.[29] Other historians have begun to focus on the
role played by the political parties in mobilising new constituencies of interest during the post-war years. This has resulted in a re-examination of the
relationship between formal politics and the electorate, together with a
transformed understanding of the meaning of 'the political' itself.[30] Like
many of these studies, much of the writing in this volume is also revision-
ist in that it critically engages with existing historical paradigms in order to
suggest fresh avenues of enquiry and new perspectives. However, in assembling the collection we have also been influenced by a more specific agenda.
This has been the issue of modernity and the extent to which Britain's

negotiation of various modernities after the war might offer a profitable way of charting the history of these years.

It has become a truism that few ideas are more troubled than the concept of modernity. A cursory glance at the literature reveals that there is no historical or sociological agreement about the meaning of the term. Most of the difficulties centre on the status of the concept itself. Because of its hybrid character — straddling history and the social sciences — modernity appears both as the 'subject' and 'object' of discourse. It is at once a philo-sophical and epistemological category relating to questions of temporality, spatiality and the way knowledge is ordered, but it is also used to designate a more specific range of historical phenomena over time. Modernity has been viewed as the project unleashed by the Enlightenment — a project fuelled by the faith that science might liberate the west from want, and reason might diminish the power of religion. In its political guise it has been linked to the rise of the nation state and its attendant modes of bureaucratic organisation, along with the political structures which accompanied the advent of mass democracy. In social and economic terms modernity has been associated with the transformations brought about by industrialisa-tion and urbanisation. As a cultural phenomenon, what Marshall Berman has called the 'modernity of the streets', the focus has been on how moder-nity organises experience and orchestrates conflicting structures of feeling.[31] Peter Osborne has drawn attention to the way in which these two uses of modernity have been promiscuously intermingled in recent discussion. This paradoxical doubling has made it so appealing, and so problematic a category, for those at the interface of history and the social sciences.[32]

Initially, however, our turn to modernity was more prosaic. As histori-ans we were aware of the extensive debate which placed Britain at the forefront of a series of long-term modernising projects, dating from the seventeenth and eighteenth centuries. Britain was, after all, the first nation to develop the structures of recognisably modern forms of statehood.[33] It was also, arguably, in Britain that a society based on the importance of fixed, hereditary social orders first gave way to one dominated by modern class structures. As Harold Perkin has demonstrated, Britain's status as a modern society in all its manifestations has an extensive history.[34] However, in addition to that *longue durée* there was also a more specific and delimited project for the modernisation of Britain in the mid-twentieth century. After 1945 there were clear and identifiable languages of modernisation (accompanied by adjacent terms such as 'the new' and 'the future') occurring across British society. After the war an extensive series of debates about the possibility and the consequences of modernising Britain appeared to be taking place. While these undertakings were not new, their convergence in the early post-war years makes it possible to identify this period as one in which the modern emerged as a key signifier and a general referent. The contributors to this volume address particular aspects of this modernising project. Hence our understanding of modernity is neither universalist nor epochal. It is rather designed to explore the complex and differentiated circulation of the idea of the modern through conjunctural analysis. In this we have been encouraged by those commentators who have sought to delimit the global usage of modernity. In a suggestive essay written shortly before his death, Raymond Williams defined the period after the Second World War as one in which notions of the modern became more self-referential. As Williams expressed it, the modern shifted its reference from 'now' to 'just now' or even 'then'. Williams argued that in a British context modernity could be fixed within its own temporal schema, and that the years after 1945 were a period during which the modern became increasingly conscious of itself.[35]

This attempt to bring into sharper focus the characteristics of specific periods or moments of modernity is a distinctive feature of Anthony Giddens' exploration of the concept. Giddens' writing speaks to the historian more directly than many sociological commentators precisely because his work addresses particular phases within modernity. In particular his idea of 'high' or late modernity, characterising the current phase of modern institutions and life experiences, has been especially useful in thinking through the contours of the post-war years.[36] Late modernity is marked by an intensification of many of the basic traits of modernity as these are increasingly inserted into the global mechanisms of culture, communications and systems of production. Moreover, the period of late modernity is for Giddens characterised by accelerated processes of self-reflexivity, both in relation to the project of modernity itself and in relation to one of its key ingredients — the ways in which the self is ordered and experienced.

The idea that in twentieth-century Britain the discourses shaping the human personality have undergone a qualitative transformation, as well as a quantitative expansion, has recently been given extensive coverage across widely different historical traditions. One distinctive genre of intellectual history has traced the ever-more complex dilemmas confronting the post-Victorian liberal intelligentsia in their efforts to reconcile a traditional commitment to public service with an ever-expanding realm of private intimacy.[37] While liberal intellectuals continued to negotiate the public sphere in the middle decades of this century, their sense of who they were and their relationships to each other were transformed, not only by the forces of mass culture and democracy, but also by the fragmentation of their own sense of self in comparison with their Victorian counterparts. Noel Annan has defined 'our age' — the educated male élite who came of age and went to university between the end of the First World War and the early 1950s — as characterised by a belief in the greatest private freedom, expressed through a language of secular pluralism.[38] A very different understanding of these expanding forms of selfhood, informed by the historical project of Michel Foucault, has focused on the production of individuality in the post-war world in terms of the exercise of modern technologies of power. The management of the contemporary self, shaped by the discourses of the therapeutic state, became a coherent project after 1945. Building on earlier strategies, often derived from the traditions of nineteenth-century philanthropy and social science, it was in the 1940s and 1950s that the personal and subjective capacities of citizens entered into the calculations of government. Within education, infant and maternal welfare, propaganda, voting behaviour, as well as in the areas of the family and married life and among the socially recalcitrant, the interior lives of citizens became an object of public scrutiny.[39] Taken together, these two different forms of intellectual history have charted the changing manifestations of social selfhood. In addition, historical studies in autobiography during the period and since have revealed how these social scripts were lived out, and often with heart-wrenching contradictions.[40] What this body of work has identified is not only that conceptions of the human personality have multiplied and fractured in the mid-twentieth century, but that the principal mechanisms for constructing and experiencing the self have also undergone sustained transformation.

Moments of Modernity traces the emergence of these forms of reflexively organised selfhood across a wide range of fields or domains. The volume opens with a re-examination of one classically orchestrated account of self-determination in the 1950s, the grammar school boy. Peter Bailey's autobiographical narrative of a Coventry adolescence in the 1950s revisits a number of the classic tropes of post-war British social history. For an educationally aspiring young male, from a skilled working-class family, growing up in one of the centres of post-war affluence, modern selfhood was on offer in two distinct and competing forms. It was shaped by the formal structures of a meritocratic education system and by the new leisure industries, with their characteristically American points of reference. Yet as the best autobiographical studies always reveal, the ways in which these discourses were actually lived out begin to highlight some of the complexities of the modern in post-war British society. At the level of subjective experience the future was frequently compromised by the weight of the past — in Bailey's case by the legacy of late-Victorian working-class respectability and its cultural and sexual proscriptions — while the contemporary rhythms of an American-led popular culture were inflected with the historical cadences of the English Midlands. Bailey's seriously comic exploration of these themes underlines a more general point. Whether at the level of subjectivity, or in terms of the discourses moulding it, there was not one experience of the modern; rather, there were plural versions of modernity, which often jostled for attention in the same psychic space. In the area of advertising and the consumer industries, within formal politics, or in the field of sexuality, those personae which were emblematic of contemporary subjectivity were multifarious, frequently fashioned out of the languages of the past. Martin Francis' study of the 'politics of restraint', which formed the dominant code of social honour for forward-looking Labour politicians in the late 1940s and early 1950s, was in part a reworked version of nineteenth-century bourgeois masculinity. Similar historical legacies are evident in Frank Mort's study of the post-war advertising industries. Likewise, Chris Waters' analysis of the making of the modern homosexual demonstrates how much this persona was forged out of earlier sexual philosophies.

What all of these studies in self-making demonstrate is a point which can only be arrived at by a historical method. Such dramatisations were not the result of some over-arching meta-logic of the late modern epoch, nor were they simply voluntaristic acts of self-determination; they were dependent on specific policies, targeting sensitive groups of social actors. It is one of these classic accounts of education for selfhood which Carolyn Steedman opens up to the scrutiny of cultural history in her study of state-sponsored autobiography. Sociological commentaries on the genesis of modernity have defined the autobiographical narrative in its many variants as the core of self-identity in modern life.[41] But the importance of Steedman's study lies in its insistence on subjecting these large-scale claims to historical investigation in a particular setting. After 1945 the British education system instituted a very specific version of teaching selfhood as creative self-expression in schools. Official versions of this democratic critical practice were driven by a coalition of intellectual forces, prominent among which were Leavisite literary critics and educators, as well as teachers. At the heart of this policy lay the insistence on the psychological benefits of enforced self-narration for the working-class child. The limitations of this particular version of social democratic progressivism have been well-rehearsed. However, what Steedman's article also highlights are the alternative political subjects of modernity which were forged out of this post-war pedagogy, based as it was on an understanding that the 'subaltern could indeed speak'.[42]

This emphasis on the complex intersection between official versions of the modern self and personal life-experiences provides insights which deepen our understanding of post-war modernity. Waters illustrates this point in his account of Peter Wildeblood's struggles to define himself as a homosexual — struggles in which he drew on and reworked the dominant languages of sex. Waters also demonstrates a more general point about the relationship between normal and pathological constructions of subjectivity, namely that modern ideas of normality have emerged out of a concern with forms of conduct perceived to be troublesome and dangerous.[43] Pat Thane's study of population politics points to a specifically feminine version of self-determination, arguing that post-war demographics opened up the space for a new generation of women to imagine a future world not wholly dominated by motherhood and childcare. And it was not only progressive versions of identity which worked in this way. In his story of the closing of the imperial moment, Bill Schwarz insists that the process of becoming modern can turn on the telling of old stories which serve to compensate for contemporary dislocations. In the 1950s, conservative modernities were frequently lived out as powerful recidivist projections of selfhood which consolidated an explicit sense of white Englishness.

The conditions which orchestrated these various forms of subjective expression did not follow any single or unilinear logic. Here again historical research delivers important qualifications for an overly sociological approach to modernity. However, one major influence shaping subjectivity was the power of experts and their knowledge. Indeed, the expansion of professional expertise has been cast as a defining feature of the post-war years. In 1945 the political philosopher Evan Durbin announced that without a proper understanding of individual psychology many planned government reforms were doomed to failure.[44] The subsequent twenty years witnessed the proliferation of experts across a wide variety of areas. These were the individuals who could provide the 'proper understanding' which Durbin called for and thereby contribute to the efficient operation of an increasingly technocratic society. Such men and women were frequently portrayed as the torch-bearers of modernity. Their contribution was explored by C.P. Snow in his seminal address, *The Two Cultures and the Scientific Revolution* (1959), and they were also celebrated by Fabian historians of welfare in their studies of the benign influence of the civil servant.[45] Contemporary popular culture, however, told a told a different story about these experts, exposing them to ridicule. This was particularly evident in the 'Carry On' films of the 1950s, a long-running genre of high farce which lampooned the human frailty of doctors, teachers and other professional types.

Since the 1950s the position occupied by these professionals has been the subject of widely differing forms of analysis: from the confident progressive accounts of the immediate post-war years, often influenced by sociological functionalism, through the Marxist critical perspectives of the 1970s and 1980s, to more recent Foucauldian studies.[46] Without engaging with the specifics of these debates, we would identify the period from the middle of the war to the mid-1960s as one that witnessed a quantitative expansion of experts and their forms of knowledge. This was on a scale that was quite as significant as earlier moments of professional growth, such as the 1830s and 1840s or the years before the First World War. Yet, in contrast to those previous periods of professional hegemony, there were important differences. The terrain on which the post-war professionals operated was significantly broader than it had been in the earlier moments of expansion. It extended well beyond the sphere of 'government', or even 'the state' in its expanded, Gramscian sense. By the 1950s the authority of experts had become central not only to economic management and social policy, but also to the areas of cultural taste, the urban and rural environments, consumer behaviour and the psychological well-being of communities.

The importance of the expert in driving forward a vision of the future is central to many of the essays. Peter Mandler and Becky Conekin focus on the role of professionals in two key areas in the 1950s: urban planning and contemporary design. Noel Whiteside, Nick Tiratsoo and Mort trace emergent forms of expertise in the spheres of industrial management, labour markets and the consumer marketplace respectively. Thane assesses the work of a broad coalition of politicians, policy-makers and researchers to predict and oversee demographic change. Many of the stories of these intellectuals follow plot-lines familiar from early periods of British history. Progress and modernisation were spoken not in one single voice, but usually by a loose and often uneasy chorus of professional forces. More often than not their recommendations were not the disinterested expression of expert judgment, but rather reflected the ambitions and the *habitus* of particular interest groups. Conekin's evocation of the earnest young men with double-breasted suits, brigade ties and pipes who mounted the Festival of Britain as an improving educational project is one of many instances of such coteries in action. Frequently these intellectual cadres circulated knowledge which was promoted as central to national culture, character, or even national survival. Frequently too, evangelical professional zeal was qualified and checked, by politicians or by the ruder noises of popular resistance. Such scenarios are familiar from a longer history of professional society.

In addition to these familiar rituals, expert interventions in the period after 1945 also worked to promote new social settlements. In particular, professional knowledge was instrumental in reconfiguring a number of nineteenth-century dualisms, such as the relationship between the public and the private spheres, between the state and the private sector and between social responsibility and individual freedom. William Beveridge's expansive outline of the post-war welfare state, *Social Insurance and Allied*

Services (1942), was one of the most coherent attempts to strike a new balance between the state, the family and the individual, but there were many other noteworthy interventions of a related type. The Wolfenden Report's shockingly pragmatic reformulation of the boundaries between public and private morality in 1957 (ostensibly in relation to male homosexuality and female prostitution, but in fact with far-wider social implications) was another milestone in this process. The redefinition of meanings and boundaries was also powerfully at work within political culture. The efforts of a new generation of social democratic and liberal intellectuals in the United States and Britain (as well as those from the New Left) to redefine the political itself in response to the exigencies of the post-war world marked an important process of revision.[47] As both Francis and Mort make clear in their contributions, the greatest challenge posed to formal politics in the late 1950s was from the cultural and psychological reverberations of affluence and prosperity.

In all of these instances the role of post-war expertise was fundamentally concerned with the dissemination of a set of norms of conduct governing how the individual was to function in a society which for the first time was acknowledged to be essentially secular. By no means all of this was new to the period after 1945. Let us take arguably the two most influential post-war intellectual influences: Freud and Keynes. Both of these figures were formed in an earlier conjuncture of 'modern times'. But their respective contributions to the mapping of psychic and economic life were taken up and reworked by their followers after 1945 in ways that make it possible to characterise this period — and not an earlier one — as distinctively 'Freudian' and 'Keynesian'. A major influence of both figures lay in the promotion of styles of individual and economic management which were less formulated around fixed systems of value and more around what the French sociologist Jacques Donzelot has termed the partial floatation, or relativisation, of principles of moral and material life.[48]

Thus far our exploration of the modernity of post-war Britain has been conducted primarily in domestic terms. Our emphasis on the defining features of this period — professional expertise, the new social subjectivities and pathologies, the reconstruction of political culture — is at least partly familiar from established historiographies. Yet the idea of modernity shatters the comfortable boundaries demarcating the histories of nations.

Conceptually modernity has been formulated as a global idea, an attempt to theorise the dynamic, expansionist properties of a new world system. Within this understanding the nation itself is seen as one of the concomitants of the modern order. Benedict Anderson has insisted that nationalities as well as nationalisms are imagined communities of interest, the historical product of a particular discursive field underpinned by modern systems of intellectual power.[49] Once again social and cultural theory provides some of the most suggestive accounts of these transformations. Here modernity refers to the multiple shifts in knowledge and in material culture which involve the reorganisation of time and space. A characteristic feature of these phenomenon are those disembodying mechanisms which project the coruscating experience of modern life.[50] High modernity involves precisely the development of genuinely global systems of social relations whereby, for the first time in human history, society can be imagined and lived at a distance. This is the progressive, international story of modernity. But these expanding horizons are not neutral; the interlinking of social events and human capacities are understood to be part of an aggressively universalising history of human development.

The connections between modernity and colonialism here are critical. The idea of the non-contemporaneousness of geographically diverse but chronologically simultaneous times, which are elaborated as the corollary of colonial expansion, serve as the basis for western-centred narratives of 'progress', 'modernisation' and 'development'. All of these conceptual frameworks carry with them a cosmopolitan intent. As Zygmunt Bauman has emphasised, western modernity constitutes itself as the 'given', unmarked unit of history, constructing a binary opposition between itself and the problematic 'marked' side, which is only comprehensible in terms of its distance from western myths of advancement.[51] Such insights point to modernity's repressed 'other' and have the capacity to unmask the very foundations of the project, revealing its origins in an international world order (and an epistemological regime) founded on colonial domination.[52] Paul Gilroy has called for the history of the modern to be reconstituted and retold from the 'slaves' point of view. His radical questioning of the tidy and comfortable understanding of modernity — focused as it largely has been on the European metropolis — involves an inversion of the conventional cultural history of the centre and its margins. Gilroy's idea of 'the Black

Atlantic', which offers both a material and a symbolic account of the
modern black experience, involves a radical reconstruction of the conceptual history of modernity which has the capacity to shed light on the
formation of the west itself.[53]

How does this theoretical repertoire impinge upon the history of post-
war Britain? The obvious but nonetheless important point is that the
British experience of modernity is part of a much wider international
formation. The long-term legacy of Britain's premier position as an
imperial power is a central part of any account of the years after 1945.
Historians have traced the international ramifications of British decolonisation, but its effects on social life at home have yet to be examined in detail.
Schwarz explores the closing of Britain's imperial moment for what it
reveals about the imaginative fictions of English white ethnicity, which were
consolidated at the very moment when the empire was unravelling. In this
context 'learning about race' involved inhabiting a frontier mentality,
which translated the settler tropes of imperial frontiers — in South Africa
and elsewhere — into anxieties about the urban frontlines at home. Thane
in her study shows how even in the late 1940s worries about the domestic
birth-rate were never far removed from a concern about the cultural reproduction of British ideas, traditions and institutions throughout the
Commonwealth and the world.

In the post-war years the international dimensions of modernity were,
however, not reducible to the rapidly shifting relations between the old
imperial powers and their dominions. The world order which came into
being at the close of the war continued to mark out sharp differentiations
among and between the 'advanced' nations. In this respect the impact of the
Cold War, projecting two massively competing versions of the future, was
of paramount importance. But in Britain other influences were also noteworthy. *Moments of Modernity* examines two of these: the impact of
'continental' modernisms and the pre-eminent influence of the United
States. At a cultural level the European faces of modernity — at times
Scandinavian, at other moments French and Italian — played a major role
in shaping the views of many post-war arbiters of taste and aesthetic
judgement. Such versions of cultural value frequently had their origins in
the early twentieth-century moment of high artistic modernism, but their
accelerated impact on the public culture and policy of 1950s Britain was

marked.[54] Tony Crosland, who himself encapsulated many of these 'progressive' values in his own personality, repeatedly wove together lifestyle images of Sweden and France in his efforts to transform the puritan sensibilities of British politics and civic life.[55] In this volume Mandler and Conekin explore two versions of continental modernism. In both cases their respective accounts point not only to the way in which the European-inspired discourses of planning and design were championed by particular fractions within the cultural élite at home, they also draw attention to the extent to which these influences were transformed, and at times countered, by specifically British or English versions of commerce and culture.

American models of economic development and of modern mass society have exercised a paradigmatic function for entrepreneurs and cultural intellectuals for much of the twentieth century. However, it was the political and economic task of reconstruction facing the war-torn societies of Europe which intensified the impact of the American way of life. After 1945, almost all of western Europe took American society as a major point of reference, either to provide a positive vision of the future, or against which to define alternatives. Whether considered advantageous or not, modern life in Britain after the war was inextricably bound up with the material provision and the cultural symbolism of the United States. Many influential studies of this Anglo-American dialogue have been conducted on the terrain of popular culture and Bailey continues in this tradition in his study of the influence of American jazz on English provincial youth.[56] Yet much less is known about the actual impact of American systems of production and consumption on British business and commerce during this period. For too long the voices of those liberal intellectual critics who stressed the growing stranglehold of American material culture over Britain have been privileged. Tiratsoo and Mort break with this tradition and focus on the debates about American influence as they were played out among British industrialists and retailers. Their respective studies of industrial management and advertising reveal the ambivalent responses of many British business leaders to economic systems pioneered in the United States.

The British experience of modernity after 1945 was never a linear history of progressive advance. Perhaps the most striking feature of so many of the modernising projects pioneered during this period is that they were continually compromised and contested. British modernity was always a balancing act between innovation and tradition. Many of the essays in this volume address the nature of these compromise settlements, which were particularly important in the spheres of economic management, aesthetics and planning and social policy. Historical research highlights these nuances, which are much more than nuances of detail, in a way that grander sociological studies generally do not. Taking a longer perspective, it is possible to characterise these compromises as standing within the broader traditions of English ad hocery and the orchestration of change under the guise of continuity, which have their origins in the distinctive character of nineteenth-century liberalism. In the post-war period the recent continental experience of totalitarianism under the dictators made that search for compromise all the more urgent. Our understanding of Britain's 'deferred modernity' is that it was partly founded on the strong associations of Fascism and Soviet-style Communism with modernism in the British experience.

David Marquand and Anthony Seldon have recently suggested that 'the historiography of the last fifty years is still in flux' and that 'the patterns and contours of post-war British history have been strangely hard to define'.[57] To reiterate our own perception of this state of affairs, it is in part the result of the highly compartmentalised nature of the history of the years after 1945 and the inability of scholars to speak to each other across disciplinary lines. It would be too simplistic to propose the present volume as an answer to these dilemmas; nor, as we have insisted, do we wish to privilege the story of the post-war engagement with modernity, erecting a new grand narrative under which all aspects of recent British history can be subsumed. Our ambitions as editors are more prosaic, though nonetheless specific. They are to use the idea of modernity to focus a conceptual debate about the significance of this period, to move beyond a comfortable empiricism and to initiate an interdisciplinary dialogue about the ways in which contemporary history might be written.

At the close of the millennium it is perhaps an historical truism to state that we continue to live in the shadow of this mid-twentieth-century moment. Yet the period does indeed articulate a 'history of the present' in more than a rhetorical sense. The idea of modernity confronts us as its heirs, demanding a socially engaged response. In a contemporary situation where many commentators on the postmodern celebrate the passing of the modern world, the importance of the continuities, as well as the differences, between our own present and this period of the near past are especially important. Our own reading of the history of early post-war Britain suggests that the various projects of modernity are far from finished, though they have entered a different phase. The authors of these essays adopt differing stances towards this modernising agenda. Some view the period as essentially one of failed modernisation, which, had it succeeded, might have transformed British society in beneficial ways. Others gloss modernity as a discourse of regulation, while a third group remain studiedly neutral about its implications. The social project of modernity remains incomplete and open-ended. The study of its historical significance and its application to twentieth-century British history has really only just begun.

1. Jazz at the Spirella: Coming of Age in Coventry in the 1950s

Peter Bailey

This is a tale of adolescent bricolage, of learning to play jazz piano in a room full of corsets. It is set in what now seems an antediluvian world: before television, before rock music, before permissiveness. Yet its subjects would have had no difficulty in recognising modernity, as understood both then and now. This personal account is based on teenage diaries, whose production must derive in part from the encouragement of a modern self-awareness in post-war education that Carolyn Steedman also examines in this collection.

Expanded opportunities in education and welfare were part of Labour's new social order, of which Coventry — the phoenix city arising from the ashes of the blitz — was the provincial flagship. No one growing up in Coventry in the early 1950s could be unaware of the material evidence of a city being comprehensively rebuilt according to the blueprints of modern planners and architectural modernism, accompanied by a fervent rhetoric of progress and renewal. The same mix of exhortation and congratulation extended to the city's manufacturing industries whose post-war success was hailed as testimony to Britain's recovery as a modern economy and to the virtues of efficient management and a trained workforce. These models of civic renewal and the engineered life were the official narratives of a rational and orderly modernity, devoid alike of risk and romance. 'Coventry', exclaimed a psychologist, reviewing my youth, 'where they live life to the thousandth of an inch!'

What registered strongly by its absence was that complementary yet conflicting strand of modernity that Marshall Berman characterises as 'a mode of vital experience', a continuous adventure historically realised amid the 'possibilities and perils' of big city life and its street-bred excitements.[1] If such a world was not to be had at first hand in the Coventry of the 1950s, it was a vivid imaginary presence in the popular culture of the United States of America. For the young in particular, American film and music projected a countervailing pulse of modernity that held the promise of freedom, adventure and pleasurable disorder.

Since the inter-war years, Coventry's reputation as a prosperous and progressive modern industrial city had been shadowed by charges of a philistine materialism and an obsession with work and wages that denied a fuller life. After 1945 such reservations were momentarily crowded out by dynamic images of reconstruction and a thriving car industry. Plentiful jobs and rising wages swelled the town with immigrant workers and Coventry was quickly restored as the nation's boom town — 'the Klondyke city of the Midlands'.[2]

When I first learned of Coventry's boom town image I had difficulty reconciling this with what I knew of the city. My model of a boom town was indeed that of the Klondyke and the Wild West, besides which Coventry was incomparably tamer. There were no bordellos in Broadgate, or shoot-outs in Corporation Street. Whatever fortunes were made were not obviously fabulous. This was certainly a town of car-makers, but bikes and buses provide the memorable images of town traffic in the early 1950s: dense surging columns of pedalling workers released from the factories at the end of the day; long snailing queues of workers, shoppers and school-children waiting to board the bus home. The top deck of the number 7 with its thick cigarette haze was the closest I got to gunsmoke. But I was bound to be disappointed, for Coventry was not a frontier boom town but a suburban boom town. It was a city of mostly prudent adventurers seeking the bonanza of their own suburban home and its comforting accessories, secured through savings and a mortgage, rather than the lucky strike or the hold-up.[3]

My parents provide a pre-war example. After a long courtship while savings were accumulated, they married and bought their own home in one of the new private suburban estates developed in the housing boom of the 1930s.[4] The mock Tudor terrace house was a dream come true, particularly for my mother who had lived with parents and siblings in a cramped working-class house until she was over thirty. 'When the new carpet and suite arrived from Lewis's,' she told me, 'I thought I'd died and gone to Heaven!' This in contrast with her wedding night, 'when your dad wore red pyjamas, and I thought I was going to Hell!' Heaven and hell were somehow reconciled, and I was born in the new house in 1937 to a stable and affectionate couple. My father was an electrician, a skilled worker in an aircraft factory busy with rearmament orders. Though the war did something to bring people together, life among the largely first generation homeowners of our suburban enclave remained predominantly domesticated and inward-looking. Few, if any, wives in the families of our acquaintance went out to work. The men from this sample worked in shops, offices and factories across the city, but when they came home they mostly stayed there. Significantly, as it proved, the domesticated male like my father was, however, often an absentee figure, for the heavy demands of overtime working, both during and after the war, extended factory hours into the evenings and weekends.

We were a respectable family who nonetheless liked a bit of fun — that slender zone between repression and excess. After the war, as rationing lifted, family and friends were invited to the occasional weekend tea-party with some elementary games and music-making. Mum at the piano and Dad at the banjo ('Jess and Cec') played mostly musical comedy hits and 1930s 'novelty numbers'. Significantly, there were no electricians' songs. With this musical inheritance I was 'put to the piano'; that is, virtually bolted to the stool daily from the age of ten practising classical pieces for a succession of exams, the hurdles and prizes in an unfolding obstacle course of measured and certificated cultural improvement.

Meanwhile, having passed the eleven-plus I was being put through a further succession of exams at the local grammar school. As a beneficiary of the 1944 Education Act, I was being force-fed another diluted version of élite or genteel culture. Real gentlemen and scholars would come down from Oxford to encourage us, opening with the inevitable Latin tag: 'You'll remember it was Virgil who said, etc.'. Our teachers would nod in self-congratulatory acknowledgment. I was uncertain of the wisdom but impressed by the style. At King Henry VIII School scholarship boys like myself were now in a majority; there were none of the severely traumatic discrepancies between the worlds of home and school recorded in other accounts from this period.[5] Perhaps I was less disturbed by any difference in codes because of a readiness to assimilate the manners of my elders and betters as a necessary competence rather than as defensive colouring. In this I did well enough to secure the accolade of the headmaster, who wrote in his letter of reference for my application to Oxford, 'Bailey is a gentleman', thus implicating Bailey more deeply in the dialectic of pretension and insecurity which attended the transient in the English class system.

As yet, however, class, like the school history I was reading and writing about, was something that happened elsewhere; it was intuited rather than lived out. A largely one-class city with no obtrusive evidence of any upper or lower strata to frame its population of 'ordinary' people, Coventry seemed classless.[6] My father was a wartime shop steward, but the work that defined his craft and his class were invisible to me. Politics were seldom talked about. Our regular newspaper, the *Daily Mirror* — 'Britain's One and Only Independent Newspaper of the Left' — protested at the barriers of class but decried class warfare and talk of capitalism as the enemy: 'We are not trying to destroy anybody; we are trying to readjust so that we can become as privileged as the privileged people'.[7] If no more than an apprentice gentleman, I was already privileged for someone of my class background. With a grammar school education I was on my way. Yet such advancement was only dimly perceived at the time, and was poor compensation for the effort involved. By comparison, friends from the supposedly inferior local secondary-modern school enjoyed a social and sexual utopia. They were enviably free from homework, enjoyed the promiscuity of mixed classes, left school early, got jobs and earned good money for regular nights out. Adolescent restlessness at these inequities generated minor delinquencies such as a little festive shoplifting, but it was jazz that offered a licensed deviancy from the norm.

I liked the idea of jazz before I actually heard any. Older boys talked of it in an entranced but knowing manner: it was infinitely superior to 'commercial' popular music; it was American and exotic but had its homegrown heroes; it came with a history, a mythology and a literature; it was collectable on record; it was playable on the piano; my parents would not understand it; it was different.

I was one of an increasingly numerous body of converts to a music already firmly domesticated in Britain.[8] On its arrival following the First World War, jazz had been denounced as degenerate and alien (that is,

black and American) and a threat to civilised culture (white and British).
But by the 1930s it had found a dedicated minority following among the
middle- and lower-middle class young, who listened studiously to
American recordings in private houses or suburban rhythm clubs. During
the war a growing jazz public received fresh encouragement from the New
Orleans revival. Revivalist or traditional jazz was inspired by the American
left, which sought to rescue an indigenous popular culture from commer-
cialised swing music. The aim was both to promote forgotten black jazz
veterans and to inspire white musicians to reconstruct the original sounds
of the mythical birthplace of jazz. Yet almost simultaneously young black
musicians in the States were rebelling against established forms and white
appropriations with the wholly new sounds of bebop or modern jazz. The
traditional jazz of white copyists chugged along exuberantly through
well-formalised variations on familiar melodic and harmonic material.
Modern jazz was looser yet more intense, foregrounding lengthy solo
explorations whose angular lines and disconcerting harmonies were
sustained by a more irregular beat. The fans became divided with an
almost Cold War intransigence between traditionalists and moderns, the
'hot' and 'cool' schools of jazz. In post-1945 Britain, it was traditional jazz
that commanded the more numerous following as the existing audience
for jazz swelled with working-class youths, university and art college
students, and returned servicemen. Significantly, jazz fans were also learning to play the music for themselves. Thus there was already a flourishing
provincial jazz scene of local bands and local clubs when I enlisted as an
ardent traditionalist in the early 1950s: 'Jazz Boom in Midlands' was one
report from 1953 that seemed an appropriate annunciation.[9]

For all the reverence accorded its American progenitors, British traditionalists invested their jazz with a distinctively native inflection. The
earliest bands, notably George Webb's Dixielanders, formed in Bexleyheath
in 1943, pursued authenticity with an almost evangelical zeal. While playing with what Humphrey Lyttelton noted as a 'belt and braces' application
reminiscent of the brass band movement, this band of mostly working-class
amateurs from a local factory accepted their technical deficiencies as something of a prerequisite for the ardent primitivism they sought to recapture.
'Band expression', rather than 'solo expression', was the only correct chan-
nel for the spontaneous improvisation that distinguished true jazz from its

commercial approximations. Such earnestness reminds the historian of a Victorian mutual improvement society, though it probably had more immediate origins in the cultural seriousness of wartime Britain. Putting the band before the individual also resonated with the collectivist ideals of the post-war social order. The Webb band was briefly sponsored by the Young Communist League, but jazz musicians in general were more partisan about their music than about politics.[10]

Not all traditional jazz in Britain conformed to this austere and doctrinaire artisanal model. Jazz was after all good-time music. There was dancing and drinking, though far from total hedonism. It took the visit of the Australian band of Graeme Bell in 1948 to reintroduce dancing — a vital original function of jazz long disdained by British *cognoscenti* as an obstacle to aesthetic appreciation and a reminder of the effete spectacle of the ballroom or palais. Dancing couples proliferated, bringing a new flamboyance — and a greater number of young women — to the local jazz scene. A proper appreciation of the music also made for a temperate crowd and several prominent jazz venues were unlicensed. But partiality to drink could become as much a bond as the music, particularly for musicians in the more successful bands who by now constituted something of a professional sub-culture, defining themselves against the rest of the world and the more tedious of their followers, the 'squares'. The puritan prescription in British revivalism was reinforced by Ken Colyer, the forthright proletarian who made the pilgrimage to New Orleans, but there was a cavalier or bohemian element that had brashly infiltrated its ranks. Mick Mulligan, one of a number of public schoolboys drawn to jazz, was notably careless of purist orthodoxy and decorum. His band played in the looser, more suspect Chicago style — the 'white' sound of Spanier and Condon; it was also, as their one-time agent Jim Godbolt records, 'the top drinking band'. Another public school maverick was the band vocalist, George Melly, who essayed the bravura style in song, drink and promiscuity. With one foot in the art world and his other parts generously discharged across a wide area, Melly was the most egregious example of the new jazzman as 'raver'.[11]

For the most part, however, the traditionalists were different but not delinquent, though journalists continued to hunt for sensational copy. The general atmosphere, maintained Humphrey Lyttelton in his 1954 account of these pioneering years, 'was tweedy and pipesmoking': the frontispiece of his book showed this best known of bandleaders (and old Etonian) relaxing at home with his wife. In the same year *Picture Post* visited a basement jazz club in Soho. There were no drugs, no alcohol, no prostitution, but the crowd was reportedly 'abandoned', the band 'apoplectic'. An accompanying shot of 'frenzied' dancers caught a woman in the audience knitting.[12]

For traditionalist fans it was the modernists who were the real delinquents. Those who took up modern jazz or bebop were mostly young professional musicians trying to accommodate their enthusiasm for the new sounds with making a living in the better dance bands and West End clubs.[13] Their mecca was New York, not New Orleans. Joining bands on transatlantic liners — 'working the boats' — enabled a handful of aspirants like Ronnie Scott to make it to 52nd Street and immerse themselves fully in Charlie Parker's bebop revolution. The British disciples were soon as hooked on the stylistic codes of bop as they were on the music, assuming its sharp suits, dark glasses and 'jive talk', the latter readily assimilated to a sardonic native (often Jewish) wit. Drugs were a further borrowing from the States, though there were few hard users among British musicians, who did little more than experiment with what were archly referred to as 'naughty African-type Woodbines'. Modernist manners were thus generally more worldly and metropolitan. When traditionalist trumpeter, Dickie Hawdon, an ex-Leeds Grammar School boy and respectable provincial, crossed the line to join Tubby Hayes' modern band of East End and inner-city Londoners in the mid-1950s, he thought himself fallen among thieves.[14] To traditionalist fans, the modern musician with his 'hip' style and superior technical accomplishment was a facile professional with no heart, a kind of musical spiv or wide boy, ritually scorned as a 'dirty bopper'. In reply, the traditionalist was assailed as a 'mouldy figge'.

As the professional jazz world expanded and musicians of both stripes came to play with more assurance, there was a growing impatience with these categorical divisions. Other musicians besides Hawdon crossed over (from both sides), while Lyttelton became a forceful advocate of a broad church 'mainstream', drawing on the music's varied inheritance and employing the best talent in any idiom. Yet among fans and lesser practitioners the pressure of cultural identity continued to sustain the contest of styles between ancients and moderns. *Picture Post* had likened the modernists to a Cadillac, traditional jazz to a galloping horse, and a cluster of associated images fall readily into place. The modernists were streamlined city slickers in suit and tie, the traditionalists galumphing and shaggy in a studied disarray of sweaters, duffle coats and beards. For the latter the bucolic motif was sustained in their dedication to Merrydown cider and a remarkable enthusiasm for cricket (exemplified in a musicians' team — The Ravers XI). Certainly there was a greater freighting of Englishness in the traditionalists' rearticulation of what had been defined as quintessentially American music.[15]

If the master narrative for jazz fans of all persuasions was nonetheless set in America, it was an America of several different faces. Modern jazz drew its identity directly from contemporary America and the proto-beat mentality of the jazz musician as anarchic outsider. America for the traditional fan was a land of arrested or romanticised modernity set in pre-1917 New Orleans or Prohibition Chicago. Its contemporary equivalent was most likely to be California, where white revivalist bands were most active. It was from this latter model that British traditionalists came by their fixation with the banjo and its associations with that other musical topos, Dixieland. The banjo with its rigid neanderthal clank was the ball and chain of homegrown rhythm sections.

The jazz world into which I was inducted was sectarianised, anglicanised, yet enthralled by its various Americas. By the summer of 1953 I was writing school journals extolling the sublime purity of New Orleans jazz. I had obviously been reading Rex Harris, author of the purists' bible, *Jazz*, a Penguin handbook of 1952 that went into several reprints. An optician from Kent, Harris was a fervent promoter of the 'renaissance' that was the revivalist movement, the rebirth of jazz after the 'empty thirties', 'the long and wearisome years of swing' and 'American commercial exploitation'. His purism was unforgiving. Thus, we read, Coleman Hawkins had forfeited his claims to the jazz pantheon by playing the saxophone, not the clarinet.[16] Bebop was awarded a scant page; Johnny Parker (Lyttelton's pianist) was acknowledged, but not Charlie Parker.

As a new recruit to the jazz boom, I was buying records, to be played at first on friends' machines, for at home a record player was regarded as a substantial purchase for somewhat doubtful purposes. Nonetheless within

'White Negro', Porridge Foot Pete, Coventry Jazz Club, Railway Hotel, January 1956, in the author's collection

the year I had a record player of my own, a dozen or so 78s and a covetous consumer's eye on the new long-playing records. Rab Butler's 1953 budget made my acquisitions easier with reductions in the purchase tax on discs, record players and instruments. I was part of an already growing market among 'youngsters in their teens' reported in the *Melody Maker*, the weekly trade paper for dance band musicians that was giving increasing coverage to jazz. My diary noted record shops 'full of boppers and their girls'.[17]

As a neophyte I devoured jazz history, of which Harris provided plenty. Again without having first heard the music, I identified early with Jelly Roll Morton, the New Orleans piano virtuoso, bandleader and accomplished all-round rascal who flourished in the 1920s. His nickname, we read with interest in Harris, 'connoted sexual prowess'. The names of other heroes of the classic period were similarly exotic — Pine Top Smith, Blind Lemon Jefferson — and it was on this model that my best friend and I transformed ourselves into jazz celebrities. He, a trumpet player, became Deaf Rhubarb Blenkinsop, myself, on piano, Porridge Foot Pete. Thus equipped we dedicated ourselves to living out the authentic jazz myth, destined of course for an early death, in keeping with the careers of the legendary jazz greats whose genius was cut off in its prime by drugs, alcohol, or what we fervently hoped would be other excesses. To this end we hoped to recruit some young neighbourhood housewife for the role of our favourite fantasy blues singer, Naked Nellie Bloggs.

We learned how to play the music itself, progressing from earnest if ragged jam sessions at home to providing interval music at the Railway Hotel, the rundown pub that was Coventry's traditional jazz venue. I played my first paid jazz gig in October 1955 just before I left school. With A levels completed and Oxford entrance secured, I then waited three months for call-up into the army for National Service. There were more gigs, Porridge Foot and Deaf Rhube cut a private record, and there was a trip to London to play a jam session at the Cy Laurie club (of the *Picture Post* report) before sleeping out on the Embankment. I grew a beard and thought I might be an existentialist, though one still subject to the tyranny of the last bus and quizzing by bemused parents. Trying to explain to my mother (who was early into cultural studies) how you went about playing jazz, she replied, 'Yes, but what does it mean?'

Studies of jazz in the inter-war years in Britain suggest some answers.

According to Eric Hobsbawm (writing under his jazz alias Francis Newton), its following of predominantly lower-middle-class males was motivated by a revolt against respectability and upper-class culture. 'Culturally self-made men', they adopted jazz as their own intellectual discovery. Simon Frith has identified a similarly defensive yet aspiring petty-bourgeois intelligentsia whose intellectualism was complemented by an urgent desire for spontaneity and emotional ignition — 'playing with real feeling' — the quest of the archetypal bourgeois suburbanite dogged by deep male fears of being 'inauthentic', or having no feelings at all. Frith's prime exhibit of this mode of masculinity is the poet Philip Larkin, a schoolboy in the pre-war years, attending the same Coventry grammar school as myself, though a name unknown to me during my time there.[18] Hobsbawm took his analysis into the post-war period when jazz became a more obtrusive signifier of protest for the 'angry young men' of literature, though the note of rebellion was, he found, more muted among its expanding general public. A personal history gives a more specific inflection to the complex determinations of cultural self-making for the jazz bricoleur of the early 1950s, particularly in the playing of the music, which was rarely part of the pre-war experience.

'The jazz life saves me', reads my diary for 26 February 1954. From what? From servitude, tedium and repression would seem to be the answer, recorded with doleful and exaggerated relish. Listening to and playing jazz was a release from the relentless demands of homework and school — 'work, work and more work'. Jazz, with its fantasy destinations in New Orleans, Chicago and Soho basements, filled the otherwise tedious intervals between schoolwork in a city whose lack of cultural amenities was most pronounced for the young (among the first groups I played in was the Weary City Jazz Band). This was escape or withdrawal rather than revolt — consolation not ululation. But jazz in the 1950s was still, as Hobsbawm put it, 'a rude word' that was a protest in itself. Yet the note of protest could be as much consonant as dissonant with prevailing values. Intellectualising the music, through the study of its history and claims for its aesthetic status, made it another examinable subject aligned with the sacred canon of the great god, GCE (General Certificate of Education). Addressing our sixth form discussion group, I represented jazz as exciting and different, exploiting the rude word to secure a kind of avant-garde legitimacy in the eyes of academic elders, while clamping it into a new orthodoxy. It was, of course, myself as much as the music that I wished to register as exciting and different, bidding for recognition within limits defined by the system.

The 'real feeling' sought by a previous generation of British jazz fans was defined in terms of spontaneity and uninhibited emotional and physical expression. In remarking on his 'unspent youth' in Coventry, Larkin signalled the strong subtext of sexual frustration. In this discourse the truly fulfilled other was the black man, the 'American Negro', the authentic progenitor of jazz and the exotic embodiment of its rhythmic intensity and open sexuality. Thus jazz was invested with the displaced yearnings of the 'white Negro', Norman Mailer's projection of the 'subjective black man' under the white skin, who might be infused with the mythical virility and abandon of the racial other in the shared identity of the 'jazz musician'.[19] As a still-oppressed proletarian, the American black was also the object of class sympathy. As it was, however, these identifications remained mostly in the head. Other than on record, the only black person I met in Coventry was a barber who spoke to me in the thick local accent which, much to my embarrassment, I was having to recognise as my own: 'Ow dya loike yer 'air cut?' No jive talk here, no instant cultural and political fraternity. Despite the disappointing encounter with the black Figaro, my romanticised image of jazz as an authentic music of the people continued to generate an earnest if cheaply bought liberalism.

Playing jazz could bring acute pleasure. Much of the music we produced was inept and lumpish but, as the diary records, there were moments of 'superb exultation ... when you really rock and capture the complete attention of the crowd'.[20] Such epiphanies had to be conjured from the complex triangular dynamics of the individual musician, the band, and the audience. Playing in a band, executing a skill, fashioning a product, did provide some kind of artisanal satisfaction. Learning and exchanging a musical language and its insiders' trade talk was like induction into the 'mysteries of the craft' denied to the solitary proto-academic. At the same time, trade competence had to be meshed with that of the other performers and balanced against the less calculable risks of live performance and the mantra of 'improvisation'.[21] It was this allegedly spontaneous element that endowed the music with a superior aesthetic aura. New Orleans jazz had a democratic and primitivist appeal, yet paradoxically served a cultural élitism among its petty-bourgeois snobs. We craved applause and attention, yet disdained the common herd. They were 'peasants'; 'they couldn't tell a B flat from a bull's foot'. We were men of the people yet artists and bohemians, vulgarians and sophisticates at one and the same time.

Yet it was a marked feature of the British jazz world that pretensions of any kind — prelapsarian purity, ideological piety, aesthetic affectation — were undercut by a distinctive if hybrid humour. My self-awarded musical alias as Porridge Foot Pete was plainly an absurdity that mocked any assumptions of artistic parity with authentic American jazzmen. We delighted in saluting each other as 'Dad', Bruce Turner's wry anglicisation of the black American address, 'man'.[22] The parodies owed something to British music hall, wilting on stage in the 1950s, but still current on radio, where the style was leavened with the surrealism of *The Goon Show*. George Melly's blues singing came with music hall inflections and borrowings from the parallel traditions of American vaudeville.

For Porridge Foot Pete, the greatest of absurdities lurked at home in the front room where the group of schoolfriends first rehearsed around the piano. It was here in this latterday parlour with its other apparatus of respectability that my mother ran her part-time business as corsetière for the Spirella company, taking measurements and orders for ladies' 'foundation garments', an appointment discreetly announced by a plaque on the wall outside. This, we told ourselves gleefully, would assure our place in jazz history, looking forward to the day when Jazz at the Spirella would be as legendary as sessions at Mahogany Hall, Condon's or Birdland. But Spirella was not really that incongruous a conceit for, while corsets were inherently comic, they represented the inescapable other in our lives, adding further sexual freight to the jazz identity.

'My life is jazz and sex', I wrote as a sixteen-year-old; 'I get a fair amount of one but none of the other.'[23] This familiar enough tale of adolescent male frustration was heavily imprinted with atavistic Victorianism. Despite the public furore over the *Kinsey Report* on female sexuality in 1953, direct acknowledgments of 'sex', that incandescent term, were significantly few at home. One mutually discomforting exception was my father's lecture on masturbation, in language not far short of Victorian proscriptions against the loss of 'vital fluids'. I was what the novelist Brian Aldiss called a 'hand-reared boy' and thus beset with physical as well as moral anxieties. The guilty act was coded in the diary (*la croix*), then penalised with the self-imposed sentence of twenty-four hours' bad luck. I was still under the spell of Baden-Powell's *Scouting for Boys* (the other major text in my life with Rex Harris's *Jazz*), which prescribed cold baths and brisk exercise as antidotes to 'beastliness'. The great scoutmaster and moral *generalissimo* had further advice under 'Courtesy to Women': 'Don't lark about with a girl whom you would not like your mother or sister to see you with'; 'Don't make love to any girl unless you mean to marry her'.[24] 'Make love' was another omnibus signifier, an elastic term implying everything from larking to fucking, an almost inconceivable progression for someone consigned to the apartheid of a single-sex grammar school.[25] But virginity, however reluctant, won commendation at home. 'You've always been a very moral boy', said Mum with approval, as damning an accolade as being pronounced a gentleman. I knew, and my diary knew, that I was secretly a 'cad', a wanking cad masquerading as a decent, manly chap. 'I'm afraid my girls have to be loose or angelically crushworthy' was the inescapable corollary, an unwitting echo of the Victorian dichotomy separating stereotypes of magdalen and madonna.[26]

What relief from these anxieties could be found in jazz? I had not then read the verdict of Theodor Adorno, Frankfurt School theorist and formidable jazz-hater. Writing under the pseudonym of Hektor Rotweiler, he declared that hot jazz provided only the illusion of freedom. If anything, he continued, its sexual message was one of castration, 'combining the promise of liberation with its aesthetic denial'.[27] As it was, my hitherto cloistered talents as a parlour pianist were now happily transferred to the more dramatic setting of the pub and the bandstand, where I enjoyed the fraternity of other tentative dissolutes and some extra pocket money. True, the local jazz scene was less satisfying in assuaging more specific adolescent anxieties. Nobody wrote or sang 'Acne Blues' or 'Masturbators Moan'. Naked Nellie Bloggs failed to materialise and there were no groupies. Perhaps Adorno had a point.

The traditional jazz world of my experience was a predominantly heterosexual, defensively masculine, beer-drinking subculture. Yet women loomed large indeed in the male jazz imaginary. Mere auxiliaries on the dance floor and scarcely figuring as musicians, they might yet attain recognition in impersonation of their honoured role in jazz mythology, the woman as blues singer. The greatest of these was Bessie Smith, the black 'Empress of the Blues' who sang directly and movingly of the pain and pleasure of sexual love. The blues lay at the heart of 'real feeling'. Female vocalists were few in British bands and were not likely to do any better than male instrumentalists in capturing the 'black' American sound. Yet men's wishful thinking could recast them as the 'real thing'. As a schoolboy, George Melly had written to his mother that he would only marry a black woman, 'preferably Bessie Smith'. When he reviewed the Northern Ireland singer, Ottilie Patterson, on her London début with the Chris Barber band in 1955, a visual conceit assimilated her to this ideal. For the British male this was as much corporeal as vocal. 'Out of that prim-looking little figure', Melly reported breathlessly, 'roared the fierce noble voice of an enormous Negress singing the blues.'[28]

In our eyes, as in Melly's, authentic women blues singers only came in one size. The favourite of more sophisticated jazz savants, Billie Holiday, simply failed to qualify, either in voice or body. Blues singers were big, a fact that moved us to laughter as much as admiration, rendered helpless at images of exotic bulk. The sense of welcome erotic intimidation was relayed in the conventional appellation of the blues singer as the 'big mama', familiar American argot in which mamas and babes doubled as lovers. On the record cut by Porridge Foot and Deaf Rhube I played and sang my own (highly derivative) composition, 'Missin' Mama Blues'; on the reverse of this lament we strutted through 'I Want a Girl Just Like the Girl that Married Dear Old Dad'. A staple in the British revivalist repertoire was 'Mama Don't Allow': 'Mama don't allow no jazz band playin' in here/But we don't care what Mama don't allow, we're gonna play jazz any ole how'. Young men rehearsing a music of protest and desire, we were all, it seems, defiant mother-lovers.[29]

Images of Bessie Smith competed and conflated with those of other fantasy figures, the well-upholstered ladies of my mother's Spirella corset catalogues. An American company, already well established in Britain, Spirella was somewhat uneasily updating and expanding its product line in the mid-1950s. Considerations of health and durability (the earliest Spirellas were advertised as 'unbreakable') were subordinated to a new emphasis on fashionability and glamour, if in conservative tones — 'this has nothing to do with the shallow pated glamour girl as such'.[30] While newly targeting the young, Spirella still catered to its more traditional core market, the carriage trade of older women of 'fuller figure'. The style of illustrations was changing in the mid-1950s, but those I remember best were of models of a streamlined stoutness who, with a faint echo of the seaside postcard, seemed a hangover from the 1930s. For whatever age or size, the Spirella look still depended on a highly engineered body to achieve its compromise between science and nature. The literature detailed a formidable apparatus of straps and buckles, 'anchorage points', 'lockable zips' and 'trolley suspenders'. As mechanical fetishism this was arresting enough, but still more so was the acknowledgment of the unruly and imperfect body underneath the heavily fortified shell. In instructional manuals for the corsetière, breast types were classified, from scant to pendulous. This latter feature was much desired in visions of the mythical Naked Nellie Bloggs; it was also a source of considerable humour. From within its neo-classical sheath, the carnivalesque body was struggling to get out; *Venus naturalis* contested with *Venus celestis*. While pictures of corsets and their contents constituted a form of soft porn for the teenage voyeur, the Spirella model was less muskily erotic than Bessie Smith. Yet she too was a big mama, her maternal sexuality perceived as both threat and invitation, its tensions indulged and dissolved in nervous laughter. For me, Spirella woman was the unspoken 'white Negress'.

In spring 1956, the army shipped me out to Singapore and I was temporarily lost to jazz; in the same year Elvis Presley and Bill Haley arrived in Britain on record. At this time traditional jazz and a new satellite, skiffle, were briefly recruited to the pop scene, aggressively promoted as 'trad'. A jolly music complete with bowler hats and other gimmicks that alienated its original fans, 'traddy pop' withered in the early 1960s under the onslaught of rock, native and American.[31] Jazz of all kinds subsided into a minority interest, putting many of its musicians out of work while securing its increasing status as an art form. Though there were further stylistic upheavals, sectarianism waned.

Where it has been recognised at all by social historians or cultural critics, the jazz world of the early post-war years has not had a good press, its claims to any radical or subversive impact now firmly discredited. Yet in

'White Negress', Spirella Magazine, *February 1956. Illustration provided courtesy of the First Garden City Heritage Museum, Letchworth*

the mid-1950s, Ken Tynan identified jazz as nurturing 'an instinctive Leftism' that drew on related allegiances to drama at the Royal Court Theatre, CND, higher education and folk music. In John Osborne's *Look Back in Anger*, playing at the Royal Court from 1956, the anti-hero Jimmy Porter plays jazz trumpet as part of his oppositional persona. A passion for jazz informed the writings of other angry young men from the Movement, notably Kingsley Amis and John Wain, whose fictional male protagonists paraded their jazz enthusiasms as calculated insolence in the face of high culture.[32] Such protests now seem too limited and self-regarding on the part of authors whose left-liberal sympathies soon soured into a curmudgeonly conservatism, perhaps viciously so in the case of Larkin and Osborne. A close friend of Kingsley Amis, Larkin shared and compounded Amis's well-known misogyny and homophobia. Such associations have so contaminated the image of jazz in Britain that it has more recently been abominated as 'a suburban, reactionary, racist, middle class phenomenon'. This is an intriguing reversal of earlier demonisations.[33]

Radical politics is not the only measure of significance for an historical appreciation of subcultures. Though some supported the worthy causes of the day, jazz musicians and their fans of the 1950s were not in the vanguard of any aggressive new cultural politics.[34] (Twenty years on, two leading trad bands were happy enough to play for Mrs Thatcher's campaign for the Tory leadership.) Yet the post-war British jazz scene had a distinctive energy and sound of its own, generating a utopian allure in vivid contrast to the insipid commercial popular culture of the day. The jazz world was a collective improvisation in a larger sense, whose do-it-yourself music constituted an alternative culture for the first uneasy beneficiaries of the post-war settlement, educationally advantaged but culturally displaced. However tame it may now seem in retrospect, it was a micro-model for the more explosive youth music cultures of later generations.

Perhaps more importantly, jazz also furnished the materials for a more satisfactory sense of self. It constituted an area of self-acquired competence and knowledge, free from obvious institutional control and the official agendas of the city and its industries. The self-consciously literate dimension to my enthusiasm both emulated and mocked the élitist ideals of the school and formal education. The jazz world licensed an agreeably disreputable *alter ego* and an undemanding sub-heroic masculinity. Jazz also brought fantasy closer to home. It was, however, the home that sustained the most constricting of competing cross-identifications for the aspirant jazzman. Here was the prime site of respectability and a prolonged and disabling dyadic dependency on the mother common to the upbringing of many young males of this generation. Home life (like the Spirella corset) was only slowly learning to bend with the times.[35]

This account registers none of the severe alienation that produced the spectacular and critically engrossing subcultures of later years. By the side of the punks, Porridge Foot Pete is no more than the Adrian Mole of his day. But for me the anxieties of coming of age in the early 1950s come back forcefully enough. Whatever the exaggerations of the diary and its bid for a romantic exceptionalism, the personal experience of which it tells has some wider reference. Jazz at the Spirella was an exercise in modernity of a distinctly conservative and English kind. It was fuelled by fantasies from the hyper-modern other world of America, yet contained by the claims and dependencies of welfarism and its own strongly self-regarding national culture. The reach for 'vital experience' found expression in a cautious adventurism that was characteristic of the period.

In the 1950s I dreamed of going to the States, but adventure took me, cautiously, to Canada and to Winnipeg, another rather flat midlands city. Still playing jazz (if now something of a dirty bopper) I continue to feel that excitement happens somewhere else.

2. State-Sponsored Autobiography

Carolyn Steedman

The idea of a 'State-Sponsored Autobiography' — the claim that there actually was such a thing — is a partial answer to a large question about the post-war years in Britain; and that large question itself has to do with historically determined ways of thinking and feeling. Indeed, the idea of 'modernity' itself, which this collection interrogates, implies that there is some conclusion to come to about the relationship of selfhood to social structure and social change. If ways of being a person, and ideas of what a person is, are appropriated and learned differently in different historical epochs, then they are also taught. This chapter is concerned with the ways in which the subject of British modernity was instructed, and made a matter for instruction, in the years after 1945.

Questions about modernity and selfhood press themselves because it is becoming increasingly clear across the historical disciplines that practitioners believe past forms of cognition and affect are to some extent retrievable, and that it is one of their jobs to interrogate them. The historical interrogation so far conducted has been mainly to do with written texts (as this one will be), and has focused on the eighteenth century. In John Mullan's felicitous formulation, for example, the eighteenth-century novel of sensibility enabled you to learn about feelings. 'In a culture in which the art of being an individual involved learning how to have feelings', he says, 'the best kinds of fiction made for the best tuition.'[1] In Elizabeth Cox's discussion of epistolary fiction from a slightly earlier period, the letter and the letter-narrative are texts that bring into being 'the modern body-subject... that notion of the self as represented and bounded and what it does and makes'.[2] The novel composed of letters makes this bounded and private thing public, able to be appropriated and used by others. It can have this effect as epistolary fiction because letters themselves, pieces of text that are most intimately connected to biological bodies, operate this way, in social worlds.[3] Roger Chartier summarises two decades of his own work concerning the selfhoods that were learned from written texts in the eighteenth and nineteenth centuries, with a call for 'a social history of the uses and understanding of texts by communities of readers who successively take possession of them'.[4]

The tacit agreement then, among a number of cultural and social historians, is that, since the early modern period, varieties of literature have delineated varieties of selfhood and feeling and that these models and patterns have been grasped, appropriated and used by some readers. We are not entirely clear about the way in which this has happened, in different times and places, but are in some kind of agreement that it has. Nor are these assumptions restricted to the realm of self and affect. Linda Peterson, for example, has described the endurance of hermeneutic autobiography well into the secular world of the nineteenth century. The practice of writing that we most readily associate with seventeenth-century Protestantism, in which interpretation of the life-story was understood to be of greater significance than its story-content, is seen at work by Peterson in many nineteenth-century autobiographies. A writer's concentration on *meaning* rather than *event*, on *significance* rather than on *what happened*, are thus in her argument, evidence of a particular form of cognition in the past.[5]

It is autobiography — the writing of the self — that is in question here, and the way in which, in the second half of the twentieth century, autobiographical writing became 'a "genre of choice", for authors, audiences and critics .... '[6] Anthony Giddens describes a 300-year development in the West, by which personhood and self-identity have come to be comprehended as 'the self ... reflexively understood by the person in terms of her or his biography'.[7] In his *Modernity and Self-Identity* (1991) 'autobiography' is conceptualised not so much as a form of writing, nor as a literary genre (though it is, of course, both of those things), but rather as a mode of cognition. The process of actually writing an autobiography, of getting it published and having it read, is seen as a minor variant of more general 'autobiographical thinking'. In this 'broad sense of an interpretive self-history produced by the individual concerned', says Giddens, '[autobiography] whether written down or not ... is actually the core of self-identity in modern life'.[8]

The connections between autobiographical writing and the emergence of the modern self are particularly well established in British historiography. All major twentieth-century accounts of the self in society, whether they be historical or literary in focus, make the implied connection between the processes of individualisation and the act of writing. The historical developments that are usually evoked in accounts like this are, first Protestantism, and second an early and relatively sophisticated print-culture in England, operating in conjunction with a relatively high literacy rate.[9] A new historical account of autobiographical practice in Britain from 1600 to the present day could learn from these earlier histories of the seventeenth and eighteenth centuries and could consider habits of self-narration as taught and learned activities. It could pay some detailed attention to the way in which practices of writing are recommended, prescribed and actually made matters of instruction in different historical epochs. My focus here is specific and concentrates on the massive programme of teaching selfhood and self-expression in operation in British state schools since the end of the Second World War. Key developments of the 1950s and early 1960s are the subject of this chapter, though some material has to be drawn from the 1970s, when commentators looked back ten and twenty years, in order to write the history of a new form of selfhood still taught to children in schools. The argument has to move some years beyond the precise timeframe of this book because we are still in this moment of modernity, still becoming its subjects and telling ourselves.

'Creative Writing' and the Cultivation of Post-War Selfhood in the Schools

'Creative writing' developed in British state primary schools from about 1950 onwards. By the late 1970s it was a timetabled lesson (and sometimes made emblematic of an entire pedagogy) for all primary school children. As a practice it was promoted by 'progressive' educationalists, in training colleges and in schools, and was endorsed by Her Majesty's Inspectors of Schools. The famous *Plowden Report* of 1967 gave the practice unqualified support.[10]

The Plowden Committee provided its own history of progressive education and reported on the astonishing changes that had taken place in educational practice since 1945. The Committee suggested that 'perhaps the most dramatic of all the revolutions in English teaching is in the amount and quality of children's writing'. It reported that:

> the code of 1862 required no writing other than transcription or dictation until Standard VI ... In the thirties, independent writing in the infant school and lower junior school rarely extended beyond a sentence or two. Now ... there is free fluent and copious writing on a great variety of subject matter ... Its essence is that much of it is personal and that the writers are communicating something that really engaged their minds and imaginations.[11]

Teachers and other educators of the 1950s and 1960s rarely used the term 'autobiography' or 'autobiographical writing' to describe this kind of practice. What they meant by using the term 'creative writing' was a kind of ethical self-cultivation, to be achieved by children through the use of the written word. 'What Is Good Children's Writing?' asked the journal *Use of English* in 1952. It was writing that released 'the younger child's inner creativeness'.[12] It was not particularly expected that the child would write in his or her own voice, about his or her own life (though this kind of writing developed rapidly from the early 1960s onwards). What *was* expected was that the child would be 'involved', by being presented with subjects that allowed him or her 'to draw on first-hand experiences, which are relevant to the life he lives, or which stimulate and release his imagination to a lively and sincere response'.[13] What mattered was that 'sincere response', which in the early years of the period under discussion was understood to be dependent on the teacher's gift to the children of 'vivid first-hand experience'.[14]

The stakes were very high and the cultural mission of the English teacher of very great significance: one account from the 1970s looked back over the past twenty-five years of English teaching, and spoke of its 'ambitious heart'.[15] In 1973 the Head of the English Department at a rural secondary modern school drew on the work of Lev Vygotsky, G. H. Mead and the new cultural anthropology of Jack Goody in order to perform the same kind of historical exercise, and to express the hope:

> that in encouraging [children] to the practice of writing about things
> that concern them, for readers who are concerned about them, and
> thus helping them to find the individual selves they have become, we
> may also be helping to protect them from that extreme awareness of
> individuality that we call alienation. Thus may education compensate
> for society.[16]

Moreover, teachers and educationalists — like this Head of English — had
access to an explanatory history of their classroom practice. They placed
what they were doing with children in the tradition of English studies
inaugurated by F.R. Leavis in the 1930s under the auspices of the
Cambridge English School, and disseminated through the journal *Scrutiny*.
Even Ministers of Education were able to rehearse this history by the
1960s. In the summer of 1964, Edward Boyle congratulated the journal
Use of English on twenty-five years of existence, saying that it was 'one of
the good things which we owe in the long run to the Cambridge English
School'.[17] A few years later a head of English at a Somerset secondary
school filled in the publication history of this movement:

> Although it is difficult to define, there now seems no doubt that there
> is a 'New English'. It perhaps took tangible form with the publication
> of *Reflections* in 1963, and received semi-official recognition with the
> Schools Council *Working Paper No.3, English*, in 1965 (HMSO). But this
> was only the crystallisation out of what had been in suspension for
> many years. *Culture and Environment*, first published as long ago as
> 1933, was possibly the key book: the young men who studied this in
> their sixth-form days have now become heads of English Departments
> and writers of English books.[18]

He went on to note that 'The interaction of personalities in the movement
is significant: for example, it is not just chance that both Esmor Jones, the
first Secretary of NATE (National Association for the Teaching of English),
and David Holbrook were both at Downing College, Cambridge, when Dr
Leavis was English Tutor there'.[19]

F.R. Leavis' and Denys Thompson's *Culture and Environment* asked secondary school children and their teachers to scrutinise a tawdry Americanised culture from the perspective of a traditional, organic community. In its pages the traditional community was invented by listing the prose works of John Bunyan, late nineteenth-century accounts of change in rural life like George Sturt's and the Hammonds' valedictory histories of labour and loss.[20] It was written by the Cambridge academic and former elementary school teacher in the space of three months, in only one of the significant 'interaction[s] of personalities in the movement' that this Somerset teacher noted.

Frank Leavis, the long 'moment' of the journal *Scrutiny* that he edited, and the relationship between textual and political practices that he supported, has recently been written into histories of cultural Marxism in post-war Britain. Dennis Dworkin describes the formation of the Birmingham University Centre for Contemporary Cultural Studies in 1964 as an attempt to 'use the methods of literary criticism to understand popular and mass culture and to develop criteria for critically evaluating specific forms'.[21] This practice had a long gestation period outside the academy. Writing for schoolteachers in the journal *Use of English* in 1950, Raymond Williams recommended a series of books to use in classrooms with children pursuing what he called 'Culture and Environment Studies'. He made overt reference here to Leavis's and Thompson's book of 1933, which he assumed his audience would know well, explaining that 'Literary criticism is the informing discipline of the studies as a whole ... "Culture and Environment" involves an extension of this kind of analysis and judgement to a variety of cultural forms'.[22] *Culture and Environment*, published in 1933, was the first of many 'significant encounters', between critical and political practices, between schoolteachers and academics, in the formation of cultural studies. The assumptions and practices that Dworkin describes were worked out long before 1964, and often in the English classroom.[23]

In the 1960s, in the histories of English familiar to schoolteachers, the name of I.A. Richards was at least as important as that of Frank Leavis. This was in part a result of the astonishing permeation through the education system of the critical practice he inaugurated at Cambridge in the 1930s.[24] Richards had concluded his *Practical Criticism* of 1929 with the assertion that 'the lesson of all criticism is that we have nothing to rely upon in making our choices but ourselves', arguing that 'the whole apparatus of critical rules and principles is the means to the attainment of a finer, more precise, more discriminating communication'.[25] *Practical Criticism* was a university class reader and a manual for university teachers, showing examples of responses to poetry that had emerged in Richards' Cambridge pre-war seminars. There were no names and dates attached to the poems that students were to study and discuss: the reader was to come to the text without preconceptions, bringing only him- or herself to the act of response. Denys Thompson later attested to the great changes that this critical practice brought about, and to 'the fact ... that Richards has been the main influence in changing the method of studying literature in schools of most kinds'.[26] Comparing the Cambridge English examination papers of 1963 with those of 1925, he said that 'a knowledge of history, social background, linguistic origins and Aristotle, had ceased to be tested'.[27]

Thompson approved of this change, which by the late 1960s had spread far beyond the walls of ancient universities. In 1973 the University of London regulations for GCE (General Certificate of Education) English mentioned 'liveliness of response and sincerity of interest' as the paramount considerations in assessing sixteen-year-olds' examination answers.[28] Pupils were expected to show evidence of 'a personal response', and examiners were often to complain about the 'lack of genuine personal response', and the 'received opinion evidenced'.[29] Methods for assessing genuineness of response were made precise:

> The evidence of a thoughtful response, of a candidate's having imaginatively 'lived through' the experiences of the text, is often provided by the careful, in some cases instinctive, choice of verbs, adverbs and adjectives with which the description of a character or an episode is presented. Such answers come alive.[30]

This methodology was adopted as a democratic critical practice throughout the school system — for each child possessed the rich resource of his or her own critical response, and was not dependent on the unequal distribution of interpretative devices (on actually *knowing* something about history, or a literary tradition). Simultaneously, of course, it defined most responses as inadequate. For *Practical Criticism* came accompanied by other manifestos of Cambridge English. In his pamphlet of 1930, *Mass Civilisation and Minority Culture*, F.R Leavis had put forward a claim for the study of literature which later became the mission statement of *Scrutiny*. He wrote that:

> in any period it is upon a very small minority that the discerning appreciation of art and literature depends ... only a few who are capable of unprompted, first-hand judgement .... Upon this minority depends our power of profiting by the finest human experience of the past. Upon them depend the implicit standards that order the finer living of an age. In their keeping is the language ... upon which fine living depends ... By 'culture' I mean the use of such a language ... [31]

There are several accounts of the way in which 'a very small minority' was given a missionary task by Leavisite criticism, which involved sending a hand-picked band into the educational system to organise resistance to advertisements, movies, American milk-bar culture, women's magazines and pulp-fiction.[32] However, there are no detailed accounts tracking the movement of personnel from the Cambridge English School to the secondary schools and then into the training colleges, to educate the aspiring teachers of primary school children from the 1930s to the 1970s. In the absence of that information, it is best to rely on the histories which do exist: of the impact of Leavis' and Thompson's *Culture and Environment*, and the direct use by school teachers of *Scrutiny* and Leavisite principles of criticism in their daily classroom practice, from the mid-1930s onwards.[33]

These ideas were also transmitted to the classroom by the journal *English in Schools*, which Thompson edited from 1939 until 1949. Later, it became *Use of English* (still under Thompson's editorship, funded by the Bureau of Current Affairs). The Bureau was partly sponsored by the Carnegie UK Trust in order to 'stimulate and "service" the study of Current Affairs in discussion groups'. Its single issue pamphlets on topics of interest ran from September 1946 until 1953.[34] The paradigms of post-war English classroom practice were set out in the bureau's groups, as they established the basic framework of talk, literature, civics and self-exploration for the discussion of all topics throughout the war years and after.

The taught and learned practices of the self, promoted through English teaching in schools in the post-war years, were connected, in as yet unex-

amined ways, with the reformulation of class politics in Britain. In particular, autobiographical narration fed into forms of political analysis and
action which focused on the lived experience of working-class people. In
this context a more or less official pedagogy of creative writing in schools
needs to be considered in relationship to the post-war expansion of a
whole range of social projects, conceived in different registers and different voices: adult education, the development of the worker-writers and
community publishing movement (and thus an astonishing flowering of
working-class autobiography in the 1970s), the rapid growth of community
theatre, the folk movement and its deliberate forging of a sense of community between past and present narratives of the poor, the practice of oral
histories of the working class, the development of the History Workshop
movement, and, towards the end of the 1960s, the practice of conscious-
ness-raising in the emergent women's movement.[35] All operated on the
assumption that the subaltern *could* speak; that through articulation in
spoken or written words the dispossessed *could* come to an understanding
of their own story.[36] That story — that life — could by various means, be
returned to the people who had struggled to tell or to write it, and be used
as basis for political action.[37]

Teachers' own education in self-understanding through the process of
writing can also be seen as an early aspect of this same historical development. In some training college archives lie autobiographical fragments
which were once part of an interview and selection process. The practice
of asking applicants to write about themselves seems to have developed in
the mid-1950s, and to have been formalised by 1960. In one college,
students had to write two pages about: 'a) Your home — father's and
mother's work; brothers and sisters: home life — its advantages and difficulties: the problems of leaving home. b) Your desire to teach ... etc'.[38] The
point of the exercise was that eighteen-year-old trainee teachers might learn
to connect their own stories of childhood, and their own desires, to those
of the children with whom they were to work. This was an ethical preparation that we can see codified in Peter Abbs's *Autobiography in Education*
(1974), which he described as 'an introduction to the subjective discipline
of Autobiography and of its central place in the education of teachers'. The
book juxtaposed the writings of training college students with extracts
from the autobiographical writings of Rousseau, Wordsworth, Coleridge,

Gorky and Jung among others. Through reading them, and then writing, the student would 'embrace parts of his childhood' and reach an 'enhanced affirmation of the self'.[39]

Working-class Autobiography and its Implications

Autobiographical practice did not develop first in the training colleges. Rather, it seems to have emerged in the schools, in the years after the Second World War. There is an extremely telling example of it at work in Valerie Avery's *London Morning*, first published in 1964. *London Morning* was written in 1955 when Avery was fifteen, in her English class at Walworth High School, at the instigation of Harold Rosen, her English teacher. Rosen later became Professor of English at the University of London Institute of Education and is best known for his militant opposition to theories of linguistic deprivation, derived from Basil Bernstein's work on elaborated and restricted speech-styles, distributed by social class. In the 1950s and 1960s Rosen was a secondary school teacher and a leading member of the progressive English teachers' organisation, the National Association for the Teaching of English.

London Morning described a family's progress from the Old Kent Road, where Avery grew up, out to the new working-class housing estates. Interviewed in 1982, Avery remembered that:

> Gran and Granddad had moved to a prefab in Peckham, and now all our neighbours were leaving the Old Kent Road to go to distant places ending in 'ham' for some reason: Bellingham, Downham and Mottingham — suggesting fresh country air and grassy pavements.[40]

The book ended with that move. In its last pages it became a mourning for a lost way of life, and an elegy.

London Morning presented itself as fictionalised autobiography. Told for the main part through dialogue recorded in dialect, it drew a good deal on a central tradition of British working-class autobiography, particularly that derived from music hall: the playing of 'Life's Comedy', where the warm, rumbustious, disorganised life of sprawling families was told through a wealth of incidents that provoke laughter and tears, both at the same time.[41] There is nothing surprising about *London Morning* then, except that it was written by a girl of fifteen, in a classroom — and its subsequent publishing history. It was reprinted twice in the 1960s, and in 1969 reissued as a class reader to be studied as literature, alongside William Shakespeare, Jane Austen, and the Georgian poets, in the secondary school English class.[42] The extent of *London Morning*'s dissemination was not as important as the pedagogical and political autobiographical principles it embodied: that the dispossessed were enabled to tell their story and to come into consciousness of their self through the practice of writing. Subsequently, the story was to be returned, not just to the child in question, but to many other children too, so that they might also come into a sense of self.

London Morning and its publication history was the apotheosis of a common classroom practice. In 1952, a teacher working with nine-year-olds reported that he always said to the children, "'When you write, remember it is for someone to read and enjoy'". He then went on to describe how 'corrected copies of some of the more interesting efforts were typed out, so as to appear more like the stuff in a printed book'. He was particularly concerned to inculcate what he called a kind of 'animism' — getting the child to imagine itself as another person or thing.[43] Indeed, we ought to consider the proposition that an entire autobiographical pedagogy originated in the Old Kent Road, for that is where this primary school teacher was working too, a few years before fifteen-year-old Valerie Avery was encouraged to produce her own book.

Yet it was class rather than location that mattered. Whilst creative writing was an educational method recommended for all children, it was deemed particularly appropriate for the supposedly inarticulate, the dispossessed and the deprived, for what in other times had been 'the children of the poor'. It was they who particularly needed to be freed to share 'their hopes, fears, interests, needs' in this way and, through writing, to reveal to their teachers 'much of the social context in which they lived'.[44] Working-class children could be helped by being asked to draw on the resource of their own experience, their own babyhood and early childhood, in order to tell the story of the self, for the lack of a sense of self was a deprivation among all the multiple ones they suffered.[45] Once told, the story of the self nearly always had the power to move the adult reading it. As the Plowden

Committee reported in 1967, 'the best writing of young children springs from the most deeply felt experience', and 'is nearly always natural and real and sometimes has qualities which make it most moving to read'.[46]

As the epitome of these educational and autobiographical practices, *London Morning* can be read in other contexts of self-writing. The writing of fictional and real 'scholarship girls' of the 1950s and 1960s, who recorded their progress away from working-class backgrounds towards the golden city of higher education as Val Avery did, suggests that the genre needs to be investigated in terms of a sociology, or historiography, of literary forms. Maureen Duffy's *That's How It Was* (1962), Margaret Drabble's *Jerusalem the Golden* (1967), Jeanette Winterson's *Oranges Are Not the Only Fruit* (1985), and Judith Grossman's *Her Own Terms* (1989) prompt questions about the rise and fall of such forms, about the needs and desires of writers and readers, which are expressed in their circulation and consumption, and about the popularity of stories told in a particular way, organised in one fashion rather than another, ending the way that they do. A history of the autobiographical form, as a structure both for enunciating the self and also as a mode of cognition, may help the historian to understand more clearly the relationship of literary forms, and social forms; to understand that to write a history of literary forms, even in a very partial way, is to contribute to a history of societies.[47]

There already exist extremely rich and detailed accounts of progressivism in Britain, its adoption as a more or less official educational ideology, and the personal sense of mission felt by many of its adherents.[48] The productions of children from the Old Kent Road — the nine-year-olds imagining themselves in 1952 as some other kind of person, some other kind of thing; the fifteen-year-old filling the London County Council exercise books with her extraordinary autobiography three years later — can, in individual cases, be directly attributed to the pedagogical convictions of teachers working within a progressive framework. But there has been relatively little discussion of writing compared with other creative forms in this pedagogical practice, and of the way in which a child's personal, creative, and autobiographical output was understood as the epitome of the process of growth through self-expression.

In investigating this form of autobiography the historian ponders, first of all, the enormity of the enterprise. In the post-war years in Britain, out of all the continuous, first-person prose narratives produced in any one day in British society, the vast majority of it came from children, writing in their news books or diaries in the primary school, and in all the forms of creative writing encouraged in the lower secondary school. It was not until well into this century — in the post-war decades — that our now taken for granted assumption was established: that the first word a child learned to inscribe was his or her own name. It was a dramatic and striking change, in historical terms, to take the 'I', the self, the named individual, as the focus of writing for educational purposes. The assumptions discussed here, about the perceived power of autobiographical writing to shape and form human subjectivities, were not educational ones alone, though their educational promulgation raises the most compelling historical questions precisely because the practice was so vast and the practitioners so articulate.

These questions of autobiography and narrative as learned and taught — as *required* — formulations of the self, return the historian to interrogate further the question of modernity. In particular the strategy of self-narration forces us to confront modernity's over-extended chronology. They must make us wonder about what kind of moment of modernity we are in, and whether it is not so long a *durée* as to lose all usefulness for historical enquiry. In *Poor Citizens* (1991), David Vincent gives a more specific reading of such issues, in exploring the relationship between the poor and the state in twentieth-century Britain. He suggests that families came to be seen as poor when they could no longer keep their stories private — were forced to tell them to Poor Law Relieving Officers and Boards of Guardians (later, Social Security officials) in order to obtain state benefits, to Schools Attendance Officers, schoolteachers, policemen; to Uncle; to the corner shop when trying to get tick ... to a neighbourhood that had the most sophisticated repertoire of devices for reading the marks of poverty inscribed on bodies, clothes, ways of moving through the streets.[49] We have seen that a concomitant development of this enforced autobiographical mode in the second half of the twentieth century was the encouragement of children's stories by an agency of the state, so that a recuperative selfhood might be given to the deprived.

Enforced autobiography is nothing new, and has a history at least as old as Protestant spiritual autobiography of the seventeenth and eighteenth centuries. The emerging modern administrative state in England demanded, however, that it was in fact the *poor* who told their stories, in vast proportion to their vast numbers, from the seventeenth century onwards: the story you told of your life before the magistrates administering the Poor Law in order to gain your settlement; the variant you would supply as a woman, if you were to claim any maintenance from the father of your bastard child; the narrative given before other judges in other courts of law; the details taken of all your life if you were in any way to gain the sympathy and the dole of the philanthropic organisation. These enforced narratives of the poor made their way into the novel and other forms of fictional writing, and became one model of what a life was, or might be.

This longer history of state-required and state-demanded narration shifts our perspective on the autobiographical practice of the 1950s and 1960s. But any conclusions about its development in the period 1945 to 1964 must be framed by a consideration of what was new about it, as well as by the perspective of a *longue durée* of enforced self-narrative. Beliefs about the psychological benefits of writing the self in six-year-olds (and fifteen-year-olds) in classrooms, the assumption that writing allowed a recuperative selfhood to be developed in working-class children, must be considered in conjunction with new practices of self-narration outside the school and the political uses to which these working-class stories were put. These technologies of self-dramatisation emerged in the moment of modernity that this book discusses.

3. The Commercial Domain: Advertising and the Cultural Management of Demand

Frank Mort

In *The General Theory of Employment, Interest and Money* (1935), in a passage shortly before his famous formula specifying the relationship between employment, investment and consumption, Keynes reviewed both the 'objective' and the 'subjective' factors which influenced the propensity to consume. Under the rubric of objective influences Keynes listed a familiar range of economic variables. But his consideration of subjective factors influencing demand tempted him for a brief moment on to cultural territory and specifically on to the field of human motivations:

> There remain the second category of factors which affect the amount of consumption out of a given income — namely, those subjective and social incentives which determine how much is spent ... These eight motives might be called the motives of Precaution, Foresight, Calculation, Improvement, Independence, Enterprise, Pride and Avarice; and we could also draw up a corresponding list of motives to consumption such as Enjoyment, Shortsightedness, Generosity, Miscalculation, Ostentation and Extravagance ... Now the strength of these motives will vary enormously according to the habits formed by race, education, convention, religion and current morals ... In the argument of this book, however, we shall not concern ourselves ... with the results of far-reaching social changes or with the slow effects of secular progress. We shall ... take as given the main background of subjective motives to saving and consumption respectively.[1]

Keynes here suppressed the field of social and cultural change, and the vagaries of the human personality, in the interests of economic theory. Yet the relations he articulated at this point in one of the classic accounts of modern economics — about the connections between economic progress, secular ethics and the cultural and psychological motivations of individuality — were issues which resonated throughout the post-war period. A characteristic development across the industrial societies of Europe and North America in the mid-twentieth century was the proliferation of knowledge and technologies for connecting economic activity with the field of culture and human relations. Both the advocates and the opponents of this strategy highlighted a vision of modern industrial society in which commerce and culture were now inextricably linked. Anthony Giddens and Zygmunt Bauman have argued that a defining feature of 'mature' or 'late' modernity was the new equilibrium forged between the economic and the cultural domains. This relationship had far-reaching effects, not simply on what was written and spoken about in official public culture, but on the ways in which modern subjects lived out a sense of who and what they were.[2]

Historians have documented these changes via the concept which lies at the heart of Keynes' own theory — the idea of consumption. In a British context the intensified impact of consumption has become enshrined as one of the master-narratives of the 1950s and early 1960s. Together with economic growth, full employment, political consensus and the rise of the welfare state, it has been used as one of the basic building blocks to tell the story of post-war society. Yet in as much as the term is liminal, crossing the boundaries between economics and culture, between material life and the moulding of human wants, arguments about the precise significance of consumption have varied enormously. Economists and economic historians have foregrounded the impact of Keynes' own strategy of demand management, understood in the context of the offensive against socialist versions of the command economy, the move to fiscal regulation and the stabilisation of post-war international trade.[3] Business historians have highlighted the shifts in productive organisation and output which underpinned the upsurge of consumer demand. Flow-line assembly, deskilling and standardised product design have been understood to provide the infrastructure of that quintessentially modern form for the dissemination of goods — the mass market. In Britain, arguments about the coming of a mature consumer society, or the society of affluence, have often been tied to a still broader polemic about the impact of 'Americanisation'. There has been a widespread assumption that, during the 1950s, British business increasingly looked towards the advanced techniques of selling derived from the United States. The growing role of advertising and marketing — those twin engines of modern consumerism — has been at the heart of such accounts; commercial culture has been identified with a distinctive secular ethic which achieved its most developed forms in North America. A generation of political historians (often themselves part of the culture of post-war social democracy) has pointed to the ways in which formal politics defined consumption as part of the new post-war settlement, via a focus on rising living standards and the achievements of consensus and social progress.[4] Finally, sociologists and cultural historians, during the period and since, have examined the impact of changing consumption patterns on key groups targeted by the consumer industries. The relationship of affluence to regional and generational change within working-class communities, its effects on women's roles and experience and on the crystallisation of new youth identities, has been studied almost obsessively.[5] Taken together, these histories have embraced a general thesis; namely, that from the early 1950s British society entered a new phase of economic organisation and management which had far reaching effects on social and cultural life.[6]

The purpose of rehearsing such widely differing accounts is not to engage in a detailed appraisal of their approaches. It is rather to emphasise the point which Keynes touched on but drew back from elaborating: that the story of post-war consumption in Britain has been a multiple history which has ranged across the fields of economic policy, political calculation and the social and psychological management of the secular self. Yet therein lies an acute historical problem: the persistent tendency to over-generalisation. At once part of a thesis on industrial and commercial restructuring, about the character of the new political settlement and the recomposition of class, gender and generational identities, consumption has been mobilised as a composite and synthetic term. It has been used to tell multiple stories about the nature of change in post-war Britain.

Faced with this burden of over-generality, recent work on consumption has moved towards a more concrete and grounded focus.[7] Such an approach has treated consumption practices as sectorally specific. It has also distinguished between different moments in the consumer cycle and

between different levels of knowledge and experience: commodity manufacture and product design, advertising and marketing, together with the
projections of selfhood and social fantasy which have been seen as such a
central feature of the post-war cultural landscape. Tracing the various
practices which shaped the circulation of goods has enabled more mean-
ingful comparisons to be made across different sectors of the consumer
economy. It has also projected more complex patterns of historical change
than those presented under the rubric of post-war affluence or the coming
of the 'consumer society'.

The story charted here confronts three interlinked themes which have
dominated debate about British consumption in the 1950s and 1960s: the
crystallisation of a mass market in goods, the impact of American methods of entrepreneurship on British business and the professional culture and
social imagery of the advertising industry. These are not simply issues of
economic development, they also chart the cultural history of commerce
during these years. In so doing, they have the potential to historicise
grandiose sociological claims made about the connection between
consumption and modernity. The cultural ramifications of bulk methods
of selling, the international flows of commodities produced by the expansion of world trade and the versions of subjectivity carried by commerce
— such questions need to be investigated concretely as well as philosoph-
ically, at particular points in time and in limited settings.

The Coming of a Mass Market?

'Mass distribution marts, the logical outcome of machine and mass production, are a boon and a blessing to the people.' This was the claim made by
Montague Burton, chairman of the largest British menswear clothing
multiple in 1935.[8] In their heyday, from the 1930s to the early 1960s, such
firms displayed many of the characteristic features of Fordist enterprise,
embracing batch production which provided the infrastructure for the
crystallisation of mass consumption. Household names such as Burton's,
Hepworth's and the Fifty Shilling Tailor dealt in huge runs of standardised
products, apparently serving a uniform market. Backed by a hierarchical
and centralised business culture, these companies organised their retailing
on a national scale. The quintessential product of the menswear sector, the

suit, has been read as an emblem of mass society, projecting an image of collective masculinity which paralleled other representations of gendered culture during the period: workers at the factory gate, the trade-union meeting, the football crowd.[9]

On closer inspection, however, menswear retailing provides an eloquent testimony to the partial and extremely uneven character of the British transition to mass consumption. Though Montague Burton lauded the arrival of the mass market, the picture inside his firm told a different story. Size, scale and nationwide coverage were certainly characteristic features of Burton's performance. The company's precise market share is not recorded but, from the 1930s, Burton's was the largest manufacturer and retailer of tailored menswear in Britain.[10] Even as late as 1961, in the opinion of the Economist Intelligence Unit, Burton's remained the 'biggest brand name in men's suits'.[11] In terms of market position, the 'tailor of taste' lay almost in the dead centre of men's clothing retailing. Obviously distanced from the genuine bespoke trade of London's Savile Row and upmarket competitors like Aquascutum or Simpson's, Burton's claims to taste and affordable elegance also differentiated it from firms such as the Fifty Shilling Tailor, where the emphasis was almost exclusively on price. Occupying prominent sites, with over 600 branches across Britain, Burton's shops were landmarks in town and city centres during the post-war years. With characteristic fittings in marble, oak and bronze, designed to connote quality and solid worth, the atmosphere of a Burton's shop was unmistakable.[12] Such local details were centrally controlled from head office in Leeds, where business managers and even the chairman himself paid minute attention to window displays, opening hours and the routine of the working day.

Yet underpinning this form of retailing were a series of commercial arrangements which cut against the corporate model. These were to be found both within the manufacturing process itself and in Burton's approach to the consumer. During the inter-war years menswear had become increasingly dominated by two related changes: the growth of large-scale factory production and an increasing number of branch tailors retailing their own product — what was known in the trade as 'multiple tailors' selling 'wholesale bespoke'.[13] In reality, Burton's suits were factory made under strictly standardised procedures. Customers' individual measurements were fitted to predetermined shapes and sizes: long thin, medium, short portly, etc. These were produced as templates for cutters, to facilitate batch production. There was no direct personal contact between tailor and customer, no hand-finishing, nor was a Burton's suit truly made-to-measure. Consequently, the taste leaders of Savile Row never tired of pointing out that Burton's was in fact a counterfeit tailors.[14] Yet the firm continued to imitate the genuine bespoke trade, especially in its approach to customers. 'Sir' was measured by Burton's salesmen with all of the ritual to be found in a traditional tailoring establishment. This ideal of dignity and decorum was epitomised in the preferred profile of the company's salesmen. The art of salesmanship was to be approached with high seriousness. All excess was to be avoided through restraint and quiet good manners. As Burton's famous memorandum to staff counselled: 'Avoid the severe style of the income tax collector and the smooth tongue of the fortune teller. Cultivate the dignified style of the "Quaker tea blender" which is a happy medium.'[15]

It was this personalised stance which also guided Burton's policy on advertising. A company which was dedicated to mass retailing clung steadfastly to a local strategy for advertising and marketing as the most effective way of reaching its customers. This stance flew in the face of contemporary business philosophy, which underlined the importance of mass selling techniques for goods produced in bulk, on the grounds of cost effectiveness and national coverage.[16] Until well into the 1950s, Burton's attitude to commercial communications was overwhelmingly local, with advertising positioned as close to the point of sale as possible. The window display, the role of the salesman, the location of the store on the high street, together with announcements in the regional press, these were seen as the most effective forms of promotional culture. Guidelines issued from head office to the branches repeated these formulae endlessly. The impression made on customers by a well-dressed shop window could not be matched:

> A well-dressed window is a greater selling force than a newspaper and other forms of publicity combined. To neglect the greatest selling asset ... is unworthy of a progressive businessman ... the shop window is better than a picture, for the prospective customer sees the original. Ten thousand words could not convey the same description that a good window does.[17]

The superiority of direct techniques of selling was emphasised over national publicity. The shop front conveyed an immediate sense of visual excitement, an atmosphere of variety and an invitation to purchase, which advertising could not hope to match. Burton's argument was that adverts only created verisimilitude; the tangible reality of commodities on display was the major selling asset. The point is important because the composite blueprint of national advertising, as the medium disseminating commercial information under the conditions of mass consumption, has over-simplified the structure of British business. Traditional techniques of retailing remained central for many firms during a period which witnessed a large-scale expansion of their market share.

The varied dynamics of so-called mass consumption become even more apparent when they are read alongside the promotional imagery which was circulated in the menswear market. From the 1930s to the mid-1950s, selling techniques relied on one clearly identifiable icon. This was the image of the gentleman. The emblem dominated the advertising of the clothing multiples and also shaped the approach to customers on the shop floor. The gentleman represented the peculiarly negotiated discourse of modernity preferred by many British entrepreneurs. At Burton's he was a hybrid; a retailing compromise between traditional codes of social honour and more up-to-date, democratising influences. The gentlemanly conception of masculinity was formal and fixed. The ideal was of full adult manhood, indeterminate in age, but secure in position. In press advertising and pattern books, Burton's gentleman appeared in a variety of milieux — about town, as well as on the way to the office — but his standard pose was always upright, if not stiff. He was depicted either solo or in dialogue with other men, linked by the bonds of a shared masculine culture. In manners and self-presentation this was a decidedly English world-view. It was taken as given that the gentleman always appeared correctly dressed, for clothes were a public sign of social esteem.

Burton's gentlemanly type was in part the legacy of nineteenth-century languages of class. Clothes as an expression of status, manners as visible markers of distinction, these rituals were grounded in a vertical model of class relations. After 1945 there was a more democratic tinge to the marketing of men's clothes. Burton's gentleman was now projected as a variant of 'John Citizen'. Depicted serving in the armed forces, or against the municipal landscape of the town hall, he was quite literally 'everyman', demanding clothes for his particular role in life.[18] In menswear at least the coming of mass retailing drew on forms of aristocratic symbolism, reworking them for a general public. Historians investigating commodity culture in West Germany and Italy during the same period have identified similar compromise patterns of commercial modernisation.[19] They point to the fact that the so-called paths to mass consumption were plural and diverse and that the pace of transformation was often extremely uneven. There was no single model of change.

The Americanisation Thesis

Arguments surrounding the advent of modern consumer society in Britain have revolved not only around blueprints of economic development, but also around an even more grandiose thesis. This has charted the impact of American business methods and their related forms of commercial culture. Variants of the so-called 'Americanisation thesis' exercised a paradigmatic function for entrepreneurs, as well as for intellectual critics of commercial culture, for much of the 1950s and 1960s. The United States introduced many of the major technological innovations associated with the mass market in goods and was also cast as the centre of diffusion for some typically modern consumer products. In the aftermath of the Second World War almost all of Western Europe took American mass society as a major point of reference — either to provide a positive vision of the future, or against which to define alternatives. By the mid-1950s in Britain these debates revolved around one specific medium — the power of advertising.

In the Spring of 1956 Lt. Colonel Alan Wilkinson led the British delegation to the '4As' advertising convention held in Sulphur Springs, West Virginia. A doyen of the profession and an ex-president of the Institute of Practitioners in Advertising (IPA), Wilkinson made frequent trips to the United States. He was continually impressed with the 'powerful and all-pervading influence of advertising on the American scene'.[20] During his visit he noted how every American, from President Eisenhower down, was advertising-conscious. The industry had helped to shape the American national character and had made a major contribution to the country's very high standard of living. Advertising was central to the American vision of the future, Wilkinson continued, encouraging an immense vitality and a dynamic urge 'to go forward — to improve — to extend and enlarge'.[21] No visitor could help but benefit from a fortnight in the company of the United States' advertising élite. Wilkinson's advice to British colleagues was that they should visit the USA as soon as possible, and that they should visit it often.

Wilkinson's panegyric was a characteristic expression of British advertising professionals' pro-American stance during the post-war period. More often than not such sentiments were bound up with a positive commitment to the progressive forces of modernity, and especially to a secular ethic of material progress. In the years during and immediately after the war British advertisers weighed into the debate over economic and social reconstruction, offering their own vision of a dynamic future. Invariably, their language took its cue from American cultural symbolism. Countering socialist visions of the planned economy, the young agency man, Robert Brandon, believed that the post-war growth of British advertising, along similar lines to that experienced in North America between the wars, was critical for the economic modernisation of Britain.[22] Frank Bishop, assistant general manger of *The Times*, writing in *The Ethics of Advertising* (1949), looked forward to the expansion of the industry as part of a future utopia, in which for the first time in human history 'material needs may be adequately met for all mankind'.[23] Once again, Bishop's prototype for this revolution was the United States. In the 1950s, with the growing impact of psychological theories of consumer motivation, American advertising was endowed with an even greater power — to reshape human character. The most notorious of these interventions was made by the Austrian émigré, Ernest Dichter, who managed his own Institute for Motivational Research in New York and who believed that contemporary American advertising was leading the way in the progressive modernisation of human nature. Frequently, such arguments were shot through with a free-market defence of commercial techniques of persuasion, in the face of what Dichter himself claimed was the 'present historical struggle between free-enterprise and Communism'.[24] As Dichter saw it, the battle for American hegemony lay not in the field of missiles and the conquest of space, but in the conquest of the emotions of the people of the world.[25] Though Dichter's theories were never adopted in Britain, his emphasis on the political and psychological power of advertising frequently was.

The reverse of these optimistic visions of an American future were the periodic critiques of consumerism launched by British and other European intellectuals. Such assaults had already crystallised during the inter-war period, with the affirmation of distinctive traditions of Englishness in the face of the perceived invasion of American popular culture. They had been spearheaded by the intellectual forces of English literary criticism, represented by figures such as T.S. Eliot and Frank and Queenie Leavis. Denys Thompson, himself a member of the Leavisite Scrutiny movement, in his polemic against the excesses of press advertising, *Voice of Civilization* (1943), set the tone for post-war critiques of American commercialisation. Making a familiar ethical distinction between real and false needs, Thompson singled-out advertising for stimulating artificial wants and for creating illusion rather than providing information.[26] American-style advertising was in danger of replacing literature as the formative influence on British culture, Thompson argued. Paraphrasing D.H. Lawrence, he noted that the great mass of the population was now 'living according to the picture', rather than being guided by more sustained intellectual influences.[27] Reversing the arguments disseminated by the industry, Thompson concluded that so-called democratic advertising was dangerously close to the propaganda of the dictators.[28]

These essentially liberal critiques of advertising formed the mainstay of the counter-attack against consumerism throughout the 1950s and early 1960s. J.B. Priestley and Jacquetta Hawkes' travelogue to Texas and New Mexico, *Journey Down a Rainbow* (1955), exposed the 'American style of urban life'. For Priestley in particular, the United States was 'now the great invader' — the country which for most of Western Europe 'pays the piper and calls for most of the tunes'.[29] His famous characterisation of the American society of 'Admass' — 'my name for a whole system of increasing productivity, plus inflation, plus a rising standard of material living, plus high-pressure advertising and salesmanship, plus mass communications, plus cultural democracy and the creation of the mass mind' — resonated on both sides of the Atlantic. There was a working alliance between such critiques and blueprints for the reform of consumer culture emanating from the Labour Party in the 1950s, especially from its Fabian and Co-operative wings. Fabian proposals for a tax on advertising and measures for greater consumer protection, continued to weld together ethical and moral critiques of American-led consumption with attacks on the economics of waste.[30] It was this double set of arguments which provided the rationale for the new consumer-rights groups emerging from the mid-1950s.

British responses to American forms of modern consumerism should not simply be read as negative critiques. Placed alongside the enthusiastic commercial endorsements of material culture, they are best understood as part of an extended discourse on the dynamics of mass society — its systems of provision, its mobilisation of wants and the mechanisms for constituting social relations. In Britain, this discourse was usually given a national inflection; fixed as part of a commentary on the American way of life. The difficulty is that such cultural commentaries appear myopic when they are read against the actual business relations developing between Britain and the United States during the post-war period. Closer inspection of this dialogue points to an altogether more complex relationship between British and American understandings of consumer society. The history of British television advertising in the 1950s provides a striking case in point.

The arrival of commercial television in Britain, in September 1955, brought to a head an already heated debate among public intellectuals about the creeping effects of consumerism. Television advertising was viewed by its opponents as ushering in an American culture of mediocrity, hidden costs and sinister methods of persuasion. Anxieties were compounded by the aggressive expansion of American-owned multinational advertising agencies in Britain, via a series of acquisitions, mergers and take-overs.[31] Vance Packard's exposé of American selling methods in *The Hidden Persuaders* (1957) seemed to confirm existing apprehensions about the new commercial medium.

Yet as reviewers were quick to note, the first night of commercial television in England was a modicum of decorum and restraint. Scenes from the inaugural ceremony at London's Guildhall were followed by Sir John Barbirolli and the Hallé Orchestra playing Elgar's *Cockaigne* Overture.[32] There were speeches from Dr Charles Hill, the Postmaster-General, and from the quintessentially establishment figure of Sir Kenneth Clark. At 8p.m., the cameras visited Associated Broadcasting's own television theatre for variety, featuring established music hall and television personalities such as Reg Dixon, Billy Cotton and Elizabeth Allen. It was during this programme that viewers saw their first commercial. As the young Bernard Levin described it for the *Manchester Guardian*: 'A charming young lady brushed her teeth, while a charming young gentleman told us the benefits of the toothpaste with which she was doing it'.[33]

On the whole, British advertisers remained sceptical of techniques imported from New York's Madison Avenue, not on account of any cultural hostility, but for sound business reasons. John Hobson, founder of the influential John Hobson and Partners agency and later a President of the IPA, noted how the producers of early television commercials quickly grasped that British audiences demanded a style of advertisement which was not provided by the American 'hard-sell' model. Hobson observed that: 'American experience and examples were not altogether helpful ... the hammer blow commercials of [their] Agency men were not considered suitable for the British public, who, it was thought, would not welcome this degree of hard sell in their living rooms'.[34] This acknowledgment of cultural specificity — that markets could not be treated entirely as multinational entities — had already been taken up by the Conservative MP Ian Harvey in his free-market defence of advertising, *The Technique of Persuasion* (1951). Harvey observed that advertising was international only in principle and artistic form; national and local characteristics made it essential to vary the appeal and the methods in which the appeal was made.[35] According to the British agency, Crawford's, a company with a reputation for a stylish, art-directed approach in the 1950s, it was precisely the mismatch between American selling methods and the British character which drove domestic agencies to develop their own approach to commercial communications. Aggressive selling shifted goods for a time, Crawford's remarked, but ultimately such methods set up their own forms of resistance in the minds of many consumers. As Crawford's pontificated, this was because, to Europeans, American commercials lacked good taste.[36]

This emphasis on the distinctiveness of the UK market was upheld by many British businessmen who admired American commercial methods. Montague Burton travelled widely throughout North America in the immediate post-war years, assiduously noting the benefits delivered by modern consumer society.[37] But, as we have seen, his own firm retained selling techniques which were unlike American approaches. His successor at Burton's,

Lionel Jacobson, concluded in 1957 that American systems would not work easily in British markets.[38]

There is a further difficulty in portraying the international dimensions of British business during these years simply in terms of an Anglo-American dialogue. This is the continuing importance of the Commonwealth. Commonwealth markets accounted for the largest proportion of Britain's export trade until well into the 1960s. Such exports included not only key consumer durables, but also commercial forms of knowledge. It was British expertise which was instrumental in setting up the Australian television network in Sydney in 1957, while many of the leading British advertising agencies established bases in the white dominions.[39] The reverse of this dialogue was the image Australia and Canada occupied (quite as much as the United States) in the imagination of a generation of post-war working-class migrants, as lands of democratic plenty and consumer abundance.

What this story reveals is a more complex pattern of international business than American hegemony in world markets. Though the United States loomed large in the imagination of domestic entrepreneurs and cultural critics, the distinctiveness of the British economy and its forms of commercial culture, together with the continuing importance of imperial preference, were also stressed. In this context, the British advertising industry emerged as a new expert grouping, claiming not only the ability to read the dynamics of consumption, but also the psychological dimensions of national character.

Advertising and the Reflexive Self

Anthony Giddens, addressing the characteristics of late modernity, has identified a significant recent shift within western societies around the changing conception of identity. For Giddens this sea change has essentially involved a movement from the external projection of character, operating in the public world, to the idea of the self as constituted inside the personality with internal referents. The net effect of this process has been to produce social selfhood as a reflexively organised endeavour, which extends deep into the individual.[40] A key mechanism for connecting the self-reflexive individual to society has been the growing impact of styles of life, or lifestyles. Giddens' concept of lifestyles has been more broadly conceived than its understanding by the post-war consumer professionals; it has embraced all those spheres of everyday life in which individual appraisal has displaced more external rules of authority. This idea of the reflexive self is important for understanding how the expansion of commercial advertising in the 1950s was driven by a modernising project, whose ultimate aim was the reshaping of human character.

Institutionally, British advertising grew rapidly in the early 1950s. But professional discussion about its importance had preceded the expansion of the industry by more than a decade. Emerging out of political economy, this earlier debate had produced a cultural reading of economic life which was dedicated to a new form of governing and imagining the self. Unlike the expanding theories of maternalism, child welfare and social deviance, the classic terrain for this development was not the state but commercial society.

Economic theorists, such as Pigou and Marshall, had denounced advertising as a misuse of productive resources, because it introduced an added burden of hidden costs for manufacturers and consumers alike.[41] But during the 1930s and early 1940s, a new breed of economic commentators, influenced by theories of imperfect or monopolistic competition, focused on the advantages to be gained from extraneous interventions into the market. Advertising's role in stimulating demand for consumption goods, in regularising output and flattening the booms and slumps of the trade cycle, thereby contributing to a general lowering of prices and an increase in quality, were among the standard themes announced by the new apologists for promotional culture. The majority of these writers were influenced by Keynesian critiques of the deficiencies of demand and its effects on the real economy during the inter-war years.[42]

The point about these economic commentaries was that they pointed inexorably to issues which classical economics could not or would not answer. Almost imperceptibly, they moved into the domain of culture and psychology. As Bishop saw it in 1944, the products of one manufacturer were never quite the same as those of another.[43] Variations in taste and subjective preference drew the consumer into complicated decisions of discrimination and choice. Such an acknowledgment led to an even more significant point which implicitly refuted one of the basic tenets of economic theory. It appeared that where consumption was concerned the concept of *homo economicus* — rational, calculating and always perfectly informed — was far from true.[44] Consumers were usually equipped with imperfect knowledge of the market-place and were easily influenced and persuaded. Writing at the height of the Labour government's austerity programme, the young economist Edward Laver concluded in 1947 that, even for those on small incomes, 'biological necessities' (such as food, clothing and shelter) accounted for only a portion of their incomes. With the rest consumers invariably sought to buy 'psychological satisfaction' and to express their personalities.[45] From an economic standpoint advertising could be seen to create utility by 'moving and arranging minds'.[46]

It was this questioning of some of the basic tenets of economic theory which opened the space for an expanded reading of consumer behaviour. In the marketing discourse of the 1950s the consumer emerged as a highly complex entity, by no means the passive tool of the advertisers.[47] Consumers needed to be mobilised, their tastes and desires mapped and future wants predicted. Here psychological theories loomed large. In 1958, British advertising and marketing came out strongly critical of the excesses of the American methods of subliminal advertising, on the grounds both of their suspected ineffectiveness and their immorality.[48] But this injunction did not involve any wholesale jettisoning of a psychology of consumer behaviour. Advertising and marketing in the late 1950s were a promiscuous mixture of expert knowledge derived from sociology, literary criticism, psychoanalysis and the burgeoning field of market research.

Hobson's own company was at the forefront of efforts to match advertising's message to the social transformations which he believed had been set in train by the post-war upsurge in demand. Hobson himself was a gentleman-player in the industry. A Cambridge English graduate, he was fully aware of the aesthetic potential of advertising. His influential text, *The Selection of Advertising Media*, first published in 1955, acknowledged that the profession was 'still an inexact science'. Hobson believed that, in addition to a battery of quantifiable data on markets and audiences, agencies also needed much 'more complete knowledge on the workings of the mind and the emotions'.[49] The critical element here was what he termed the 'atmosphere' of the message. Atmosphere essentially involved subjective indicators, involving the mood of consumers and their emotional response to products. While other features could be measured, 'atmosphere' demanded a more 'intuitive and perceptive' approach. Such arguments opened the space for an enhanced role for creative artists, especially copy-writers and art directors, within commercial processes.[50]

Attempts to read the psychology of consumers were given a more comprehensive and scientific gloss in the pioneering work of 'motivation research'. This was a characteristically British response to the excesses of American consumer psychology as represented by figures such as Dichter. Rather than pronouncing on the cultural future, motivation researchers insisted that their aims were much more prosaic: to supplement the knowl-edge of the manufacturer and the advertiser in their task of selling goods. According to Harry Henry, research director of McCann Erickson's European arm and a pioneer of motivational techniques in Britain, this approach was not an attempt to dupe the consumer, but to understand more fully the 'why' of consumer choice. Like Hobson, Henry was a char-acteristically hybrid intellectual. A pre-war graduate of the London School of Economics, he had served Montgomery during the war as a Statistical Staff Officer. Responsible for the Hulton Readership surveys from 1947 to 1953, he entered commercial market research in 1954. Henry was keen to emphasise that his methods did not champion one single social philosophy. Eclectic in form, they borrowed from clinical psychology and the other social sciences, as well as from behaviourism.[51] Such techniques — which might include group discussions, in-depth interviews, as well as more specific tests to measure the personality — were especially important for gauging the impact of branded products, where the image or the person-ality of the commodity was all-important. Henry believed that the impact of television advertising was creating a situation in which image rather than reality was critical to purchasing choice.[52]

A spate of celebrated television and press campaigns, for commodities as diverse as cars, cigarettes, food products and lager beers, testified to the impact of the new formula. Running through them were the three themes which dominated commercial advertising in the late 1950s and early 1960s. These were the triple utopias of modernity, sex and status, expressed through an expanded conception of the personality of key groups of consumers. Advertisements designed by the London Press Exchange for cars and motor fuels were characteristic early examples of this genre. Their

'Katie and the Cube', J. Walter Thompson television advertising for Oxo Ltd., 1958

Strand cigarette print advertising, London Press Exchange for W.D. and H.O. Wills, 1960

1963 account, 'Getaway People', for National Benzole, carried the message of 'petrol for the with-it people', the 'people who did good things'.[53] While their vision of the new Ford Anglia car, produced in the same year, was anchored by the caption 'Beauty with Long Legs', accompanied by an image of a veiled and aloof woman, with bare midriff. A different language of modernisation, which was driven by changing patterns of class and family life, was evident in J. Walter Thompson's long-running narrative about 'Katie and the Cube' for Oxo Ltd. Beginning in 1958, the agency told an ongoing tale about the domestic adventures of a young modern house-wife and her husband Philip — individuals on the lower rungs of the executive ladder, who were decidedly 'semi-detached people'.[54] While each of these campaigns was different, what characterised all of them were their efforts to suggest associations between modern people, commodities and a distinctive quality or style of life.

Among Hobson's contribution to this genre were two commercials addressed to younger men. His company's acquisition of Ind Coope's Double Diamond pale ale account from the London Press Exchange in 1963 involved an upgrading of the product. The traditional format of beer advertising (what was dubbed the masculinity of the saloon bar) was displaced by more modern codes of manliness. 'Double Diamond — the Beer the Men Drink', pictured men in a world of 'affluence and jet-age leisure': surfing, parachuting, water-skiing and mountaineering.[55] A different variation on contemporary masculinity was adopted in the agency's Strand cigarette advertising for W.D. and H.O. Wills which appeared three years earlier. Here, the individuality of the 'youth generation' was captured by an atmosphere of 'loneliness'. What John May, a member of Hobson's team, who coined the successful slogan 'You're never alone with a Strand', suggested was a 'hyperconsciousness', an 'entirely independent way of living' among the young.[56] Drawing on the 'loner' theme pioneered by Hollywood cult figures such as Marlon Brando and James Dean, the actor in these cigarette commercials was shot in a variety of states of solitude. In one Strand advert he was filmed leaning against the wall of London's Chelsea Embankment, in another standing on a deserted Brighton beach. In both cases the settings reinforced what May termed a symbolic style of independence.

Atmospheric advertisements of this type reflected the soundings taken by market researchers about the shifts in post-war consumption patterns. Here we confront the wider cultural factors which were shaping the advertising industry's modernising project. Hobson's own musings on the marketing criteria used to analyse social class were informative in this respect. Acknowledging that the conventional five status gradations, A to E, remained a touchstone for the industry, he nevertheless insisted that class categories were in urgent need of revision. Hobson was emphatic that class now needed to be understood not simply as an economic indicator, but as a cultural variable, involving ways of life or 'lifestyles'.[57] Moreover, markets and consumer preferences were complicated by the emergence of what he termed 'special-interest groups', defined by age or by leadership position within the community. Hobson's point was reinforced in a report issued by the Market Research Society's working party in 1963, which concluded that growing professional confusion about the issue of class was also the result of its ever-expanding reference points within the social sciences.[58] Such findings paralleled the work of New Left thinkers like Raymond Williams and Edward Thompson on the cultural ramifications of class. But these commercial pronouncements probably had a closer affinity with liberal sociology and social democratic politics on both sides of the Atlantic. David Riesman's writing on the contradictions between forms of the 'outer directed' as opposed to the 'inner directed' self, Daniel Bell's fascination with an economy which had produced display as a critical marker of personal esteem, and Tony Crosland's efforts to reshape the culture and psychology of the British Labour Party in line with post-war affluence — taken together these projects marked attempts to confront the new relationship between culture and commerce.[59] In all of them an expanded sense of personal selfhood was acknowledged as a necessary part of the future.

Conclusion

This movement towards an enhanced role for individuality under the conditions of post-war demand was not the result of some smooth meta-logic of the late modern epoch. It was dependent on much more specific strategies. It is here that we return to the problems of over-generality attendant on many of the accounts of consumption and modernity with which we began. The management of post-war affluence was formed at the intersection of a number of commercial and intellectual systems of entrepreneurship. In Britain, as in the United States, this process was characterised by the growth of knowledge and expertise dedicated to understanding the modern consumer economy. Conducted on the terrain of commercial society rather than through the state, this process was humanised and psychologised by the figure of the consumer, who represented an expanding bundle of motivations and aspirations. But British advertisers and retailers were characteristically eclectic and pluralist in their epistemologies. Their acknowledgment of national markets and psychology, as well as the international dimensions of trade, makes any simple appeal to the Americanisation of British economic or cultural life during the 1950s appear misplaced. Moreover, our excursion into the organisation of the clothing sector revealed how much the process of modernisation was piecemeal and *ad hoc*. Methods for producing and circulating key consumer goods, together with their attendant cultural symbolism, rested as much on traditional technologies as on any coherent blueprint for the future. The paths to mass consumption need to be rethought in the light of these particularities.

We might do well to return to Keynes' own speculations about the dynamics of the modern economy. As Keynes was well aware, 'demand management' (the term favoured by his own disciples, the post-war politicians and policy makers) was much more than a process of macro-economic regulation. Essentially, it involved the construction of a set of programmes for orchestrating the fields of economics and culture. This is an ensemble which could provisionally be classified as the commercial domain. Less systematised than the traditional public sphere of government and social administration, it focused on the management of persons and families and, crucially, on the cultivation of the secular self. British liberal intellectual traditions and social democratic politics in the mid-twentieth century were reformulated in a forced dialogue with this commercial project. It represents a modernising impulse in which economics, culture and conceptions of the human personality were deeply intertwined.

4. Towards a Modern Labour Market? State Policy and the Transformation of Employment

Noel Whiteside

A case for the establishment of a modern labour market can easily be made for the post-1945 era. The late 1940s witnessed the emergence of the managed economy, endowing government with powers to regulate levels of economic activity, to stimulate growth, to generate prosperity and full employment — banishing the mass unemployment, job insecurity and poverty which had characterised the inter-war years. Economists and new forms of macro-economic expertise colonised the heart of the policy-making process, setting an agenda for post-war reconstruction, identifying specific, objectively measured criteria for analysis. The success of wartime controls and the subsequent adaptation of Keynesian theories legitimated state interventions to counteract market failure. The achievements of this new economics signified a benchmark on the road to human progress; unemployment became considered obsolete. The assessments on which new strategies were based thus transferred labour markets and their performance from the private to the public sphere, requiring their integration into an economic construction of the national interest. Furthermore, state guarantees of full employment were supplemented by an universalised system of state welfare, based on the 1942 Beveridge Report. Welfare legislation constructed the parameters of a national labour market, shaped according to gender and age; the employment contract became established as a legal foundation for individual social rights.[1] In this way, labour market status joined family structure within legislation which formally defined obligations to social support.

The definition of a modern labour market rests on an assumed uniformity in the nature of employment, combined with universal rights for all workers — to social insurance benefits when sick or out of work, to a decent pension at the end of a working life (retirement age was legally specified for the first time in 1946) and to paid holidays. In addition, workers had the right to negotiate collectively the terms and conditions of their employment. The modern labour market was founded on full employment and the rationalisation of all types of work into a five- or six-day working week throughout the year in all sectors, from coal mining to the welfare services. It aimed to reconcile two, possibly conflicting, objectives: that waged work should be the basis for securing an acceptable standard of life and that all productive potential should be utilised to full capacity, promoting collective prosperity. Rationalisation of work practices into full working weeks served both of these aims, by reducing uncertainties and variation in earnings and by apparently guaranteeing the deployment of labour resources in the most economically efficient manner. Growing acceptance of Keynesian theories, together with the post-war Labour government's preference for a state-managed economy, permitted labour market modernisation to be inserted — albeit implicitly — into official programmes of post-war reform. As government influence within the economy was radically enlarged during the post-war years, through the extensions of social welfare and nationalisation as well as through new strategies of economic management, state regulation became a major force for encouraging labour market modernisation. In so doing, government came to confront working patterns and practices — established by specific market conditions, by tradition or by negotiated industrial agreement — which recognised considerably greater variation in the nature and conditions of work than was implied by these new norms.

Accounts describing the triumph of strategies to secure uniform labour markets, within new structures of employment and social protection, only depict one side of a more complex picture. Both the emergency of war and the problems of post-war reconstruction positioned work practices directly under official gaze. Shortages of materials and manpower and the exigencies of the post-war export drive placed the British productive machine under unprecedented strain. Debates about full employment reached beyond issues of job security and social welfare; labour markets became central to macro-economic concerns over industrial performance. The genesis of more elaborate statistics legitimised state scrutiny of how manpower was to be deployed and utilised. Manpower budgets had permitted the rational use of labour resources during the war and offered the prospect of more sophisticated manpower policies after it. Post-war shortages encouraged a focus on the new question of productivity; this permitted criticisms of previously agreed work relations and working practices. Taken together, such policies marked an invasion of the hitherto private realm of employment which, while seen as broadly acceptable during the war emergency, provoked conflict and dissent once peace was restored. The new approach was strongly associated with the promotion of productive rationalisation, the advocacy of mass production techniques and American manufacturing systems characteristic of the post-war period. In this extension of the role of the state, similarities can also be observed with reform debates of the Edwardian era, which had aimed to secure industrial efficiency through a politics of decasualisation and the abolition of 'sweating', also involving the ideas of — the much younger — William Beveridge.[2] As in the Edwardian years, labour markets and their apparent deficiencies became an object of public and professional scrutiny.

By the 1940s, legitimate state intervention in the economy had undergone a dramatic change. The successful implementation of this economic programme of modernisation, however, demanded the acceptance by established interests (employers, workers, financial institutions) of the theoretical terms within which objectives were now being discussed — namely the internalisation of macro-economic modes of labour market analysis and co-operation in the achievement of these new common objectives. For this to happen, existing diversities in labour management, in economic co-ordination, in working conventions and agreements had to be brought to conform with the expectations established under new political and economic orthodoxies. To explore the creation of a modern labour market, it is thus necessary to examine the role of the state as a proponent of economic and social modernity — not only in terms of policy development (the historian's usual preoccupation), but in terms of the acceptability of official interventions and their success. Modernity could only succeed if its frames of reference were universally internalised, securing change in employment practices and the legitimation of external intervention shaping such changes.

The attempted translation of official economic strategies into new labour market practices forms the subject of this chapter. Here, the reality of a modern labour market becomes contestable. Four areas of employment in both the industrial and service sectors of the economy were each subject to varying degrees of state regulation after the war: the cotton industry, the docks, the coal industry and the National Health Service. All were officially considered central to Britain's recovery and all were subject to efforts to rationalise employment. Retrospective illusions of homogeneity in the post-war labour market are the product of macro-economic analysis: illusions reinforced by official statistics, themselves based on categories which form an integral part of the institutions of macro-economic policy. Such measurements do not necessarily signify a transformation in labour markets, merely a transformation in the way governments wished to understand and analyse their operation.

If this analysis is correct, the belief that the state could ensure full employment and manage labour markets as part of its agenda of post-war modernisation must be seen as a socio-political construct, specific to this historical period. In the context of chronic and continuing post-war labour shortages, full employment and managed labour markets became entangled with the broader aim of securing maximum output from limited manpower resources. The post-war labour market must be examined in its broadest context, within the social, industrial and political ideologies that gave full employment its meaning. For the clash between state, industry and labour over issues of modernisation exposed the limits of state authority and the orthodoxies it promoted. This proved to be an invisible limit to economic modernisation in Britain, beyond which the state's writ could not run. The construction of new forms of social knowledge — and the creation of new agencies to promote them — ran up against established and accepted systems of labour management, which were resistant to external intervention. The determination of working practices through collective bargaining in heavy industry dated from the nineteenth century and was the legacy of early industrialisation. Collective bargaining by trade offered a paradigm for labour regulation in all sectors and the post-war union movement, with the co-operation of the Labour government, wished to secure its survival in established strongholds and its extension into new worlds of employment. Subsequent conflicts over labour market modernisation came to reflect not only disagreements over working practices, but also disputes over who had the authority to determine them. As a result, the remit of manpower policies became the site of politicised conflict.[3]

Transforming Employment in Mid-Twentieth-Century Britain

Compared to the United States and Germany, British manufacturing firms in the mid-twentieth century were small, under-capitalised and highly reliant on workforce skills in the manufacture of high-quality products for export. The appearance of bigger firms in the inter-war years involved the transfer of financial control over small units, but this did not generate rationalisation or modernisation of production as such. Fordist systems of manufacture and employment were not common and their introduction remained controversial. British industry, unlike American industry, did not rely on a domestic mass market for its products and needed the flexibility to respond to varied orders from overseas. Industrial structures and distinct export markets together shaped the different conventions of employment characterising specific industries, regions and products. Employment was far from uniform; norms, expectations and working practices varied widely.

Different branches of industry developed specific strategies to meet fluctuations in demand. In some trades, unemployment — experienced as gaps between jobs — was endemic. Ship-building and repair, construction, the docks — all traditionally paid above average wages to compensate for idle time. Other industries (clothing, furniture, local government services, cars, bicycles) fluctuated according to season as well as the state of trade. Here, extensive subcontracting allowed manufacturers to externalise the risk consequent on changing demand, blurring distinctions between employer, employee and the self-employed. In coal, cotton and textile engineering, employers shared work among their skilled operatives when trade was slack; short-time working allowed the services of workers essential to business to be retained, pending a revival. During the inter-war slump, employers in coal, textiles, iron and steel and oil refining, among other trades, formed trade associations which met the crisis by fixing prices, apportioning output and sharing markets between member firms, thereby preventing cut-throat competition driving some out of business altogether. This strategy received government support in the form of tariff protection and — in the case of coal mining and cotton textiles — legislation to encourage these industries to close the least efficient pits and mills, thus removing excess capacity. This failed to have the desired effect; small, low productivity units survived — an illustration of the ability of industrialists to bend policy to serve their own ends.

During the inter-war recession diversities in labour management meant that the workforce did not divide into two discreet categories — the 'employed' and 'unemployed' — even though official statistics suggested otherwise. Under-employment and short-time working muddied any clear-cut distinctions.[4] High levels of unemployment stimulated diverse responses; the strategy of each industrial sector reflected traditional responses to the threat of slack trade. Wherever possible trade unions protected their members against redundancy by negotiating manning levels, job demarcation and working practices to protect the livelihoods of the maximum possible number of workers.

The consequences of inter-war unemployment did not vanish with the advent of war. Labour surplus transformed into labour shortage, but established trade practices were only suspended on the understanding that they would be restored when hostilities ceased. After the First World War, the shortlived boom had deteriorated into prolonged recession. After 1945, many trade unionists remained wary of official promises to sustain full employment. They preferred to use industrial muscle when required to reinforce manning levels, job demarcation agreements, apprenticeship numbers and to safeguard the legitimacy of formal collective bargaining and shop-floor regulation in shaping the world of work. Industrial labour's support for full employment thus translated principally into demands for job security. This did not necessarily involve any rationalisation of working arrangements; questions involving the deployment of labour within firms remained the province of collective bargaining, immune from external interference.

Much has been written in recent years about the failure of post-war reconstruction in the context of Britain's long-term economic decline. The post-war Labour government has been criticised for preferring investment in welfare and defence to the desperately needed reconstruction of British industry, as well as for allowing short-term economic interests — specifically the maintenance of full employment and the protection of union rates of pay — to outweigh longer term needs in the field of industrial policy.[5] Economic post-war constraints on policy restricted the programmes of reconstruction and modernisation promoted by the Labour government.[6] Shortages of men and materials focused official attention on the low productivity of British industry, when contrasted with its American counterparts. Post-war dollar shortages constrained the import of sorely needed raw materials, particularly steel. Hence the goal of higher productivity, central to official economic strategy, sought to get more output from old plant. This focused attention on work practices. Growth was to be promoted through industrial reorganisation and the rationalisation of manpower, requiring industry to abandon established working conventions and agreements.

During the 1940s, government intervention into industry was unprecedented. Government became the chief purchaser (and distributor) of essential raw materials and foodstuffs, the chief customer for war goods of all types, regulator of industrial disputes, director of manpower through Essential Work Orders (which gave the workers involved a guaranteed weekly wage). It also established the Joint Production Committees in engineering and munitions and oversaw the extension of national collective bargaining.[7] After the war, the promised restoration of pre-war practices was progressively delayed while the Attlee government actively pursued a policy of industrial modernisation. The Board of Trade set up official working parties to report on modernisation strategies for specific industries. Following the introduction of the European Recovery Programme and Marshall Aid, the Anglo-American Council on Productivity (AACP) funded visits by both sides of British industry to the United States, in order to raise awareness of advanced manufacturing methods and hence to make the British economy more competitive. Numerous official reports offered endless critiques of established production systems and labour management practices. The American economy offered a template of modernity, particularly in its systems of standardised mass production in key industries. Government declared that the newly nationalised sector would serve as an example to private industry, demonstrating how Britain could adopt new management methods to boost productivity.[8]

The impact of these initiatives was, however, strictly limited. As the AACP noted, British workers worked as long and as hard as their American counterparts, but continued to produce much less. Moves to rationalise production were not always well received on the shop floor. Fears of a return of the inter-war recession (when state-sponsored rationalisation had spelt price cutting and speed-up for some and redundancy for others) helped fuel suspicion. The TUC supported the Labour government loyally, but had little hold over rank-and-file members. In the context of labour shortages, which continued throughout this period, a combination of poor labour management, inefficient layout of plant and the ready availability of alternative work impeded progress and raised levels of labour turnover — a development which was not conducive to higher productivity. While resistance to TUC directives has recently been attributed to the politicisation of the shop stewards (particularly in engineering), it appears likely that rising militancy stemmed from a variety of factors — the potential transfer of authority in determining work practices being prominent among them.[9]

Private employers resisted official intervention in all forms, interpreting this as an initial step on the road to nationalisation and direct state control. The immediate post-war years witnessed buoyant demand for British exports. This made it hard for employers to identify excess capacity and — being cash rich — it also rendered them relatively immune to government blandishments to close defunct plant, which took the form of grants to promote industrial restructuring. The large number of small family firms which were directly threatened by policies designed to promote amalgamation and mass production, argued that the government had no right to direct the management of private business. While advice in the shape of working party reports was acceptable, direct worker involvement in management — through joint production committees — was not. The proposed introduction of development councils to rationalise key industrial sectors was vehemently opposed by those trade associations which had fought during the previous decade to protect small business, not to oversee its destruction.

Industrial cartels, such as the trade associations, came under direct attack in 1948 and 1956 when anti-monopoly laws reached the statute book. This legislation was designed to promote competition and to destroy those protective agreements, negotiated within associations, which guaranteed prices and market share for all members. Trade associations helped protect small business from official policies designed to secure rationalisation into larger productive units; their removal was not politically feasible. Government relied on trade associations to enforce production standards and price controls as well as to co-ordinate marketing, all vital in the immediate post-war years when raw materials were in short supply. Hence legislation to destroy cartels protecting 'backward' firms had limited effect.[10] Although American policy (in trust-busting tradition) aimed to eradicate such constraints on trade, British and other European governments pursued this goal with minimal enthusiasm. In Britain some associations and federations transformed themselves into amalgamations — concentrating financial control and externalising government interference, without necessarily rationalising productive capacity. While the press was arguing by the mid-1950s that workers' restrictive practices were to blame for low productivity and Britain's comparatively slow rates of growth, surveys of industrial employers found little agreement about whether working methods constrained output and still less about how a restrictive practice might be identified.[11] The AACP — in so far as it commented on issues considered properly the province of collective bargaining — found restrictive practices among industrial employers much more alarming than those prevalent on the shop floor.[12] Industrial complacency (for want of a better term) combined with strategic decisions to constrain the introduction of American methods in the private sector of British industry. With limited Americanisation and standardisation, can we argue that Fordist modes of employment were ever prevalent? Did the state have greater success in promoting rationalised forms of employment in the quasi-public and nationalised sectors of the post-war economy?

The Cotton Industry and Post-War Modernisation

Cotton textiles, one the oldest industrial sectors, was among the Labour government's chief candidates for modernisation and was initially endowed with a central role in Britain's post-war economic reconstruction. The inter-war years, a period of prolonged decline, had already witnessed a number of official attempts to eliminate excess capacity and modernise the industry. The *Clynes Report* of 1930 had recommended extensive rationalisation in the spinning section. These recommendations had been implemented at the depth of the slump, provoking strikes and disruption. Progress was limited, not least because the new initiative coincided with the collapse of world markets. Thereafter, local cartels had guaranteed that the pain of recession was spread fairly evenly. It was only at the outbreak of war, with the establishment of the Cotton Control Board in 1939, that 200 of the 450-odd spinning mills closed for the duration of hostilities — with employers compensated and the labour force directed elsewhere. By 1943-4, when 'deconcentration' was under discussion, the Cotton Board, ignoring the demands of the United Textile Factory Workers Association for the nationalisation of the industry, presented post-war plans to elimi-nate excess capacity in weaving and finishing.[13] The post-war Working Party on the Cotton Industry followed this up with extensive recommen-dations for the amalgamation of firms, the establishment of a central marketing company, the introduction of double-shift working and the replacement of antiquated machinery with modern plant, imported from Germany and Japan as part of enemy war reparations.[14] Stafford Cripps, as President of the Board of Trade, reinforced this initiative in 1947 by offering £15 million in grants to amalgamations of spinning firms willing to rationalise their holdings.[15]

Although employers in the industry conceded the foundation of a Development Council, there was no rush to take up the minister's offer.[16] The industry was working flat out to meet existing orders and employers looked askance at any proposal to eliminate less productive plant. In these circumstances, excess capacity was hard to identify; mill owners contended that the diverse demand from overseas markets made rationalisation a distinctly risky strategy. Furthermore, the cotton unions generally argued that changes in established working arrangements were conditional on re-equipment. The problem was not union obstinacy, but the different circumstances of the cotton towns. The industry had persistent recruitment problems after the war.[17] It had inherited a reputation for low earnings from the inter-war years, when short-time working had been virtually endemic, and now more attractive work opportunities existed elsewhere. Married women formed a large proportion of a workforce accustomed to arrang-ing reduced working hours around domestic obligations; they had little incentive to conform to the full working week required by rising post-war demand. Production issues thus focused on a newly identified problem of absenteeism, which was essentially the consequence of changes in the industry's requirements, not changes in workers' behaviour. Both the unions and Board of Trade officials agreed that if married women's conditions of work were altered they would leave the industry altogether. Most of their husbands had returned from the armed forces to well-paid jobs; the pressure on these women to earn wages was less than the pressure to queue for rations at the shops. A survey in 1949 showed absenteeism in the mills standing at around 10 per cent; it was worst among married women, who explained their absences in terms of childcare problems and their desire for more leisure, not for extra cash to purchase consumer goods, which were, in any case, in short supply.[18]

Collective industrial opposition undermined the hoped-for revival of the cotton textile industry. Continuing absenteeism and labour shortages on the shop floor reflected a preference for older forms of work practice. The disappearance of mass unemployment encouraged established assumptions about gendered divisions between waged and unwaged work. Traditionally, married women worked in Lancashire's cotton textile industry because they had to, to make ends meet. After the war, additional working hours on top of the burdens of domestic responsibilities made waged work infinitely resistible, especially while post-war rationing prevented extra earnings being transformed into higher living standards. Furthermore, local employers remained determined that the family firm should retain its autonomy and resisted attempts to rationalise industrial structures. Hence productivity failed to rise.

Dock Decasualisation[19]

Casual dock work had long been considered problematic — by philanthropists, by government, by trade-union organisers — because of its close associations with pauperism and commercial inefficiency. The labour market reforms of the Edwardian era had sought to rationalise port work and to promote decasualisation. However, inter-war underemployment on the docks remained notorious; fringe casual dockers were hired for as little as a half-day and the impact of falling overseas trade was made more acute by the invasion of the general unemployed on to the docks, in search of a few hours' work. To counteract this, the dockers' union, the Transport and General Workers' Union (T&GWU), had long promoted a scheme to register all dock workers and to introduce a minimum weekly wage, conditional on regular attendance for work, funded by the industry. By 1942, Bevin, the erstwhile dockers' leader, had introduced registration and a guaranteed weekly wage under an Essential Work Order. Local joint boards administered the scheme and acted as the employer of last resort for all dockers. This system was extended into the post-war era when the National Dock Labour Board (NDLB) was set up in 1947. The legislation was viewed at the time as a triumph for the dockers' union, winning their members job security and a minimum weekly wage. Employers were forbidden to employ outsiders; they funded the guaranteed week and had to share with the union issues of recruitment, dismissal and all disciplinary matters. An efficient port transport industry was widely considered a vital element in economic reconstruction, and the reform of port labour management was essential to achieving that goal.

From the start, however, port employers opposed the scheme, while subsequent events demonstrated that new, tighter labour management also stimulated resentment among dockers themselves. In the immediate post-war years the docks were the site of extensive industrial militancy — much of it unofficial in nature — as dockers fought off the stricter labour discipline implied by the new regulations. Attempts to rationalise employment into 'regular' working weeks failed. As recruitment to the registers was frozen, fluctuations in labour demand meant that men were forced to work compulsory overtime, or were pushed into working in unfamiliar sectors of port work for lower rates of pay. While some new investment had been made on dock facilities during the war — to cope with convoys and the war emergency — the virtual closure of some ports, in the wake of the blitz, meant that new pressure was brought to bear on antiquated facilities and an ageing workforce in the post-war period. As the T&GWU formed part of the new management, unofficial port workers' committees sprang up to organise protest. The press, the official trade union, together with the Ministry of Labour, joined in condemning resistance, depicting the leaders of such actions as Communist-inspired traitors and their followers as dupes.

Faced with disruption and eager to regain control over their men, employers in major ports like London began recruiting permanent dockers and demanding compensatory cuts in the casual register. Numerous official enquiries in the 1950s and into the following decade agreed that this strategy offered a cure for the disease of casualism, while dockers protested against the extension of permanent employment in this way. By the early 1960s an unofficial Dockers' Charter was seeking to safeguard the size of casual port labour registers. Even so, the Devlin Committee in 1967 recommended that all dockers be assigned to one employer as permanent workers — a recommendation implemented amid further strikes and disruption in the following decade.

In the interim, absenteeism remained high (14 per cent in London in 1945) and productivity was problematic. In order to overcome rank-and-file hostility, employers found that invoking new labour disciplinary procedures caused more trouble than it was worth. They therefore reverted to traditional ways of improving productivity, through higher bonus payments and danger money. As elsewhere, such strategies caused labour costs to rise and this undermined productivity gains in the industry, while further discouraging the incentive to regular work. High payments proved popular; casualism and irregular working patterns survived intact — protected by rank-and-file interest to secure gains on a seller's market. As a Ministry of Labour official commented in 1951, the scheme was 'a pretence at organisation which is really no organisation at all'.[20]

Nationalisation and the Coal Industry

Like the cotton industry, chronic excess capacity in the inter-war coal mines had produced both cartelisation and the extensive use of short-time working among miners. The 1930 Coal Mines (Reorganisation) Act reinforced the move to cartels through the creation of regional boards to rationalise the industry, closing down inefficient pits, apportioning output and fixing prices among the remainder. In the event, while securing the final objective, no progress was made on the former and the industry entered the Second World War with a long tail of unproductive pits still in operation and with worksharing commonplace.[21] Further, investment in the industry in the 1930s had been minimal — lower than during the previous decade. Even the most modern pits needed more extensive mechanisation.

As on the docks, a wartime Essential Work Order gave the miners a minimum weekly wage and 'ring-fenced' employment in the industry. This constraint was not removed until 1950. In the face of much resistance from the coal owners, the wartime Coal Production Council and the pit production committees (both including union representatives) determined to concentrate production. Following its creation in 1947, the National Coal Board (NCB) continued this drive to rationalisation; planning for coal entailed determining output, wage scales and manning levels.[22] During the 1940s and the 1950s the demand for coal soared. Throughout this period, the industry experienced acute problems meeting its production targets.

The main focus for official concern was absenteeism, which rose from 6.4 per cent in 1938 to 10 per cent in 1941, rising to over 15 per cent after the war.[23] It was highest among unmarried faceworkers and underground workers: particularly among the 'Bevin boys' — conscripts sent down the pits between 1943 and 1947 who were impervious to any incentive to work regularly or hard. The industry's poor reputation as an employer generated recruitment problems in the post-war years. Those running the industry agreed that dismissals for poor attendance only made the manpower problem worse. In the context of recurring coal crises — in 1947 and 1951 — the mines became a focal point for official and unofficial enquiry to determine the cause of the problem and to effect a cure.[24]

The causes of absenteeism were various. As on the docks, traditional methods of raising production invoked higher piecework rates; young fit faceworkers preferred to clear a huge load in one shift and subsequently take time off, rather than work a regular week. The income tax levels on single men undermined the incentive of extra earnings and raised the attraction of doing odd jobs away from the pits for 'cash in hand'. The introduction of a bonus shift payment in 1948, in return for regular attendance, raised the incidence of involuntary absenteeism (a sick note excused a shift missed during the week). Coal mining virtually manufactured sickness and accidents and the pressure for higher productivity may well have increased physical risk. However, this was again complicated by the strength of established working practices. Short-time working was common among faceworkers; work had been so scarce in the inter-war years that three or four shifts in many coalfields constituted a good week.[25] As on the docks, the union tried to impose discipline, without much success. Unlike the

NDLB, the NCB had powers to restructure pay and work conditions and it attempted to use these to promote more uniform employment. During the 1950s the NCB slowly rationalised both job descriptions and day wage payment structures, in order to enforce national agreements and unify systems of bonus payments. All to little avail. By 1960 the NCB was 'writing in' absenteeism in its coal production targets and making good any deficit by importing from overseas.

The National Health Service

While the other case studies have documented old industries with well established working practices, the NHS was a new area of direct state employment, where the creation of a rationalised, modern labour market under public management might have been expected. However, efforts to establish uniform working practices and rationalised manpower deployment proved unsuccessful. The convention allowing collective bargaining to determine conditions of work was swiftly established among employees of the welfare state.

During the 1930s payment, grading and terms of employment in such public health services as existed were determined by local tradition and circumstance. Infant health unions were unable to secure a national framework for the negotiation of employment contracts and pay scales. The voluntary hospitals were completely self-governing. Here as in the many ex-poor law infirmaries, the lower grades were underpaid and overworked. Most hospital workers — even porters — were residential. Both General Practitioners (GPs) and dentists operated fee scales which fitted the local market and reflected their reputations and specialist skills. The creation of the Emergency Medical Service during the war saw the first moves towards standardisation of pay and conditions, the updating of training requirements and the introduction of more uniform systems of grading. Following the war, the NHS continued to support this policy. Several Whitley joint industrial councils were created — for nurses, for engineering and maintenance staff, for midwives and health visitors, for dentists and so on.[26] This outward appearance of smooth rationality concealed a structure fraught with internal problems. A registered nurse (SRN) might be employed in an NHS hospital, by the private sector as an industrial nurse, by the local authority as a school nurse or in a geriatric hospital. If the union could bid one sector up, the rest would be obliged to follow. Throughout the post-war years there was a chronic shortage of nurses. As a result, the Treasury was beset with problems in rationalising the pay demands from fast expanding sectors of employment, all seeking to attract recruits from a finite pool of young female labour. Primary school teaching, health visiting, nursing, social work and midwifery expanded under public sector ownership. All these professions guarded their pay differentials jealously against incursions by their rivals, and in this their sponsoring departments were as enthusiastic as the unions themselves.[27]

Unsurprisingly, the result was wage drift. From the first (much deserved) pay rise for nurses in 1948, other quasi-professionals sprang to defend established differentials. This trend was not confined to female employees. Continuing consultant shortages on the one hand and administrative shortages on the other also posed problems. To overcome the first obstacle, to flush out additional qualified labour reluctant to abandon lucrative private practice, the Ministry of Health devised part-time contracts for hospital consultants, which paid a higher rate pro rata than the full-time equivalent. By 1950, the numbers of part-time consultants had risen. A large number of these professionals converted one full-time post into two part-time contracts at different hospitals. That year, 50 per cent of consultants' wages paid by the NHS went to part-time consultants, who comprised only 30 per cent of consultants employed.[28] The higher rewards for practising medicine made it difficult for hospitals to recruit medically qualified staff as hospital administrators. Health administration was accordingly up-graded, stimulating a wage demand for parity from the National Amalgamated Local Government Officers' union in 1948.[29] To recruit dentists into the NHS, pay systems were introduced under the Spens Report in 1948, allowing income partly to reflect treatments given, thereby retaining the principle that had always dominated private fee income. Costs swiftly ran out of control; no administrators were available to check the verity of dentists' claims.[30] 'The high cost of the dental service,' remarked a civil servant acidly, ' is made up very largely of the high costs of dentists.'[31] Dentists' high remuneration stimulated discontent among GPs, and the situation was only salvaged when the introduction of dental charges in 1951 reduced demand — and dental salaries — to reasonable bounds. All this was taking place in the context of a wage freeze, which held industrial earnings down for nearly two years during the period 1948-50.

In this way, national collective bargaining diversified forms of employment while stimulating wage drift. Standardisation of working practices was further curtailed by the agreement with the voluntary hospitals, on the creation of the NHS, that their internal administration would remain unchanged. The treatment of nursing staff illustrated the point. The old system of residential employment, under strict surveillance, continued — in spite of opposition from both the Confederation of Health Service Employees (COHSE) and the Treasury on the grounds that nurses' hostels were both expensive and wasteful of potential hospital space. In an administrative structure strongly reminiscent of a convent, from which tradition it was arguably derived, every hour of the nurse's day was accounted for. Allowed no privacy and with her room frequently out of bounds to male or female friends, the nurse was taught to regard her employment as one of service and complete obedience to her superiors.[32] As nurses were not paid overtime (while domestic staff were), they took on domestic cleaning out of hours and at weekends.[33] These conditions, coupled with lower pay for residential staff, accounted for the very high wastage rate among trainee nurses. To make good the constant nursing shortages the NHS negotiated part-time working. This was popular, particularly as married women were converting from full-time to part-time jobs at the end of the war. As with the consultants, higher pro rata pay was used to encourage part-timers, a move not supported by COHSE, as part-time nurses could dictate their preferred hours of work, leaving full-timers with the dirty jobs and the unsocial hours.[34] In geriatric and mental health nursing, where post-war recruitment was particularly problematic, a number of hospitals converted nursing employment on to a daily three- or four-shift basis, using part-time payment schemes to attract trained personnel.[35]

Even as the union was negotiating another pay rise for nurses in 1952, the Treasury enforced a 5 per cent reduction in staff costs, to contain the consequences of wage drift.[36] In the early 1950s, with expenditure under strict surveillance, NHS institutions — the mental homes and hospitals for the chronic sick as well as the main general hospitals — subcontracted their cleaning and laundry work in order to cut costs. Service engineering and hospital maintenance was pooled in some large cities. The incidence of part-time work among female employees, domestics as well as nursing staff, rose between 50 and 70 per cent in the years from 1948 to 1956.[37] The establishment of national collective bargaining failed to rationalise health service employment. Far from being reshaped as modern and uniform, employment in the health sector became more diversified in the early years of the NHS; some old hospital traditions were broken, but many survived intact.

Conclusion

Post-war labour shortages generally encouraged employers to secure workers' services on a permanent basis while also strengthening union bargaining powers. The 1950s witnessed the spread of permanent work contracts, of seniority payments, of superannuation and private welfare systems. These measures were designed to discourage worker mobility in a seller's market, rewarding loyalty to the firm and raising the significance of industrial bargaining systems in determining family income and standards of living. However, such conditions had marginal impact on the rationalisation of work practices in the private and public sectors. The 1950s witnessed continuities in the nature of employment and in the rights of employers and the employed to determine conditions of work. In some sectors, regular employment expanded under the impact of nationalisation, notably in the electricity industry and on the railways. Elsewhere, higher production was bought by traditional means, especially by higher piece rates and bonus incentives. In the coal industry and on the docks, output rose without any regularisation of work; even in expanding areas of the public health services, forms of employment were diverse. While state intervention to create new mechanisms of collective bargaining was welcomed, the involvement of state officials in shaping employment outcomes was not. Free collective bargaining, however centralised and rational, reflected and sustained long-established divisions between the industrial and the political spheres. This produced a peculiarly British construction of a modern labour market, which marginalised the influence of publicly defined objectives in shaping working practices, in a manner at odds with systems found elsewhere in Europe.

This division between the political and the industrial remained problematic throughout this period. In disputes over training, wage restraint, manning levels and job demarcation, the political limitations of economic expertise were repeatedly revealed. The representations of modernity applied to labour markets document the gap between the rational ideal and common practice. Public commentary in the popular press focused on workers and their unions, condemning low productivity, restrictive practices and persistent absenteeism as responsible for Britain's prevailing economic difficulties. Such criticisms constructed full employment as the elimination of waste (understood as the absorption of slack time in productive endeavour), and the means to secure general prosperity through economic growth. The advent of full employment, universal welfare and job security was envisaged by wartime reformers as fostering worker co-operation in an economically rational, collective endeavour to ensure Britain's industrial future. The identification of absenteeism or restrictive practices described working conventions which, to the external, rational observer, impeded production unnecessarily. In economic terms, as an inter-war labour surplus was transformed into a post-war labour shortage, 'short-time working' (with employee as victim) became translated into 'absenteeism' (with employee as villain), without working practices changing very much at all. Labour market modernity vested legitimacy in a more scientific management, which challenged older principles of industrial democracy. The new language appeared predominantly in the form of observations on work practices made from outside industry, by social scientific investigators whose findings were publicised in the press. It was rarely used by industrialists themselves — except in conflict situations — when the rule book was enforced more strictly than normal.

To admit the principle underpinning such analyses would have been not only to attack existing working practices, but also the means used to decide them. The prospect of transferring authority away from the workplace was contested and the outcome of ensuing debate was to secure decision-making structures beyond the reach of both the state and the law, thus perpetuating industrial autonomy. The language of productivity was countered by reference to established custom and practice and to time-honoured working agreements. These notions were rooted in old principles of industrial democracy, dating from the nineteenth century, which rejected external assessments as unversed in the mysteries of trade and therefore unable to unravel its complexities. Both sides of industry tacitly collaborated in this reinforcement of the status quo. The defence of free collective bargaining became associated with industrial self-government. This reassertion of voluntarist principles, although appearing 'backward' in an era of European-managed economies, struck a chord within post-war public opinion, also resentful of official regulation — associating it with war shortages, deprivations and the loss of old freedoms. The new agenda of economic growth, full employment and social security was not inscribed on a blank page. Modernity was partially and haphazardly imposed over existing conventions and practices. The groundlines of later divisions and conflicts, over the proper remit of a modern economy and the expert's role in establishing it, became visible from the earliest post-war years.

The construction of British socio-economic modernity in the sphere of the labour market emerged as partial and incomplete — particularly when contrasted with other European developments. In France and Germany, the post-war integration of economic planning, social protection and ratio-nalised employment — together with the acceptance of the role of the state and the law in resolving conflict in this area — permitted a convergence of public and private interest in the type of settlement never established in Britain. The closer association between the employment contract and rights to social support in continental economies, enabled their unification within labour policies dedicated to training, to the rationalisation of manpower and to planning. In Britain, the defence of a liberal political economy rendered such integration impossible. The establishment of an agreed modern project for employment was ruptured by internal divisions between state and industry, as well as between employers and employed. These divisions perpetuated conflict, over both the principles of labour management and the role of government in deciding what these should be, fracturing industrial politics for the next thirty years.

5. Limits of Americanisation: The United States Productivity Gospel in Britain

Nick Tiratsoo

Touring the United States in 1957, the writer J.B. Priestley felt that he was viewing a new kind of society. He christened this 'Admass' and explained:

This is my name for the whole system of an increasing productivity, plus inflation, plus a rising standard of material living, plus high pressure advertising and salesmanship, plus mass communications, plus cultural democracy, and the creation of the mass mind, the mass man.

Priestley judged 'Admass' to be a 'swindle'. It provided jobs and food but little else: 'You think everything is opening out when in fact it is narrowing and closing in on you ... You have to be half-witted or half-drunk all the time to endure it.' What worried him most was that elements of the new system were already gaining ground in Europe. Indeed, there was every possibility that Britain in particular would soon turn completely into an 'Admass' society.[1]

In subsequent years many echoed Priestley's views. During the 1960s polemics like Francis Williams' *The American Invasion* (1962) and James McMillan's and Bernard Harris' *The American Take-Over of Britain* (1968) argued that American capitalism was irresistible and had already greatly transformed the British economic order.[2] The later literature on Fordism makes almost identical points, albeit in an allegedly more sophisticated theoretical way. A mode of production from America is depicted as having spread inexorably through the long post-war boom.[3] Of course, from the

1980s onwards globalisation, new patterns of consumption and the advent of flexible manufacturing systems appeared to have recast international relations once again. Nevertheless, many remain convinced that for thirty years after 1945, American influence was paramount. The British learnt about management ideas, business practices and industrial processes from across the Atlantic.[4] For good or for ill, they were in part 'Americanised'.

Such assertions need to be modified. One particular episode — the history of the United States government's technical assistance programmes — demonstrates that Americans had far less impact in Britain than many have imagined. This is a concrete way of charting one particular collision with the modern. Washington was certainly keen on promoting economic modernisation but the British were generally unenthusiastic in their responses. The problem, as will become clear, was that American prescriptions conflicted with long-standing indigenous methods and traditions. 'Americanisation' had definite limits.

The United States Technical Assistance Programmes

The blueprint for the technical assistance initiative was developed in the late 1940s.[5] Americans who came into contact with European industry at this time felt it was, by their own standards, almost entirely old-fashioned. United States manufacturers were using more sophisticated technologies and well-rewarded labour to produce an ever-widening range of consumer goods. By contrast, many Europeans shared a highly restrictionist outlook, clung to outdated machinery and treated their workers with contempt. Typically, their ideal seemed to be the satisfaction of small but lucrative markets of upper-class consumers, with the ordinary citizen all but ignored.[6] What made this backwardness particularly unacceptable to Americans was the political context. As Washington saw it, unless the Europeans changed economically, they would not be able to withstand the challenge of Communism.

Spurred on by these perceptions, the Americans believed that the only way forward was to create a sweeping campaign aimed at promoting change. Marshall Aid funds were provided to help macro-economic stabilisation. At the same time great emphasis was placed on persuading people in Europe to embrace the 'gospel of productivity'. Concentrating on efficiency was a relatively cheap option — the idea hinged upon introducing new techniques and methods, not vast expenditure on capital investment. Moreover, it was one which would almost certainly produce considerable returns. More productive manufacturing implied lower costs and cheaper prices, thereby creating the basis for self-sustaining growth. Europe might become at once a more competitive exporter and a voracious importer. There were also anticipated gains in terms of political and social stability. Employers and workers were unlikely to fight, after all, if both could receive an expanding share of economic wealth.

In practical terms the Americans prioritised certain key objectives. Most important, they wanted individual manufacturers to adopt the most up-to-date ideas possible, in design and marketing as much as in production. At the same time, they urged employers to reformulate their views about workers. Labour should be treated as one arm of a partnership and allowed to share in the productivity gains. Authoritarian concepts of intra-firm governance needed to be replaced by a 'human relations' approach, using the insights of sociology and psychology. Two further concerns stemmed from an appreciation of the conditions which would maximise change. The Americans believed that competition stimulated progress. European governments were therefore encouraged to introduce new legislation outlawing collusive business activity. Finally, there was the question of management. As the Americans saw it, European managers had traditionally been drawn from a narrow social stratum and rarely possessed either academic or technical qualifications. In future, it was asserted, this must change. Managers across the continent needed to become more professional, perhaps educated in business schools on the lines of Harvard, and in this way they would be able to play a much fuller role in modernisation.

To implement these prescriptions the Americans created or financed an overlapping set of agencies and programmes, beginning in 1948 and ending roughly ten years later.[7] The first main initiative was the Anglo-American Council on Productivity (AACP) which operated until 1953. The Council sponsored sixty-six joint employer–trade union teams to visit the United States and investigate specific sectors or particular business practices (for example, production engineering). Altogether, 956 British participants were involved at a cost of $3 million dollars. On their return to Britain, the teams produced printed reports of their findings, and some 650,000 of these were eventually distributed throughout industry. Alongside the AACP, the London mission of the American government's Marshall Plan apparatus ran its own programme of visits to the United States. It made contact with various British ministries and educational establishments to recruit suitable candidates, resulting in a further 29 teams being sent across the Atlantic. To complement this activity the mission paid for a number of British managers to study in America, devising a programme which combined placements with firms and enrolment in university courses. By the early 1950s there had been eighteen such educational programmes, involving 311 students and an expenditure of $1.3 million.

In later years, new organisations carried forward this body of work. The British Productivity Council (BPC) developed out of the AACP, while the European Productivity Agency (EPA) was created to co-ordinate initiatives on a continent-wide scale. The extent of activity continued to be impressive. Between 1953 and 1957, the EPA's programmes on management subjects alone encompassed 340 training courses, one mission to the United States, seven international conferences and forty published reports. Many projects run by both organisations stretched over relatively long periods of time.

Taken together, this was a formidable attempt to popularise American business practices and manufacturing techniques. In total, direct technical assistance probably cost $15 million, while British government spending of an associated kind may have added up to a roughly similar amount. What kind of impact did this expenditure have? One obvious way of trying to answer this question is to look at what contemporaries felt about the American efforts.

Contemporary Views of the Technical Assistance Programmes

Unsurprisingly, many of those who were directly involved in the technical assistance agencies felt that they had exerted decisive influence. Surveying the entire history of post-war productivity policy in 1956, a senior American official came to rather typical conclusions. The 'cumulative effect' of the programmes, he argued, had been 'the stimulating of wider interest in improved managerial methods and better techniques and the development of a fresh outlook on the industrial problems facing the country'. Moreover, he added, most of this had occurred *directly* because of the American government's policies:

> the employment of ... U.S. aid was necessary to strengthen the hands of those few British government officials and ... officers of trade and research organisations, and educational establishments who recognised the urgency of the need for greater efficiency and improved management but who lacked adequate moral support or financial resources to put into effect schemes that would help overcome deficiencies.[8]

Nevertheless, by no means everyone agreed with this kind of assessment. Some British trade associations — key intermediaries between the official agencies and industry — concluded that the American offensive was producing tangible results, but others remained sceptical. In several cases, member firms already had a strong interest in modernisation and so were unlikely to be overly impressed by the sudden appearance of the productivity missionaries. Elsewhere, no attempt was made to disguise the fact that American ideas were being actively disregarded. Progressive manufacturers in the bronze and brass casting industry were aware of this problem and their pessimism coloured a BPC review of 1955:

> From a cross-section of the industry ... it would seem that the adoption of new techniques has not greatly extended in the last two years, although many more firms have come to realise their value. While the more enlightened firms have continued a policy of purchasing new plant or re-considering their production programmes, others have been content to look on with an 'it costs too much' attitude or have ignored there commendations entirely.[9]

The specialist and trade press held equally heterodox opinions. Many argued that the AACP had produced valuable results, especially in changing the 'psychological climate' regarding productivity, but there were also a number of more cautious assessments. The journal *Engineering* came to the following distinctly downbeat conclusions in 1953: 'Expenditure on the activities of the ... [AACP] must be regarded as a long-term investment which will eventually pay for itself, but from which the annual returns are likely to be small'. A parallel observation was that the Americans had only interested a small minority of companies. *The Statist* declared: 'There is now a wealth of examples of what can be done but for every enterprise which has taken some trouble to improve the quality of its management — and through that its productivity — there are probably a score which have been content to carry on in a traditional way'. Evaluations of the EPA could be equally unenthusiastic, with *The Economist* dismissing the organisation as 'little known in Britain'.[10]

Surveying contemporary opinion offers no easy answers about the question of impact. The best that can be said is that there was a genuine divergence of views. When we focus on the details of the American initiatives, it becomes clear that the United States missionaries were keen advocates of distinctive techniques and methods. The following sections concentrate on three of their specific recommendations and trace how they fared in British circumstances.

Management Education

The Americans were passionate believers in management education. Individuals running firms, they argued, required a range of specific skills to carry out their everyday tasks. The most satisfactory and efficient way of developing these was by formal training. Managers needed qualifications in much the same way as other professionals. Britain had no tradition of management education at this time and so the Americans recognised that they would have to move fairly carefully if the position were to be changed. The first step in their campaign was the dispatch of an AACP team led by the prominent business consultant, Lyndall Urwick, to study American university and college courses. Not unexpectedly, this delegation returned to Britain greatly enthused with the whole idea of management education; the commitment to training across the Atlantic, it was concluded, had 'a vital bearing upon American productivity'.[11]

Over the next few years, continued pressure was exerted to persuade British business that it should follow the American example.[12] The technical assistance missionaries advocated the creation of a 'British Harvard', an institution which would be able to conduct high-level research and produce management teachers, as well as train a new cadre of qualified executives. In addition, their aim was to create several chairs of management in British universities, together with a number of new courses. Attention was focused on developing syllabuses and teaching methods, with many British practitioners being given the opportunity to examine American approaches at first hand. In the later 1950s, the EPA kept the momentum going by offering numerous seminars and conferences on aspects of management education.

The result was that many larger firms began to take the training issue much more seriously. There were also changes in the education sector. The London and Manchester Business Schools were launched in the mid-1960s, while other institutions began offering Masters in Business Administration or related qualifications. However, closer scrutiny of the evidence suggests that change was, in fact, rather circumscribed. Higher education institutions remained distinctly unenthusiastic about the new provision. Academics tended to see management studies as intellectually inferior. Moreover, much of what was on offer continued to be of low quality.[13] Nor was business fully converted to American ideals. In 1956 the management educationalist, Elizabeth Sidney, estimated that a mere one per cent of the country's managers had received 'any formal training for the job'. Fifteen years later a more systematic study reported that the position was little different. It discovered that only 7 or 8 per cent of British managers attended 'in-or-out-company courses of a week or more' during any given twelve-month period.[14] Even the most senior grades largely conformed to this pattern. A 1970 survey of directors in the top two hundred British companies found that while 9 per cent had been to business school, 68 per cent were without professional qualifications of any kind.[15] Indeed, when questioned closely, many managers clung tenaciously to the idea that management could *never* be taught because it was more about instinct than expertise. The British, it seemed, were largely happy to remain devotees of what one consultant called 'folk management', regardless of the advice that was so avidly proffered from across the Atlantic.[16]

Materials Handling

A second area of American concern centred on the general question of
industrial engineering. One of the key aspects was materials handling.
The way components and semi-finished products were moved around a
factory could have a vital bearing on productivity. One estimate for the
metals sector was that 59 tons of materials had to be handled for every ton
of finished goods produced. This might represent anything from 15 to 85
per cent of total costs, depending upon the particular process. What excited
American productivity experts was that the potential for making gains in
Britain by modernising handling seemed enormous. British companies
remained wedded to old-fashioned techniques. Indeed, brute strength
frequently predominated, with as much as 80 per cent of all movement
being done by human beings. If the country changed its methods and
started using even simple equipment like trolleys and chutes, there were
likely to be immediate gains.[17]

This was a striking message and there appeared to be several reasons for
thinking that it would be heeded. Britain had a strong and well-developed
industry, producing handling equipment of every type from conveyors
and forklift trucks to barrows. There was an informative trade periodical,
Mechanical Handling, and a regular exhibition for producers and consumers
at London's Olympia. Britain also possessed some experts in the field,
most notably Frank Wollard, an innovative practitioner at Morris Motors
and the author of a classic textbook advocating flow production. Finally,
as the Americans reiterated, innovation need not be in any way expensive;
much handling equipment could be obtained at relatively low cost.

By the later 1950s it was clear that some sectors of British industry had
taken notice of the American advice. At one end of the scale, several big
car companies introduced new transfer machinery. At the other, some
small companies were known to be enthusiastically experimenting with
better layout and techniques such as palletisation. In an editorial published
during 1955, *Mechanical Handling* declared that much progress had occurred,
reporting: 'there can be few of Britain's leading industrial firm who have
not introduced some kind of improved handling facilities within the past
few years'.[18]

Subsequent observers concluded that the extent of progress had once again been rather less than was at first anticipated. Writing in 1958, F. R. Ford, the chief production planning engineer for Austin's Midlands's area factories, produced the following rather pessimistic assessment:

> A visit to a number of different factories will, I believe, convince many people that on the whole the progress in material handling lags behind the general level of improvements in the process of manufacture. There are, of course, many exceptions such as the cigarette and bottling concerns where automatic handling has been developed to a very high degree. I am, however, primarily referring to engineering concerns, and in particular, to the motor car industry.[19]

Later studies reinforced this view. In 1974, the Department of Industry's Committee for Materials Handling established a working party to examine current practice in British industry. This focused on thirty engineering companies and reported as follows:

a) Storage and materials handling cost at the median value was found to be about 12 per cent of conversion cost ...
b) Materials handling appears to be costing many of the companies more than it ought ...
c) From the sample surveyed there was little evidence to suggest that firms engaged in engineering production in the United Kingdom are aware of the true costs of storage and materials handling ...

On the basis of these findings, the committee felt justified in urging British industry 'to take a new look at manufacture by focusing attention on materials flow as well as the production processes'.[20] A similar exhortation had emanated from across the Atlantic some quarter of a century earlier.

Human Relations

American productivity missionaries saw the human relations approach as essential for shaping the internal life of the company. To American eyes, British and European firms were often run on autocratic and unscientific lines, which ultimately contributed to their overall inefficiency. Human relations solutions promised improvements. The Americans were insistent on two principles. First, they believed in the need for teamwork and consultation at all levels of the firm. Complex problems could only be solved by joint action from different specialists within management. Involving workers in decision-making would boost morale, integrate a previously unused source of relevant knowledge and ultimately advance efficiency. Second, the Americans insisted that choices should be made on as rational a basis as possible. Too many executives acted on the spur of the moment. The enlightened way to solve problems was to appraise the facts, refer to the most up-to-date corpus of relevant theoretical knowledge, and only then to act.

Much British comment on these proposals was enthusiastic. The Attlee government had encouraged human relations thinking in industry and many civil servants in Whitehall (particularly at the Ministry of Labour) remained committed to the approach in general terms. Britain had important research bodies in the field, most notably at the Tavistock Institute. However, by the late 1950s it became obvious that, once again, the real impact of American proselytising was much more limited than the productivity missionaries had expected. The converted minority attended seminars and conferences, but the great majority of managers and directors remained uninterested.

Human relations principles had certainly not changed the internal management functioning of British industry. Many companies of all sizes continued to be dominated by charismatic chief executives, in line with the generally accepted belief that the senior manager should be 'an all-powerful, thrustful personality, whose very genius overshadows and detracts from the more modest performance of his subordinates'.[21] At lower levels, managers were organised into ranks, differentiated by varying privileges and badges of position. Outside observers were habitually astonished at the elaborate gradations. Sizeable businesses frequently operated six or seven restaurants and canteens, distinguished by price and comfort, while lavatories too were organised hierarchically.[22] One study claimed that micro-distinctions coloured virtually every activity both inside and outside the office. For example, the company car was a potent indicator of prestige:

the make and number of cylinders of cars figures largely in the mind of the social climbing employee. Another point is the reception given to him once he has his car ... does he drive up to the door (and if so which entrance)? Does the commissionaire park it for him or does he have to do it himself? Where in the car park is the precious vehicle placed? In one firm the nearer the managing director's car it is parked, the higher the employee's prestige rating.[23]

This kind of structure clearly discouraged consultation and teamworking but managers were far from eager to engage in such activity anyway. The codes which bound firms together usually emphasised duty and obedience. Much use was made of military language. The ethos of 'command and control' had permeated deep into the collective consciousness. Consequently, most managers expected to give and carry out orders rather than have their staff indulge in independent thinking. Seniors might discuss issues with juniors on occasion, but this was entirely at their discretion.

Human relations' principles were little more evident in management's dealings with the shop floor during the post-war years. Personnel managers were the great evangelists of the new approach but they had struggled to gain influence. According to a survey in 1959 the discipline was in crisis — if not 'bankrupt' then certainly 'insolvent'.[24]The problem was that personnel managers too often found themselves relegated to a peripheral role. At the British Motor Corporation, for example, they were not allowed to attend major negotiations with the unions and this seemed to be fairly typical.[25] Research by Michael Poole of Sheffield University in the early 1970s confirmed that most managers continued to attach 'comparatively little importance to personnel work, particularly in comparison with production and sales activities'.[26]

Other classic components of the human relations approach to labour were equally underdeveloped. Joint consultation in plants had spread quite widely in the 1940s but thereafter it languished. An investigation by the Industrial Welfare Society in 1961, which examined ninety-eight member firms, came to gloomy conclusions. More than half of the sample had no formal consultation machinery. About one third were using their committees merely as 'a forum for managerial announcements and employee's minor grievances'. The author of the study commented: 'There is an air of disillusionment in industry about the work of formal consultation'.[27]

Other methods of involving the workforce had similar outcomes. For example, firms were rarely willing to share financial information with their workers. The majority even balked at a basic suggestion scheme. An inquiry of 1960 reported: 'it is probable that well over 500 suggestion schemes now exist in Great Britain. It is, however, quite certain that the number of successful schemes is less than a hundred'.[28] Taken together, these examples suggest that those who took a sceptical view of American influence were probably right. The various aid programmes seem to have had a fairly modest impact on British industry. If real change occurred, it usually involved a small advance guard of already forward-looking firms, with a much larger tail almost entirely unaffected. What explains this relative failure?

Problems with the American Programmes

There is no doubt that American efforts were flawed. First, there were problems with the various transmission mechanisms used. The productivity missionaries relied upon team visits, tuition by consultants, conferences and seminars, and all of these had characteristic pitfalls. British delegates visiting America were sometimes overwhelmed by the degree of affluence they found there and failed to register much about the specifics of industrial processes. Conversely, American consultants in Britain occasionally showed great ignorance about local conditions or impatience with their 'backward' tutees. Several conferences and seminars produced little but banal or formulaic exchanges. There was also a long-standing problem relating to the selection of participants in the various programmes. The Americans were keen to exclude both known Communists on the trade-union side and the most reactionary employers, but they frequently lacked enough information to assess other candidates and this left an opening for abuse. One of those involved with the delivery of the programmes was aware of 'a small population of seminar goers and jaunt takers' who avidly encouraged these activities for purely 'personal reasons'.[29]

Moreover, there were recurring doubts about the type of knowledge that the American drive aimed to popularise. Some British commentators argued that, while the suggested prescriptions might be relevant in America, this did not make them universally applicable. The British Electrical and

Allied Manufacturers' Association journal commented:

> It is easy to be captivated by other people's methods and to ask why
> don't we do this or that; not by any means so easy to adopt and
> adjust those methods to entirely different surroundings and entirely
> different temperamental, social, and industrial problems.[30]

Particular controversy surrounded the American advocacy of the '3Ss' —
standardisation, simplification, and specialisation — since some local entrepreneurs believed that pursuing these objectives would be actively
damaging in the British context. American manufacturers faced an enormous home market which was understood to be relatively homogeneous
in terms of taste and purchasing power. Their counterparts in Britain, by
contrast, had to deal with very varied and demanding consumers, abroad
as well as at home, and this put a definite limit on the scope for the '3Ss'.
The Engineer was emphatic: 'High productivity must be sought without
necessarily and always associating it with high production, and without
necessarily carrying specialisation and simplification so far as they have
been carried in America'.[31]

The various difficulties that have been touched upon should not, however,
be exaggerated. Despite everything, the Americans were able to offer a vast
amount of information. Moreover, most of this was entirely appropriate and
applicable, and judged as such by contemporary experts. No one, for example, was to be heard arguing that Britain's traditional methods of mechanical
handling were technically preferable. Even the issue of the '3Ss' is not as
straightforward as it at first seems. Some trades were no doubt handicapped
by their markets circumstances, but few believed that this was true of industry as a whole. Indeed, journals like *The Economist* argued that the scope for
standardisation was enormous if only companies would take their production operations more seriously.[32] Equally, it is important to add that the
Americans were not advocating the blind pursuit of change. They stressed
that manufacturers should survey their markets and costs and only then
consider altering product lines. The objective, as one explanatory pamphlet
underlined, was 'to cut out *wasteful* variety, not to eliminate variety altogether'.[33] Thus, a recognition of the problems with the delivery and content
of the American programmes is not sufficient to explain the limited impact

of technical assistance as a whole. Inevitably, this throws the focus on to the British. Why where they so sceptical about what was being recommended? To answer this question it is necessary to look first at business and then at the role of particular governments.

British Management Culture and Employer Politics

There is no doubt that some British executives disliked the technical assistance initiatives simply because they were American. British attitudes to the United States were complex but rarely completely positive. The London correspondent of *Newsweek* reported that one in every three Britons were 'more or less antagonistic to anything that came from America from Buicks to businessmen'.[34] Mass Observation in the late 1940s reached similar conclusions, remarking that Americans were disliked for 'their boastfulness, bumptiousness, and baloney; materialism, get-rich-quickness, speed-before-thoroughness; and ... language and accent'.[35] Those in industry had additional reasons for worrying about the influence of the United States. Many felt uneasy about American intentions and were prepared to believe that Washington was trying to ruin Britain as a serious trading competitor. Others pointed out that the USA was not anyway a suitable model for Britain to imitate; contemporary sociological accounts like William Whyte's *The Organisation Man* (1956) suggested that there might be little to look forward to in an American future.[36]

The tensions at work here were particularly keenly felt by Britons who worked for American multinationals. The business journalist Graham Turner observed that a fair proportion of this group harboured suspicions that they had become 'quislings'. He was struck by the pervasive obstinacy of his subjects:

For the most part they remain steadfastly British in appearance and manner: none of the people I met had been Americanised to any significant extent although some freely used the jargon of American business ... Some, indeed, while accepting one-class restaurants and the absence of a whole range of cherished status symbols, deliberately set their faces against trans-Atlantic patterns of behaviour of which they disapprove.[37]

More fundamentally, much of what the Americans were recommending contradicted basic tenets of British management culture.[38] As we have seen, it was widely believed in Britain that management entailed the leadership of people, that managers were really like military generals, having constantly to inspire their subordinates. Prevarication was not admired, even if the consequences of quick thinking caused problems. Compared with this emphasis on leadership, much less was made of issues relating to technical competence. Although most believed that junior grades might need to know about specific processes and functions, they did not feel that such proficiency was necessary at the apex of the firm. Indeed, the ascent of the management ladder was popularly viewed as a movement *away* from the mundane world of specialist skills. In this spirit one leading manager told an international conference in 1951:

> a top-level executive's main job was to apply to himself a balanced cultivated life — about half his business time should be spent direct- ing his business and the other half in business activities outside, and he should, as far as his working life is concerned, confine that to the minimum. He should have long weekends ... he should play golf ... he should garden ... he should play bridge, he should read, he should do something different.[39]

Given this pattern of beliefs and assumptions, it is not hard to see why British management instinctively reacted against many of the American prescrip- tions. The Americans stressed that managers needed to be professionals, trained in their calling. The British, on the other hand, emphasised that the best place for the manager to learn was on the job — 'sitting at Nellie's knee' or 'attending the school of hard knocks'. A modicum of education was acceptable, but only if it had been attained at a public school or well- established university, institutions which were well known for turning-out 'good brains'. A similar difference of opinion existed about consultation. The American position was that managers needed to work together and consult as widely as possible. The British, by contrast, celebrated the lone leader who would stand above the fray and direct operations. Specialists like engineers and scientists might be called upon at times, but British manage- ment believed that they were incapable of thinking strategically, and so should be kept in their place. The popular aphorism 'men who can manage men, manage men who can only manage things' said much about the terms of this relationship.[40] Workers had even less claim to be heard. Typically, one British manager told a visiting American academic that if a trade-union representative came to see him about their firm's ballot sheet, 'he would kick him out of the office'.[41]

British employers had their own reasons for disliking what the Americans were advocating. The Attlee government's nationalisation programme had scarred them deeply and, even in the 1950s, they remained anxious and defensive about any measure of state involvement in industry. The American productivity initiatives were not of course judged equivalent to Labour's onslaught but they did seem to contain several unwelcome components. Employers resented being told to treat workers more seriously and worried about the American emphasis on management. Their fear here was that those who were really just servants of the firm might get ideas above their station. Few had much sympathy for the American emphasis on discussion and the exchange of information. British firms had traditionally been secretive and it was still generally believed that all commercially sensitive data should remain closely guarded. Talking about processes and performances in public, it was asserted, could only benefit competitors — perhaps the very firms of those who served in the productivity missions.

On occasion the general sense of unease provoked campaigns to curb what were perceived as the excesses of the American position. The tactics deployed ranged from non-co-operation to lobbying. Links were made to American employers' associations, so that pressure could be exerted directly on Washington agencies. As a consequence of these campaigns, American technical assistance personnel were frequently surprised at the hostility they encountered. Those serving in London concluded that some British employers' representatives were both untrustworthy and obstructive.

Government Responses

American officials believed that, given the extent of business hostility, British government support for the technical assistance programmes might well prove crucial.[42] If civil servants and politicians in Whitehall endorsed what was on offer, even complemented it with their own initiatives, then recalcitrant industrialists could be expected to take notice. However, persuading successive British governments of the need for action proved more difficult than the Americans had expected. The Labour administration of 1945-51 was largely well disposed to Washington's ideas. Generally, it had good relations with the USA and was committed to the idea that British productivity needed to be improved. Moreover, Labour had no problem about intervening in the economy; it was quite ready to use official agencies as instruments for modernising private enterprise. As a result, in the years to 1951, the American missionaries and British ministries largely worked in harmony, agreeing about ends and means.

By contrast, the years of Conservative rule in the 1950s gave the Americans rather more trouble. Conservative politicians were not keen on state-sponsored modernisation for financial as well as ideological reasons. At the same that time, the Tories fervently believed in the 'special relationship' and were sensitive about possibly offending a country which they saw as Britain's major ally. At a material level too, co-operating with the USA obviously made sense; it seemed foolish to spurn the chance of obtaining funds for projects which the government might otherwise have to finance itself. Given these different pressures, what actually occurred was a policy of drift. The Conservatives generally wound down productivity policies during their period in office, providing the least support for the American programmes they thought permissible. On the other hand, there were one or two occasions when firm action was taken. For example, the government moved swiftly and firmly to head off American pressure aimed at strengthening Britain's anti-monopoly laws, with Washington being told firmly that this was none of its business.

Conclusion

In years after 1945 the United States was indisputably the dominant economic world power. Because of this overriding position in world markets it is tempting to believe that American influence was all-pervasive. Yet simplistic diagnoses based upon notions of the international hegemony of the United States are inappropriate. The programme of American technical assistance offered to Britain during the post-war years provides significant insights into the complexities of the Anglo-American dialogue. American versions of economic modernity, based upon efficiency and the gospel of productivity, achieved only limited results in Britain. The difficulties of implementing such a programme centred on an entrenched management culture as well as on institutional resistance. In practice, British managers were relatively uninterested in both the economic and the formal justifications for industrial modernisation. They reacted negatively to American campaigns because the suggested changes were incompatible with their professional nostrums and strongly held political dispositions. Those who ran British companies continued to believe vehemently that they knew best. This story of management points to the highly compromised — and resisted — patterns of economic modernity which were characteristic of more general trends within British society in the 1950s. For their adherents in the boardrooms, traditional practices were perceived as neither deficient nor backward; rather they were understood as the very essence of managing in the British way.

6. *Population Politics in Post-War British Culture*

Pat Thane

A central and historically distinctive theme of the twentieth-century experience is the sustained reduction in the birth-rate and the general cultural acceptance that births can and should be controlled. It is an experience which divides 'modern' lives from those of previous generations and it has profoundly influenced perceptions of self and individuals' beliefs in their capacity to shape their own lives. In Britain, this change had many implications for both political and personal life. The alliance between the state and a new type of demographic expert, armed with modern statistical techniques, worked to predict population changes and developed policies to deal with those changes: the discourse produced by these experts throws up new ideas about British perceptions of national identity and of the nation's declining imperial role. Women's responses to such fundamental changes in their own lives point to new understandings of the relationship between gender, generation and the experience of the modern self.

Historians are well aware of the importance of population issues — both about the size of the population and the so-called quality of the population — in the politics and culture of some European countries in the mid-twentieth century. Concern for racial purity was most virulently practised in Nazi Germany, though sterilisation of the 'unfit' was extensively practised in the United States, in Sweden and elsewhere in the 1930s and beyond. Measures to increase the birth-rate were most vigorously, and ineffectually, promoted in France from the beginning of the century and in Mussolini's Italy. In both countries, the state promoted population growth by increasing taxes on bachelors and decreasing them for fathers.

They gave medals and small cash gifts to 'prolific mothers'. These have all been well documented, most recently by Maria Sophia Quine.[1] There has, by contrast, been less awareness of the importance of population in British politics after as well as before the Second World War.

Population Panic in Inter-War and Wartime Britain: 'The Twilight of Parenthood'

Concern about the declining birth-rate in Britain, especially the decline among the higher social classes, was evident before the First World War. Even stronger in the 1920s, it became a serious cause of panic in the 1930s, stabilised in the 1940s as a matter of quite major political concern, though with some novel features, and did not disappear from public discourse until the 1960s. It revived in the 1980s in the form of concern about the ageing of the population.

In 1923 to 1924 John Maynard Keynes and William Beveridge engaged in a public debate about fertility decline and its effects. Broadly, Keynes was in favour of maintaining low levels of reproduction, fearing that a rise in the birth-rate would exacerbate the economic crisis that was facing the western economy. Beveridge, on the other hand, was keen to encourage higher birth-rates, partly through the introduction of family allowances. He was concerned, as Keynes apparently was not, that, on a national level, birth-control was mainly practised by the 'responsible' sections of society (in all classes), thus potentially damaging the quality of the 'national stock'. In consequence, Beveridge believed that internationally the 'white races' were being differentially depleted, with alarming potential effects. He wrote in 1924:

> the questions now facing us are how far will the fall go; whether it will bring about a stationary white population after or long before the white man's world is full; how the varying incidence of restriction among different social classes and creeds will affect the Stock; how far the unequal adoption of birth control in different races will leave one race at the mercy of another's growing numbers or drive it to armaments or permanent aggression in self-defence.[2]

Beveridge was not alone in perceiving fertility decline as more than a purely personal or even an internal national matter, but as one which fundamentally affected international power relations at a time when these were exceptionally unstable. The concern of 'experts', such as Beveridge and Keynes, with demographic issues, and the attempt at 'scientific' analysis of them to underpin pressure for state action, was not a new phenomenon; it had flourished through the nineteenth century, from Malthus to the birth of eugenics. Nevertheless, modern communications enabled such views to be more widely disseminated in the twentieth century.

The 1920s fears about fertility decline reached panic levels as the British birth-rate fell to historically low levels in the early 1930s. Demography was now emerging as a distinct discipline and its practitioners were inventing statistical techniques which supposedly enabled them to attempt to predict future population levels with unprecedented scientific precision. They competed to produce ever gloomier projections, which, however cautiously phrased, some took at face value. Grace Leybourne, for example, produced widely quoted estimates that, by the early 1970s, the population of Great Britain would have fallen to 32 million (from 44 million in 1931).[3] In fact, it rose to 54 million in 1971.[4] Doom-laden studies were published, such as that by the left-wing social biologist Enid Charles, which originally appeared in 1934 as *The Twilight of Parenthood* and was reissued in 1936 as, more gloomy still, *The Menace of Underpopulation*.[5] This also contained calculations of the coming serious decline in the size of the population.

The population debate in the 1930s drew in a wide range of intellectuals and political and social activists, many of whom were to be influential after the war. Much of it took place under the auspices of the Eugenics Society, which at this time included among its membership socially concerned radicals such as Richard Titmuss and the demographer David Glass (both of them influential figures at the London School of Economics from the 1940s to the 1970s) as well as decided conservatives. The Society was a major source of funding for demographic research, although the role and meanings of eugenics in British culture in the inter-war years are far from clear.[6] Titmuss, who was to become highly influential in the development of social policy as a field of academic study after the war and an important influence upon Labour Party social security policy from the 1950s to his death in 1973, published *Poverty and Population: A Factual Study of Contemporary Social Waste* in 1938. He argued that the declining birth-rate and the resulting ageing of the population amounted to 'national suicide' and would lead to a 'decline in the mean intelligence quotient of the nation and a reduction in social competence'. 'Can we', he asked,

> maintain our present attitude to India while we decline in numbers and age ... (and India's population expands)? Can we in these circumstances retain our particular status in the world, our genius for Colonization, our love of political freedom and our leadership of the British Commonwealth of nations ... are we to bring to such a pathetic close, to such a mean inglorious end a history which with all its faults still shines with the lights of our gifts to mankind and still glows with the patient courage of the common people?[7]

One spectre haunting the debate on population was the fear that Britain was experiencing the twilight of empire alongside the 'twilight of parenthood'. Titmuss' reference to India should be read in the context of the struggle for Indian independence that was currently in progress and the protracted negotiations between Britain and India over the future constitutional relationship between the two countries. Titmuss unites regret about Britain's fading imperial role with praise for 'the common people'. His writing hints at the complex agonising of influential British liberals about the relationship with Empire in the 1920s and 1930s. Such views were widely disseminated and were summarised in a pamphlet issued to the armed forces in 1943.[8]

The population debate continued through the war. The birth-rate began to rise again in 1942, but it was uncertain whether this would be sustained. Fear about the wide-ranging ill-effects of fertility decline continued to haunt Beveridge and is evident in his 1942 report on social insurance. It lay behind his recommendation for adequate children's allowances, for, as he put it in the report: 'With its present rate of reproduction, the British race cannot continue'.[9] Population politics also lay behind Beveridge's proposal that the old age pension system should be designed so as to discourage early retirement from work: older workers were needed to compensate for the shrinking numbers of younger ones. Again, as the report spelled out: 'A people ageing in years need not be old in spirit and British youth will rise again'. In important respects population fears helped shape the emerging post-war welfare system.

In 1945 the radical social research organisation Mass Observation published the result of an investigation, *Britain and her Birth-Rate*. It endorsed the belief that the birth-rate was falling excessively, quoting an estimate by David Glass that 30 per cent of the male population would be aged over 60 by 1995, and, more cautiously, one from Enid Charles forecasting that the population of Great Britain would have fallen to only 10.4 million in 2015, of whom 53 per cent would be aged sixty or above. The authors thought it unlikely that such an extreme decline would be allowed to occur. Yet they believed there was a danger that, if present trends continued,

> the population will go on declining indefinitely and will eventually be extinguished altogether. Only those who do not like the English race can look forward to that situation ... It is quite likely that modern civilisation would simply cease to exist and a return to more primitive methods take its place. At least the conditions of such a society would be so different to anything we know now that it is impossible to imagine them.[10]

Founded by anthropologists, Mass Observation was established to explore and celebrate English culture; hence its report paid no explicit attention to the imperial and international implications of fertility decline. Primarily concerned about class differences in fertility, it concluded by surveying the 'Eugenic Prospect':

> Have we to rely on the improvident and the wishful-thinking for the perpetuation of the race? The question marks must remain. But it is difficult to find any other interpretation which fits all the contradictions which this survey brings to light ... For the eugenic future something ... is needed which will make the thoughtful breed as much as the thoughtless ... Will anything bring enough quality babies into Britain except the conviction of mothers and fathers that it will be a Britain fit for babies to live in?

Mass Observation suggested that pessimism about the future was one reason for having fewer children and its report concluded that planning for a better Britain after the war would help to increase the birth-rate.[11]

Demographic pessimism was still evident after the war. In 1948 the research organisation, Political and Economic Planning, produced the dramatic and strongly eugenist *Population Policy in Great Britain* on the implications of what it called 'the deterioration of the age structure', advocating higher family allowances to boost the birth-rate. *The Population of Britain*, a bestselling paperback published by Pelican in 1947 by Eva Hubback, an economist and long-time campaigner for family allowances (which had been introduced in 1945, but at a low level), reinforced and popularised this message. Hubback argued that the pre-war decline in the birth-rate was likely to reassert itself, leading to serious population decline. She recognised that this could be offset by immigration from central or southern Europe or, less probably she thought, from Asia. But she thought it unlikely that the latter would be welcome and she also argued that 'immigration on a vast scale is a counsel of despair, as it is a sign that we have failed to maintain the vitality and spirit to keep our own community alive'.[12]

By 1955 Titmuss was still writing about population change but had stopped panicking. He had come to recognise that what was occurring was a desirable transition from the high birth-rates, high death rates and accompanying social misery of the nineteenth century, to a more 'balanced' modern population structure made up of small families and longer life expectancy.[13] The gloomy domestic outcomes projected twenty years earlier had not come about while, at the same time, there was also a wider political acceptance of the decline in Britain's world role.

The Royal Commission on Population

The main official outcome of the population panic was the establishment in 1944 of a Royal Commission on Population to investigate demographic trends and their social, economic and political implications. This followed the publication in 1942 of a White Paper on the *Current Population Trend* which did not endorse extreme demographic fears. The work of the Royal Commission proved more difficult than anticipated and it did not report until 1949, by which time the birth-rate had stabilised, but at higher levels than those of the 1930s. Hubback, who was not a member of the Royal

Commission, intended her own study to provide a popular background to the publication of the report.

In general, the report sought to calm the grosser forms of panic about population change. Its language, however, conveyed some of the fears and expectations of the post-war world which could respectably be expressed in an official text. It also revealed how important population politics continued to be in the immediate post-war period and how far-reaching were its concerns. This was made explicit early in the report:

> with the spread of birth control, the growth or decline of population now depends increasingly on the decision of individual men and women about the numbers of children they will have. This momentous change in the conditions determining population growth raises problems that affect nearly every branch of our national life.[14]

This signalled awareness of a newly important and alarming theme: that personal, individual, choices were increasingly being made which had major national implications, that the desire by individuals to limit family size in order to cultivate other aspects of the self further threatened the nation's demographic prospects.

The report opened with an historical and international survey of population trends. This demonstrated that the populations of India and Pakistan (newly independent in 1947) were growing; the trend in China (which came under Communist control in 1949) was unknown, whilst the birth-rates of Europe, the United States and the 'white' colonies, such as Australia and Canada, were falling and apparently falling fastest among the higher social classes. The Commission accepted that an important part of the explanation for the fall in the birth-rate was the 'emancipation of women', which it was not thought possible or desirable to reverse. An important strand of argument in Britain in the 1930s, promoted particularly by David Glass, who was a researcher for the Royal Commission, had been that women had rejected excessive childbearing and that it was unlikely — and also undesirable — that government measures, such as those attempted by Mussolini, could reverse this change. The Royal Commission reinforced that line of argument: 'It may not be assumed lightly that women in the past, though they seemed to accept repeated and frequent childbearing, did so willingly and without longing for relief'.[15] It continued, approvingly: 'Unrestricted childbearing, which involved hardship and danger to women became increasingly incompatible with the rising status of women and the development of a more considerate attitude of husbands to wives'.[16] The report rejected the more alarmist predictions about the demographic future for Britain and challenged the judgments of the experts. It anticipated a more or less stable population size for the fore-seeable future, though with a shift to larger numbers in older age groups and falling numbers of people of conventional working age.

The report of the Royal Commission demonstrated a marked continu-ity with the population discourses of the early twentieth century in its arguments about the political and cultural significance of population changes. The chapter titled 'Population and the National Interest' opened:

> The industrial progress, the standard of living and the security of the British people, the development and cohesion of the British Commonwealth, the influence of British ideas, traditions and insti-tutions throughout the world may all be affected subtly but powerfully by demographic changes.[17]

The report gave these long-standing concerns a contemporary gloss. A chapter was devoted to the effect of migration upon the future labour force. It was assumed that 'spontaneous emigration' would decline as employment prospects and living standards in Britain rose. Moreover, it was acknowl-edged that the full employment conditions of the late 1940s now made it difficult to attract British-born labour for 'industries that are comparatively unattractive', such as older industries like textiles and shipbuilding which were having difficulty in attracting younger labour. The Commission esti-mated that about 170,000 young adult immigrants would be needed in the coming decade to meet industry's needs and thought it unlikely that suffi-cient labour could be recruited from Europe, despite the continuing flow expected from Ireland. At this point the report turned to predominantly cultural concerns, voicing major reservations about the quality of future generations of immigrants, their traditions and ways of life:

> Even, however, if it were found practicable to secure a net inward

balance of migration on anything like this scale we should have to face serious problems of assimilation beyond those of training and housing. Immigration on a large scale into a firmly established society like ours could only be welcomed without reserve if the immigrants were of good human stock and were not prevented by their religion or race from intermarrying with the host population and becoming merged with it. These conditions were fulfilled by intermittent large scale immigration in the past, notably by the Flemish and Protestant refugees who settled in Britain at different times. There is little or no prospect that we should be able to apply these conditions to large-scale immigration in the future and every increase of our needs would tend to lower the standards of selection.

All these considerations point to the conclusion that continuous large-scale immigration would probably be impracticable and would certainly be undesirable, and the possibility — it can be regarded as no more than a possibility — that circumstances might impel us to consider or attempt it is among the undesirable consequences of the maintenance of family size below replacement level.[18]

The lack of reference to the large, post-1880 Jewish immigration, which was rather more recent than that of 'Flemish and Protestant refugees', is notable. So too is the fact that the authors of the report conceived of the post-war New Jerusalem as no cultural melting pot. Indeed, the comments of the Royal Commission pre-figured, and legitimated, the racial tensions and restrictions on Asian and black immigration in the following decades.

The Royal Commission perceived another problem. Despite the labour shortage, it believed that it could not discourage British migration to the empire, even if this led to future dependence upon migrant labour in Britain:

the falling off of emigration might have serious ill-effects in the long-run on Great Britain and on the British Commonwealth and Empire ... continuous emigration has done much to maintain the strength and solidarity of the Commonwealth and our many ties of sympathy with the USA and if it were to cease altogether or to drop to insignificant numbers the consequence for Britain's economic future and for her place in the world might be serious.[19]

It was assumed that Britain had to be concerned not only about the population structure of the British Isles, and the quality of the 'national stock', but with ensuring that British 'stock' continued to dominate the Empire. All of this had to be achieved with a declining and ageing population. This posed a dilemma for the Royal Commission. It considered the possibility of:

> combining encouragement of emigration with a policy of selective immigration to make good any shortage that might arise in Great Britain. This combined policy has much to commend it for it would ensure that the needs of the rest of the Commonwealth for manpower were met as far as possible from people of British stock and that Great Britain with its much larger population would take on as much as possible of the problem of assimilating people of other than British stock. Again, however, we have to keep in mind that the sources of supply of suitable immigrants to Great Britain are limited, as is also the capacity of a fully established society like ours to absorb immigrants of alien race and religion.

The report urged further study of this problem in the interests of 'maintaining and strengthening the British element in the Commonwealth'.[20]

It went on to speculate on a number of 'imponderables'. These included 'aspirations and projects for European union' and the possible relationship of such a union with the Commonwealth and the United States. Whatever the outcome, the Commission concluded that:

> Undoubtedly the drift of world affairs is giving a new emphasis to the conception of Western civilisation as an entity possessing reality and value. This makes more significant the facts that the countries which constitute this civilisation have shared in large degree the common demographic experience and are confronted now with largely similar demographic problems ... while their rate of increase has been drastically reduced ... during the present century, that of some Oriental peoples has undergone a marked acceleration.[21]

This was a matter of serious concern:

[This] might be decisive in its effects on the prestige and influence of the West. The question that should be observed is not merely one of military strength and security; that question becomes merged in more fundamental issues of the maintenance and extension of western values, ideas and culture. They may also be important because of their bearing on Great Britain's ability to maintain her standing as a leading partner in this wider association.[22]

Fears in influential circles in Britain about the decline in Britain's world role were clearly expressed in the discourse about population. Equally plain was the absence of any coherent proposals for reversing it. Running through the report was the belief that there was a distinctive 'British' cultural identity and that the nation was part of a distinctive and superior 'western civilisation'. Such beliefs were not new, nor was the fear of cultural decline, which had been evident since the later nineteenth century. Nevertheless, they took on new urgency in the face of the decline of Britain's imperial and international power position after the Second World War.

The report of the Royal Commission opens up a number of themes in the history of post-war Britain, including the political question of Britain's relationship with the Commonwealth; and the more personal question of women's perceptions of the effects of declining fertility on their lives.

Who was British? The British Nationality Act, 1948

The instability of the British identity of the Empire was starkly expressed in the debates around the British Nationality Act as it went through Parliament in 1947-8.

Since the seventeenth century the Common Law had extended British nationality to the whole Empire. In principle, anyone born within the Empire was a subject of the British/English Crown and shared British nationality and identical and complete civil, social and legal rights.[23] From the end of the nineteenth century this was brought into question by, on the one hand, the growing assertion of independent national identities within the Empire and, on the other, increasing mobility of people within the Empire, together with the extension of civil and social rights within Britain. The right to vote and to qualify for new welfare benefits, such as unemployment relief, was available to all people born within the Empire.[24]

Through the first half of the twentieth century, British governments sought with increasing desperation to preserve the fiction of a unified imperial nationality, to symbolise to the world the continuing unity of an Empire which in reality was crumbling as the countries of what was increasingly called the Commonwealth asserted their independent nationhoods. The shift in terminology from 'Empire' to 'Commonwealth' was itself part of the difficult, confused, protracted process of Britain's struggle to redefine the relationship with the colonies whilst preserving it in some form.

Limits to the inclusion of the Empire-born as full British citizens were progressively defined as more of them came to Britain, often as merchant seamen, and settled. As Laura Tabili has shown, whilst demand for seamen was high during the First World War, few questions were asked about the actual birth-place of African, Asian or Arab seamen and they were readily accepted as Empire-born British subjects. With the onset of unemployment in 1920, and the emergence of open racial hostility in some British ports, many of these men found their nationality questioned by police, port and immigration officials. Fears that if unemployed they would be charges on the British taxpayer, and the reality that some of them in employment were justifiably demanding improvement of their normally atrocious pay and conditions, intensified pressures and moves to restrict their rights. Since few of them carried evidence of their place of birth, it was difficult for them to prove that they were indeed 'subjects of the Crown', born in the Empire, and not 'aliens'. Under pressure from employers and others, the Home Office in 1925 introduced the Coloured Alien Seamen's Order which effectively enabled all 'coloured' seamen to be treated as 'aliens' unless they could prove otherwise, as few could. Despite protests, this and similar barriers to 'coloured' immigrants from the Empire/Commonwealth to Britain claiming British nationality remained and intensified through the inter-war years.[25]

Such actions of the British state, together with a variety of restrictive measures on nationality rights introduced by Dominion governments, rendered increasingly evident the fragility of the 'British' identity of 'every person in the British Commonwealth and Empire who owes allegiance to the King'.[26] The last attempt to preserve this symbol of Commonwealth unity and British pre-eminence was the British Nationality Act of 1948. In this legislation Britain's weakness was exposed by the large concessions made to the Commonwealth nations. Each nation was now allowed to 'confer its own citizenship, and through citizenship of a country — and through citizenship alone — will a person become a British subject'.[27] In effect, each Commonwealth country could define who was a British subject. Significantly, they did not now even have to describe them as 'British subjects', but could choose the term 'Commonwealth citizen' and, in law, the expressions 'shall have the same meaning'.[28] The boundaries of the definition of British subject/Commonwealth citizen became still more porous in 1949 when the Republic of Ireland left the Commonwealth and its citizens who were resident in Britain retained all the rights they had held previously.[29]

The dominant language of the protracted debates in the House of Commons and the House of Lords about the British Nationality Act was not that of early twentieth-century jingoistic imperialism. The few people who spoke this language, defending British domination over the Empire, were extremely conscious that they were members of a minority. The dominant tone was a troubled awareness of the need to liberate the colonies, without shrugging off British responsibility for their disadvantages, combined with a desire to preserve the links among what was seen as a unique multicultural grouping of nations in a world in which new international blocs were forming in both eastern and western Europe. They were uncertain how best to achieve this and what the implications were for Britain's world role if it occurred. For many people it was easier to support decolonisation in abstract terms than to face up to the implications of disengagement.

The debates around the Nationality Bill expressed tensions and uncertainties about the cultural definition of and the limits to Britishness. These were to acquire increasing salience between the late 1940s and the 1960s. Aspirations to a multicultural Commonwealth sat uneasily alongside belief in the unity and homogeneity of British culture. The tension was made more acute by the increasing presence in Britain of black and Asian British people from the Commonwealth, due directly to labour shortages made more acute by population decline. Whatever the fears and expectations of demographic and political experts, it was evident that 'modern' post-war Britain would indeed be multicultural.

In the late 1940s population issues brought to the surface tensions about Britain's geopolitical position and about British cultural identity. Equally importantly, they brought into focus issues of personal identity and of new life-projections possible for women in post-war Britain.

Fertility Decline and Women's Lives

The permanent decline in the birth-rate in the first half of the twentieth century brought a major, historic shift in women's lives. For the first time in history almost all women knew that they need not be repeatedly pregnant; and that if they wished to have children they could concentrate childbirth and childrearing in a relatively few years of their lives, liberating their middle years for other activities. Women experienced a certain amount of pressure to bear more children as a result of the panic about the fertility decline, but in Britain this was mild, mainly because few people believed that a campaign would be effective.

The Royal Commission on Population acknowledged that 'intelligent and responsible women of all classes' were aware that having 'more than one or two children' was incompatible with 'living what they regard as a tolerable life'. The report continued:

> it is clear that women today are not prepared to accept, as most women in Victorian times accepted, a married life of continuous preoccupation with housework and care of children and that the more independent status and wider interests of women today, which are part of the ideals of the community as a whole, are not compatible with repeated and excessive childbearing. The question is whether they can be reconciled with an average size of family at least large enough to maintain the population.[30]

The report expressed an awareness that not only were relations among nations undergoing fundamental changes, but so too were gender relations. It went on to recommend family allowances and improved social services to enable women to combine childcare with lives of greater freedom. The language of class was as evident as that of race and eugenic terminology. The Commission was especially concerned to alter the situation in which 'a disproportionately small number of the nation's children come from the higher income groups', and the consequent danger of 'a tendency towards lowering the average level of intelligence of the nation'.[31] But it was aware that there were limits to what the state could achieve and the report thus accepted rather than resisted changing gender roles:

> Concern over the trend of population has led to attempts in some countries e.g. Germany and Italy in recent times to narrow the range of women's interests and to 'bring women back into the home'. Such a policy not only runs against the democratic conception of individual freedom, but in Great Britain it would be a rebuking of the tide. It ignores the repercussions which the fall in the size of the family itself has had on the place of women in modern society ... The modern woman is not only more conscious of the need for outside interests but has more freedom to engage them; and it would be harmful all round, to the woman, the family and the community to attempt any restriction of the contribution women can make to the cultural and economic life of the nation. It is true that there is often a real conflict between motherhood and a whole-time 'career'. Part of this conflict is inherent in the biological function of women, but part of it is artificial ... we therefore welcome the removal of the marriage bar in such employments as teaching and the civil service and we think that a deliberate effort should be made to devise adjustments that would render it easier for women to combine motherhood and the care of a home with outside activities.[32]

This conflicts with the interpretation of the immediate post-war period as one in which 'women' were thrust out of public life into domesticity; it is increasingly clear that they were not.[33] From at least 1943 the government was urging women to stay in paid work because of the predicted labour shortage. By 1949 this shortage was acute and older women who had completed childbearing were urged to remain in or to re-enter the paid labour force, though not necessarily to improve their status within it. Younger women were encouraged to stay at home and rear their children.

How did women themselves experience these changes? In theory, the knowledge that births could be limited without great personal discomfort enabled women to imagine for themselves quite different life-courses, above all to imagine a substantial period of adult life, not dominated by reproduction and childcare, which could be devoted to other pursuits. Possibilities opened up for all women for imagining new, perhaps more autonomous, forms of selfhood. But this required an immense, difficult, mental shift for the first generation of women for whom there was a real possibility of living very different lives from the previous generation.

One of the few attempts at the time to explore how women perceived these changes was carried out by Mass Observation in 1944. Investigators collecting material for *Britain and Her Birth-Rate* examined the reasons for the lower birth-rate. Mass Observation researchers interviewed women who were at home or on the streets during the daytime in a sample of London boroughs, which were chosen for their relatively high or low reproduction rates, the latter being mainly upper- and middle-class districts, such as Hampstead and Kensington, the former working-class boroughs such as Bermondsey. They sought these women's opinions about birth control and asked them what they thought was the ideal family size and why. The survey attempted to be socially representative, though research techniques at this time were crude. At best the findings are indicative and illustrative, but they are rare expressions of women's voices about these experiences.

What was notable was that the women answered overwhelmingly in terms not of the improvements to their own lives resulting from smaller family size, but of the potential gains for their children. Typical responses came from a thirty-year-old woman in Willesden, described as coming from a skilled working-class background:

> I think two is a nice family nobody wants to raise a family of sickly children. I don't think I am being selfish in not wanting more, but I've got other ideas for the children. I want them to have every opportunity so that we can be proud of them.[34]

A twenty-five-year-old woman in Bermondsey, described as from an unskilled working-class background, said:

> Well, I know the one'll be enough for me, if I get any say in it. I reckon we all feel more responsible to our kids than they did when they had

those big families — we don't want more than we can give a fair chance to.[35]

One of her neighbours, aged forty, said:

[W]e could never have done what we did for our boy if we'd had more children. He's had the best of education and we let him go right through the secondary school, he won his matriculation and had just started work in a bank when the war broke out.[36]

Most of the younger women, in their forties and younger, assumed that it was possible and desirable to plan the number of children they had. However, working-class women were more aware that 'accidents' might happen and older women seemed rarely to have been aware of birth control in their own younger days, though some had encouraged their daughters to limit their families. For example, sixty-four-year-old Mrs D. had lived all her life in a small Kentish village and had thirteen children, seven of them daughters. She was proud of her family but urged her daughters not to have more than one or two. They were all interviewed. None had more than four children and most had one, two or none.[37]

Many of the women expressed awareness of how things had changed since their mothers' and grandmothers' days, such as the skilled working-class woman in Willesden, referred to above:

it was the accepted thing when they married, it was their job to raise children and attend to the kitchen and cookery. But look around today and you see girls working on the same bench as men, they've got freedom and other interests and just home and bringing up babies doesn't satisfy them and when you can buy birth control things at practically every corner shop, that puts the seal mark to it.[38]

A twenty-nine-year-old 'D' (unskilled working-class) woman in Neasden who had no children as yet (her husband was away at war) asserted:

Every working-class woman wants her children to go one better than she started ... I'd like them to grow up in better surroundings and they should go to a better school and really have a better world. Perhaps its all nonsense but I do right inside me feel that's what I'd like.[39]

A forty-nine-year-old mother of one child in Bethnal Green said 'I come from a big family and I know what its like to get nothing'.[40]

Very few women talked about their own futures. Those who did so were middle class, such as the twenty-seven-year-old university educated woman who 'would like to have more leisure to follow up special studies, read more and attend concerts'. Similarly, a middle-class thirty-four-year-old said:

> I'd like to have one more child. Two doesn't seem a family somehow, but on the other hand I don't want to go on having children all my life. I want to be free for part of my time and have time to do other things.

The interviewer asked what other things. She was vague: 'Well at first I should just like to relax and put my feet up. There's no telling afterwards — let me have my rest first.' By contrast, a twenty-eight-year-old 'D' class woman in Willesden said:

> I don't want to do anything different ten years hence than I'm doing now. I want a comfortable home and want to make it comfortable for my husband and children.[41]

Most women thought of the fall in family size in terms of advantages for their children rather than themselves. This was the first generation in which working-class people could have some hope that social mobility might be available to their children, above all, through the education system. All women in the survey, whatever their social background, repeatedly mentioned the importance of giving children a good education: 'without no education you get nowhere — you're always looked down on'. All too often these hopes were illusory, but unlike in previous generations they had at least some substance. These women were developing new conceptions of social selfhood, of the possibilities open to people like them, but on behalf of their children rather than themselves — conceptions that it can be assumed they passed on to their children. Moreover, some of the middle-class women suggested that their own horizons were expanding and they articulated a distinctive, post-war notion of modern selfhood.

None of these women appeared to share the politicians' and social scientists' concern about the falling birth-rate, rather they expressed dark scepticism about the political motives for wanting to encourage more births. Several women made such comments as: 'They only want more cannon-fodder for the next war'. The women's own discourse about falling family size in 1944 expressed above all a hope for better living standards and greater material security after the war. These were the sentiments which fuelled the Labour electoral victory in the following year, supported as it was by a very high proportion of female voters.

These mothers aimed to encourage higher expectations in their children — their daughters as well as their sons. Daughters born in the 1940s became the new wave of feminists of the 1960s. They are often seen as reacting against what have been described as the limited lives of their mothers. But perhaps their desire for greater opportunities and autonomy was the outcome of the wider horizons which their own mothers consciously sought to offer the smaller families they reared. Daughters grew up with more confident hopes than their mothers of their capacity to control their own lives, within a new, securely established demographic regime. In this sense demographic change also influenced post-war political and cultural change.

Conclusion

The population debate of the 1930s and 1940s focused and expressed many of the central themes of Britain's incomplete struggle towards 'modernity': above all how could 'Great' Britain respond to serious challenges to her imperial hegemony and to her established international economic as well as political power? It was a debate dominated by 'experts', especially by economists who were acquiring a newly prominent role in governing circles, by exponents of the new specialism of demography, and by the growing numbers of 'scientific' social researchers. They shared a newly salient belief that careful state planning could avert crisis, though they differed about what the plans should consist of. Their influence reached a peak in the wartime white papers which offered blueprints for post-war social and economic reconstruction, notably Beveridge's plan for social insurance of 1942 and the employment policy white paper of 1944, which, inspired by Keynes, planned for full employment in peacetime, something never before experienced in modern Britain.

The enthusiasm of the experts, however, betrayed an awareness of the limits to successful planning. One face of modernity was the tendency towards uniformity — in the mass production of goods, for example, in expanding strategies of mass control (through radio, advertising, propaganda), and in the apparent capacity for centralised large-scale planning. The other face of modernity, however, was a growing emphasis on individual autonomy and the desire to assert it, the general realisation of a selfhood that was resistant to tidy planning. This was expressed in the refusal of the 'thoughtful' (that is, better-off) sections of the population to respond to pleas to sustain Britain's place in the world by increasing their birth-rate. Working people also realised that they could improve their own living standards independently of government, or expert, action by limiting the number of births. The experience of controlling birth numbers stimulated women's imaginings of wider possibilities for themselves, shaping the aspirations of their own, as well as later, generations.

The simultaneous fall in birth- and death-rates in Britain in the first half of the twentieth century fuelled the belief among many women and men that, by their own actions, they could improve their lives. It also encouraged an optimistic faith among some of the experts, especially during the Second World War, that a space was opening for effective planning of mass social and economic improvement. Finally, it gave rise to a profoundly conservative cultural pessimism among the élite about the effects of individual autonomy, about the weakening of Britain's world power and the dilution of British culture within Britain itself and within the Empire by an influx of 'unsuitable' immigrants. The power of the pessimists was to constrain the effectiveness of the optimists in the post-war world so that the transformation of Britain was slower and more painful than it might have been.

7. Disorders of the Mind, Disorders of the Body Social: Peter Wildeblood and the Making of the Modern Homosexual

Chris Waters

In January 1954 Peter Wildeblood, diplomatic correspondent for the *Daily Mail*, along with his friend Michael Pitt-Rivers, were arrested on charges of indecency with two young airmen. They were also charged with conspiring with the third Baron Montagu of Beaulieu to commit indecency with the airmen in a summer beach hut on Montagu's estate. On 24 March, at the conclusion of a sensational, eight-day trial, all three men were found guilty. Lord Montagu — who along with the film director Kenneth Hume had faced trial on similar charges several months earlier — received a twelve-month prison sentence; Pitt-Rivers and Wildeblood were each sentenced for eighteen months.[1] None of the defendants pleaded guilty to the charges brought against them. After his release from prison, however, Wildeblood took his case to the public in his book, *Against the Law* (1955), a plea for social tolerance and legal change written by a confessed homosexual.

The trial fuelled the growing debate about the status of the laws pertaining to homosexuality in Britain. It also influenced the Home Secretary, Sir David Maxwell-Fyfe, in his decision to appoint a committee, headed by John Wolfenden, to examine those laws. Given that the Wolfenden Committee recommended the partial decriminalisation of homosexuality, Jeffrey Weeks argues that the trial of Wildeblood and his co-defendants marked a crucial moment in the history of homosexual law reform. Stephen Jeffery-Poulter likewise suggests that *Against the Law* contributed to the process of reform by exposing 'the hypocrisy of the laws'.[2] In both of their accounts Wildeblood is cast as a hero who contributed to the forward march of homosexual emancipation. The story they tell is whiggish in every

Peter Wildeblood

respect: it is a story of progress, of a milestone on the long and rocky road to the 'gay liberation' of the later 1960s and beyond. Echoing these sentiments, Simon Edge, former editor of London's *Capital Gay*, considers Wildeblood's book to be a 'heroic piece of writing that changed the world' — despite the fact that very few gay men today are familiar with either the book or its author.[3] Like Weeks and Jeffery-Poulter, Edge has contributed to the image we now have of Wildeblood, an image of a crusader for reform whose trial contributed martyrs to the cause and galvanized resistance to what were held to be antiquated laws at odds with a modern society.

I do not wish to challenge such accounts of Wildeblood's importance to the post-war project of homosexual law reform. Rather, I want to suggest that by privileging the law, and by focusing on those who contributed to its reform, many commentators have often sidestepped other, equally significant, issues. For example, they seldom note the discourses within which homosexuality was inscribed, or the ways in which homosexual subjectivity was experienced, in the 1950s. As Frank Mort argues, while it is hardly surprising that the law became the main site on which struggles around sexuality and morality took place in that decade, we should not make a fetish of its operation; if we do, we will miss the 'complexity of strategies of regulation which address sexuality in its modern form'.[4] After the Second World War, many of those strategies of regulation involved a search for an appropriate language to address the problems facing society. Hence, in addition to examining the debates about what stance the law should take with regards to 'the homosexual', we also need to explore the struggles between various individuals and agencies to define what type of person 'the homosexual' was.

Peter Wildeblood contested many established definitions of 'the homosexual' and articulated a relatively new kind of selfhood. This shaped his own identity and defined the nature of those for whom legal rights were to be secured. He did not simply argue on behalf of 'the homosexual', understood as some essential and timeless being; rather, he demanded rights for a relatively new category of selfhood in post-war Britain, one assembled from many existing discourses. In order both to resist the labels imposed on him at his trial and to counter the representations of his character that appeared in the tabloid press, Wildeblood rewrote his life for

public consumption; in so doing he gave rise to a uniquely modern homosexual persona. The project of modernity in post-war Britain cannot be
fully understood without reference to the emergence of new and distinctive modes for imagining the self. Wildeblood's contribution to that process
took place against the backdrop of extensive debates about the nature of
homosexuality.

Moral Panics in the New Jerusalem

In the early 1930s roughly 400 men were brought to trial annually in
England and Wales for committing sexual offences with other men. By the
late 1940s the number had more than doubled, while 2166 men were
tried for such offences (1257 of whom were found guilty) in 1953.[5] In the
early 1950s it was not simply the increasing number of cases that fuelled
the heightened public awareness of the problem of homosexuality in
Britain, but the prominent position occupied by some of the men tried.
Within three years of the defection of the homosexual diplomats Guy
Burgess and Donald Maclean to the Soviet Union in March 1951, the actor
John Gielgud and the Labour MP William Fielding were both convicted
of importuning, the novelist Rupert Croft-Cooke was imprisoned for acts
of indecency with two naval men, and the Montagu/Pitt-
Rivers/Wildeblood trial had further exposed the existence of
homosexuality in high places.[6] The reasons for this increase in the number
of arrests for homosexual activity are complex. In part the growing perse-
cution of homosexuals by the state can be attributed to the zeal of Sir
Theobold Matthew, a devout Catholic who became Director of Public
Prosecutions in 1944 and who believed strongly that the growing visibility
of homosexuality should be halted. Likewise, the post-1951 efforts of the
Conservative Home Secretary, Sir David Maxwell-Fyfe, to clean up vice,
especially around the time of the Coronation in 1953, also needs to be
considered. Both officials' uncompromising stance towards homosexuality
was, however, also a response to broader currents of social dislocation
unleashed by the war. Their actions led Croft-Cooke to refer to the period
as one of 'sexual McCarthyism'.[7]

Anxieties about homosexual vice often surfaced in the many post-war
debates about the decline of moral standards in Britain. Moreover, those

debates were linked to a broader concern about the nation's birth-rate. As Pat Thane argues, the immediate post-war years witnessed the proliferation of studies warning of an impending demographic catastrophe. The sociologist, Mark Abrams, addressing this issue in 1945, suggested that the family, as an institution for 'biological continuity', was failing — often because new opportunities for leisure and personal fulfilment were eroding the desire for children.[8] Such concerns were also apparent in the writing of doctors who addressed the issue of homosexuality. In 1946, for example, D. Stanley Jones argued that the state should make 'the benefits that psychology has to offer' available to homosexuals because of the 'loss of potential mothers and fathers among those whose instincts have been diverted up a biological blind alley'.[9]

The complex equation of moral decline, demographic anxiety and homosexual panic after the war was also registered in the tabloid press. When, in 1953, Lord Samuel, the eighty-three year-old Liberal peer, attacked the state of the nation's morals in a speech to the Lords, he gave the tabloids ammunition for their own battle against immorality. Samuel spoke of the 'moral law' of the nation being weakened, of an increase in the 'vices of Sodom and Gomorrah', and of the need to combat the faith placed in psychiatrists to speak with authority about homosexuality.[10] Sharing these sentiments, the *Daily Mail* insisted that Samuel's speech was based on 'sound sense' rather than on those 'new doctrines of physiology and psychology which tend to weaken individual responsibility'.[11]

For such papers, it was a short step from a general survey of Britain's presumed moral decline to a detailed analysis of the role played by homosexuality in it. The *Sunday Pictorial* led the way in addressing the 'growing social problem' of homosexuality, as Douglas Warth termed it, in a series entitled 'Evil Men'. Warth asserted that homosexuality was 'an unnatural sexual vice', and he argued that, because a regime of silence 'enabled the evil to spread', it was necessary for journalists to turn the spotlight of publicity on it. What most frightened him was the extent to which an underground, homosexual subculture was flourishing in the midst of a society largely oblivious to it. While he believed that some participants in that subculture could be identified by their effeminate mannerisms, Warth argued that many could not be spotted by such visible markers of their proclivities.[12] This portrait of the homosexual who could not be recognised as such, and yet who inhabited an underground milieu of which the general public was largely unaware, served the tabloids' agenda of encouraging both the fears and voyeuristic fascination of their readers — much as the uncovering of sexual vice by W.T. Stead's *Pall Mall Gazette* had done in the late nineteenth century. Indeed, as the *Daily Mirror* put it, 'Stead's case is the classic example of how necessary it is for a newspaper to shock public opinion so that evil shall be put right'.[13]

The decade after the war witnessed the emergence of what might best be termed a tabloid discourse of homosexuality, a strategy dedicated to uncovering, naming and codifying homosexual lives for popular consumption. Not since the furor surrounding the downfall of Oscar Wilde in the 1890s had the press delved so deeply into the question of homosexuality. Nevertheless, the 'discovery' of homosexuality in the 1950s was, as it had been in Wilde's day, a contrived spectacle in so far as it depended on the prior fiction that homosexuality had once been 'hidden'. This construct served tabloid journalists well, positioning them as heroic investigators, armed with the power to disclose for the nation at large what it could not see. It also positioned them as champions of morality who could root out 'moral rot', as John Gordon, Warth's counterpart at the *Sunday Express*, put it.[14]

Despite their best efforts to defend their practices, many tabloid journalists discovered that journeys into the homosexual underworld elicited an alarmed response. As early as 1949, Dr Eustace Chesser expressed concern about the growing frankness in tabloid coverage of 'sexual abnormality', arguing that it could 'tend to cause those with a predisposition towards some abnormal activity to experiment'.[15] Such fears were widespread in the 1950s, leading the MP George Craddock to ask the Home Secretary to appoint a committee to investigate the danger to public morale caused by the publicity the press gave to 'gross and unnecessary details' in its coverage of homosexuality.[16] Little came of his request, and the tabloids continued their offensive against vice. By endorsing the role played by the state in clamping down on vice, such campaigns further legitimated the work of the Home Secretary. In addition, they fuelled debates about what was appropriate for public discussion, in so doing repositioning the discursive boundaries around the topic of homosexuality. Finally, they elicited many critical responses from a battery of self-appointed experts, individuals who attacked the various knowledge claims and representational strategies they found so distasteful in the tabloids. In short, the 1950s witnessed not only the crystallisation of a tabloid discourse of homosexuality but a parallel expansion of an alternative, scientific discourse, one that battled in the marketplace of ideas for both popular and state acceptance.

Expert Knowledge, Homosexuality and the Therapeutic State

While the tabloids began to discuss homosexuality, rarely did they use the term itself. Warth spoke of 'male degenerates', 'sexual perverts', 'men with sick minds' and 'mincing, effeminate young men who call themselves "queers"'.[17] Such journalists were roundly attacked by those with a knowledge of the latest theories of homosexuality, experts who called for greater responsibility in naming the condition the tabloids attacked. The quality press followed their lead, cloaking itself in the garb of science to counter the claims made by journalists like Warth and Gordon. In 1953 the *Observer*, ever progressive but cautious, condemned sensationalism in the coverage of homosexuality and praised the sober discussion of the topic in the Kinsey Reports. Calling for more scientific enquiry and less irresponsible journalism, the paper also printed a letter by a consultant psychologist. In so doing, it initiated a trend whereby the new experts were asked to testify against the assumptions shared by tabloid writers.[18]

If the tabloids could not be silenced, then perhaps their arguments could be countered by science; if the tabloids 'outed' the topic, then science would stake its own claim to discursive hegemony. Like journalists working for the popular press, the experts who participated in these debates also talked about the 'conspiracy of silence' surrounding the issue. However, unlike their counterparts, they asserted the importance of the latest scientific theories. Gordon Westwood, author of the first major post-war study of homosexuality in Britain in 1952, conceived of his book explicitly as an antidote to tabloid sensationalism. Like the tabloids, he claimed that the 'problem of homosexuality must be brought out into the open where it can be discussed', but there it was to be debated calmly and, above all, 'rationally and without emotion'.[19] Three years later D.J. West made the same point, writing that 'a sober presentation of the facts', debated in the light of 'modern knowledge', might end the 'conspiracy of silence' surrounding homosexuality.[20]

The work of Westwood and West was indebted primarily to the 'modern knowledge' of Sigmund Freud and his followers. West was the registrar of the Psychiatric Day Clinic at the Marlborough Hospital in London and he, like Westwood, largely rejected the older understanding of homosexuality put forward by Havelock Ellis in favour of that proposed by psychoanalysis. While Ellis had viewed homosexuality in terms of an inverted gender identity, visible in the behavioural manifestations of the invert's inner essence, Freud and his followers by and large rejected such a characterological assessment of the homosexual, focusing more narrowly on the question of sexual object choice. Like Freud, Westwood and West tended to conceive of homosexuality as a form of discrepant sexual behaviour, rather than a series of gender anomalies. They also believed that homosexuality was less an innate, congenital condition than the result of arrested development, a Freudian 'disorder of the mind'.[21]

Westwood and West worked strenuously to disseminate a modern psychoanalytic understanding of homosexuality. But they did so in a decade in which many other formulations of various sexual behaviours competed for public attention. As one writer argued in 1952, there were three commonly held views of homosexuality in circulation in Britain at the time: Kinsey's model of a continuum between homosexuality and heterosexuality; various theories of 'congenital anomaly' put forward by Ellis and Magnus Hirschfeld; and Freud's theory of the 'distorting influence of early unresolved complexes on psychosexual development'.[22]

While popular reportage remained suspicious of the claims of psychoanalysis, those claims were widely disseminated in the 1940s and 1950s. During the war psychiatry in general had made spectacular advances, particularly in the armed services, leading many advocates of psychoanalytic thought to insist on a role for themselves in the pantheon of experts called upon in 1945 to help build the New Jerusalem.[23] It was these individuals who now began to apply their training to a host of post-war social problems, particularly juvenile delinquency and homosexuality. In 1947, Kate Friedlander's pioneering work on the psychoanalytic treatment of delinquents made a case for Freudian thought in understanding the aetiology both of juvenile delinquency and homosexuality.[24] Two years later Clifford Allen published a revised edition of his study of the 'sexual perversions', reiterating that his aim was to convince readers that the antiquated work of Ellis, Hirschfeld and Krafft-Ebing needed to be replaced with the 'modern insights' of 'dynamic psychology'.[25]

Many of the psychoanalytic approaches to homosexuality put forward at this time were used to justify the need for law reform. Westwood claimed that the laws concerning homosexuality had become archaic, formulated 'long before the discoveries of modern psychology', an argument made, in the same terms, by Sir Robert Boothby in his call on the floor of the Commons for a commission to investigate those laws.[26] Nevertheless, in the battle over legal reform such arguments co-existed with those derived from the work of other sexologists. In its own call for legal reform, for example, the Moral Welfare Council of the Church of England hedged its aetiological bets. While its report spoke of homosexuality as a condition arising from developmental factors in childhood and adolescence, it also suggested that 'it may in some cases ... be innate'. Rarely did the Council use the term 'homosexual'; it favoured Ellis's notion of the 'invert', which it distinguished from the 'pervert' — the heterosexual who occasionally engaged in homosexual practices.[27]

Despite the fact that psychoanalytic models of psychosexual development were contested forms of knowledge in the late 1940s and 1950s, many urged the greater use of therapeutic techniques in the treatment of homosexuality. While writers like Westwood and West had little faith in the 'cures' that were such a major feature of post-war psychiatry in the United States, others were more optimistic. Writing in *The Lancet* in the aftermath of the Montagu/Pitt-Rivers/Wildeblood trial, for example, Kenneth Soddy called on doctors to work towards the 'prevention and cure of this unfortunate developmental failure'. He also urged the state to develop programs of 'preventive mental hygiene', contributing to the debates about how best the state might use the 'modern knowledge' of psychiatry in addressing any number of social problems.[28] Consequently, when the joint report of the British Medical Association and the Magistrates Association called in 1949 for the punishment of homosexuals to be tempered by treatment, it argued that, as courts acquired knowledge of what psychiatry could accomplish, and as opportunities for treatment expanded, so 'the practical value of psychological methods' would become more apparent both to the courts and public opinion.[29] The Criminal Justice Act of 1948 had already made some provisions for the treatment of sexual offenders, and in 1954 the Home Secretary announced that he would establish an institute where the latest psychological knowledge would be used in the care of such individuals.[30]

By the time of the Montagu/Pitt-Rivers/Wildeblood trial in 1954, the British public had been deluged with attacks on the decline of morals in general and the rise of homosexuality in particular. Moreover, experts who embraced psychoanalysis had come forward to identify the cause of the maladies and offer remedies for them. But if homosexuality was a 'disorder of the mind', as Westwood put it, it was also a disorder of the social body, as those who sought to stem the tide of 'evil men' were quick to assert. In short, despite the post-war proliferation of writing about homosexuality, no one explanatory system emerged triumphant in these years. As we have seen, the psychoanalytic understanding of Britain's post-war ills was never uncontested: state agencies remained cautious in their dealings with dynamic psychology, while traditional moralists and tabloid journalists remained hostile to what they viewed as little more than new-fangled sophistry. When Peter Wildeblood was released from jail and sat down to write *Against the Law*, he did so in a world in which tabloid, psychoanalytic and other sexological discourses of homosexuality competed with each other for attention. In quite complex ways, those discourses both constituted Wildeblood's self-understanding and were drawn upon by him to fashion his case for a change in the legal status of the homosexual in Britain.

Peter Wildeblood and the Making of the Modern Homosexual

On the first page of *Against the Law* Wildeblood declared, 'I am a homosexual. It is easy for me to make that admission now, because much of my private life has already been made public by the newspapers.' Several paragraphs later he claimed he had been compelled to offer an account of his life, trial and imprisonment because other writers had already dragged 'into the merciless light of publicity things which would have been better left in darkness'.[31] In short, Wildeblood opened his book by positioning his own story against many extant narratives of homosexuality in circulation. This point was noted by a reviewer of the German edition of the book, who praised it as an important antidote to the 'cheap language' of perversion, vice, disease and wasted energy he had encountered in the contemporary discussion of homosexuality.[32] This is not to say that *Against the Law* was untouched by the conventions of tabloid journalism. When he proclaimed that he had 'moved out of darkness and into light', Wildeblood used the now familiar tropes of secrecy and disclosure that were central to the tabloid discourse of homosexuality.[33] Nevertheless, in shedding light on his own 'condition', as he termed it, he asserted narrative authority over his life and challenged many of the representations of homosexuality he had encountered in the tabloids. Once his case had been made public, he felt he had nothing to lose by telling his own story. While neither admitting guilt to the charges brought against him nor differing in his details from the press accounts of the trial, Wildeblood repudiated many of the categories in which others had inscribed him.

Born in Italy in 1923 to a retired engineer from the Indian Public Works Department and the daughter of a sheep-rancher in Argentina, Wildeblood attended public school in England and went to Oxford in 1941. His studies were interrupted by service in the Royal Air Force, but he completed his degree after the war and soon became a regional reporter for the *Daily Mail*. By 1953 he had become the diplomatic correspondent for the paper. Arrested in January 1954, tried in March, found guilty and imprisoned, Wildeblood was released from jail in March 1955. Immediately he set to work on *Against the Law*, testified before the Wolfenden Committee and wrote several other books, including two novels, before becoming a major screenwriter and television producer.

Along with Lord Montagu and Michael Pitt-Rivers, Wildeblood was charged with committing 'indecency' with the two airmen, Edward McNally and John Reynolds. Wildeblood had met McNally in London and saw him often, exchanging letters that were later seized by the police and read as evidence at the trial. In the summer of 1952 they travelled with Reynolds to Dorset for a quiet holiday on Montagu's estate. There, it was alleged, Wildeblood, Montagu and Pitt-Rivers lavished hospitality on the two airmen, danced and drank excessively before the so-called indecencies occurred. In December 1953 McNally was arrested and promised immunity from prosecution if he turned Queen's Evidence against the three defendants, which he did. The jury found Wildeblood guilty on three counts of committing a 'serious offence' with McNally, one count of 'gross indecency' with him, one count of aiding and abetting Montagu to commit 'gross indecency' and one count of inciting McNally to commit the same.

The trial offered the press new scope for its investigations into vice. Yet the reporting remained circumspect: while the tabloids wished to shed light on the problem of homosexuality, they never offered details of the offences that took place. They expurgated the court proceedings and tried to map the essential character of the homosexual not by referring to specific acts but by offering an image of the type of person who was likely to commit them. In this their strategies were similar to those employed by reporters who covered the Wilde trials in 1895.[34] Essentially, the press projected an image of the three defendants as decadent, effete and effeminate. That image was also cultivated by the prosecution at the trial in order to secure conviction. Hence much was made of the letters Wildeblood wrote to McNally, letters that suggested characterological flaws that could be read as a sign of homosexuality. At the preliminary magistrates' hearing, the prosecutor, borrowing a line from the Wilde trials, described one of them as a 'passionate love letter, breathing almost unnatural love in almost every line'.[35] In a similar vein, when McNally spoke softly and could not be heard, the prosecutor declared, 'He has a high voice naturally'.[36] In short, the trial focused as much on the type of men Wildeblood and McNally were as on what they actually did. Consequently, witnesses were called to address their character. Edward Schofield, the editor of the *Daily Mail*, said that he had considered Wildeblood 'to be in appearance and manner rather effeminate' but that he had no 'reason to suspect anything'.[37]

Wildeblood did not conceive of himself in effeminate terms and he resisted efforts to characterise him as such. 'Everyone', he wrote, 'has seen the pathetically flambuoyant pansy with the flapping wrists ... Most of us are not like that. We do our best to look like everyone else, and we usually succeed.'[38] Arguing on behalf of a respectable homosexual selfhood, Wildeblood canvassed many of the understandings of homosexuality that were being put forward in other scholarly works. In particular, he reiterated several assertions made by Westwood. In 1952, for example, anticipating Wildeblood, Westwood wrote that it was wrong to 'imagine that all homosexuals look like "Nancy Boys"', suggesting that most 'are not physically different from the normal man'.[39] Such arguments were often put forward to counter the widespread assumption that effeminacy was a marker of a hidden, homosexual self. While at the trial much was made of those presumed markers, they were increasingly under attack, not least by Wildeblood himself. Nevertheless, although the tabloids equated homosexuality and effeminacy, they also, as we have seen, asserted that many homosexuals could not be recognised by their looks; by emphasising their invisibility journalists could more readily dramatise their danger and authorise their own quest to ferret out that danger. Consequently, Wildeblood's repudiation of effeminacy, while central to the model of respectable homosexual selfhood he advanced, could be used by the press to fuel the panic it wished to cultivate.

Not only did Wildeblood attempt to repudiate the charge of effeminacy, but he also defended his choice of partners. In his book, he argued that the main reason for his conviction was his tendency to enter into emotional relationships with younger men of a lower social standing.[40] The prosecutor made much of these transgressions of social boundaries, asking Wildeblood, 'What was the common link which bound you, a highly intelligent man and a beautiful writer, with Cpl. McNally, who started ... in the pits up at Glasgow?'[41] Wildeblood tried to justify his liaison with McNally, claiming that it was similar to many of the cross-class friendships he and others had enjoyed in the armed forces during the war. Nevertheless, apprehension about the erosion of social boundaries was a major legacy of the war and it often surfaced in the press accounts of the male homosexual and his milieu. John Ervine, one of Wilde's many post-war biographers, shared those apprehensions. He criticised the policies of social levelling he associated with Aneurin Bevan and Emanuel Shinwell, two Labour ministers, he argued, who desired a 'proletarian world' and possessed 'back-street minds'. He also believed that homosexuals threatened stable social hierarchies and criticised Wilde for seeking companions whose 'speech came from the gutter and the slum'.[42] Such fears were widespread in the 1950s, often leading to attacks on cross-class heterosexual, as well as homosexual, relationships. Echoing Ervine's concerns, for example, the social critic Geoffrey Gorer dissected the many perils of 'hypergamy', complaining about scholarship-educated working-class men who married upper-class women.[43] Wildeblood's trial thus intensified anxieties about the erosion of social boundaries, while his claim that many homosexuals paid little attention to those boundaries exacerbated fears about the moral and social chaos that might result from unlicensed homosexuality.

Wildeblood's defence of cross-class male relationships also contributed to the voyeuristic fascination in the rituals of the homosexual subculture that was a staple of tabloid reportage. At times he attempted to defend himself from attack by distancing the homosexual from the world he might occasionally inhabit: they 'do not form a cohesive or organised group', he wrote, claiming that most homosexuals were isolated from the rest of society and from each other.[44] In making such claims, Wildeblood hoped to focus attention on the individual, on the man who both repudiated the effeminate stereotype with which he was branded and remained apart from an underworld the likes of which the tabloids were eager to expose. As an astute observer of homosexual society in Britain noted, many homophobes were of the unshakable conviction that homosexuals 'are linked with each other by some mysterious bond that threatens the safety of other members of society'.[45] At his trial, Wildeblood and McNally were questioned repeatedly about the signs and signals known only to other homosexuals in their 'secret' world. Wildeblood knew that his best defence was to distance himself from that world, which he indeed attempted to do; yet he remained fascinated by it, offering a series of sketches of life in its midst in his second book, *A Way of Life*. One reviewer, who approved of Wildeblood's struggle on behalf of the individual homosexual, believed this book might undermine much of the good work Wildeblood had done. Arguing that its focus on the lives of characters in the homosexual underworld might hinder the process of reform, he termed the book a 'meretricious' rather than 'meritorious' study.[46]

Had Wildeblood acknowledged and celebrated the homosexual subculture at his trial, tabloid journalists would have been vindicated in their belief that a hidden underworld existed which needed to be exposed. Wildeblood defended himself by trying to distinguish the individual homosexual from any larger sense of community. But how did he understand the 'condition' of those individuals? What, for Wildeblood, was a homosexual? At his trial the language of 'perverts' and 'inverts' was ubiquitous while 'homosexual' was a term rarely used. The prosecution viewed McNally and Reynolds as 'perverts, men of the lowest possible moral character', while the defence argued that Wildeblood was, through no fault of his own, an 'invert' who should be treated leniently.[47] Terminological confusion was rampant at the trial, although clarification was sought in an exchange between the prosecutor and Wildeblood:

> ROBERTS: 'An invert is a man who from an accident of birth or parentage has unnatural desires, is he not?'
> [Wildeblood:] 'Yes.'
> 'Whereas a pervert is a man who, from lust or wickedness, will get desire from either the natural or from the unnatural function?'
> 'Yes.'
> 'Your character has been put in at the highest .... But are you an invert?'
> 'Yes, I am an invert.'
> 'That means to say that, through no fault of your own, you are subjected to temptations and desires to which the normal man is not subjected?'
> 'That is true.'[48]

Unlike his co-defendants, Wildeblood admitted that he was an 'invert', perhaps hoping that by adopting the label of inversion he might elicit the jury's sympathy. After the trial, however, he presented a much more fractured and unstable articulation of selfhood. In *Against the Law* he often spoke of 'inverts', rather than 'homosexuals', viewing himself in Ellis-like terms as an individual who suffered a 'tragic disability' for which there was no cure. Moreover, in his testimony to the Wolfenden Committee he mentioned Ellis by name and, like Ellis, claimed that inversion was a 'kind of anomaly' and not an illness.[49] Yet his self-understanding was not derived solely from the ideas of Ellis. In his autobiography he mapped the existence of three types of homosexuals, as he had for the Wolfenden Committee. First were the 'genuine glandular cases, the men who were in fact women in everything but body'. Here he offered a classic portrait of the invert, recognisable through his effeminate behaviour. Second were the men who seduced young boys. Finally, he argued, there were men who, much like himself, were not effeminate and who disapproved as much as he did of the other two groups.[50] It was this last group, whose ordinariness he embellished as a means of self-legitimation, that he partially understood in psychoanalytic terms. He rejected the notion that its members suffered from a complete gender inversion and instead stressed their similarities to heterosexual men in all respects except for their sexual object choice.

Despite his debts to Ellis, then, Wildeblood also spoke the language of Freud. He pondered whether or not his parents might have contributed to his 'condition'; he referred to friendships between boys that had an 'unconsciously homosexual basis'; he discussed adolescents who experienced a homosexual 'stage' before making 'the natural transition into normality'; and he claimed that homosexuality resulted from 'arrested development'. Like Westwood, Wildeblood was in part indebted to a psychoanalytic model of development: 'The first stirrings of sex in childhood, we are told, are directed indiscriminately towards all kinds of objects and persons; it is during adolescence that they are — or should be — oriented towards the opposite sex'.[51] Wildeblood also sought support for his belief that homosexuality was a 'condition of the mind' in the writings of those experts who had been solicited by the quality press to counter the tabloid discourse of homosexuality. Thus he referred to the psychiatric knowledge he had encountered in the *Sunday Times* to bolster his claim that homosexuality could be stimulated at any age.[52]

Although he made use of psychoanalytic categories in his discussion of the aetiology of homosexuality, Wildeblood remained wary of the psychiatric treatment of the phenomenon. The defence at his trial had called upon Dr John Abbott Hobson, consultant physician in the Department of Psychological Medicine at the Middlesex Hospital, to testify on Wildeblood's behalf. Hobson told the jury that Wildeblood was not a 'typical' homosexual and that because he was intelligent and willing to be treated a cure was possible. After Wildeblood was released from prison, Hobson privately qualified his statements, confirming Wildeblood's own reservations about the therapeutic panaceas being put forth by experts in courtrooms around the country.[53] Those reservations were noted by Max Lerner, author of the preface to the American edition of *Against the Law*, who argued that his experience of psychiatry made him more optimistic than Wildeblood.[54] But Wildeblood remained a sceptic and in 1962 he wrote a parody of the famous letter Freud had written in 1935 to an American mother of a homosexual son about what psychoanalysis could, and could not, offer him. In his own letter, Wildeblood argued that the 'endless confessions' extracted by the psychiatrist from the homosexual could only result in 'self-consciousness if not in downright exhibitionism'.[55] Of course, it was the endless confessions extracted from Wildeblood at his trial, eagerly reported by the tabloids, that led him to exhibit his own life, to write his own story of homosexual selfhood. Despite his reservations about psychiatry, that story was in part framed by psychoanalytic discourses of homosexuality.

After his release from prison, Wildeblood became a hero in the struggle to decriminalise homosexuality. That struggle took place on the terrain of contested knowledge: it was not merely about legal rights for homosexuals, but about the very meaning of homosexuality itself. Attempts to define the kind of person for whom rights were to be secured were central to the emancipatory project of men like Wildeblood and in this project *Against the Law* played an important role. But it was a complex, unstable text. It rejected the moral outrage associated with the tabloid discourse of homosexuality, yet was inscribed within the same binary logic of secrecy and disclosure that characterised tabloid reporting. It was informed by Ellis's belief that the invert was an untreatable 'anomaly' who should be tolerated, yet it did not approve of those individuals who displayed the signs of inversion in their effeminate mannerisms. It suggested that the respectable homosexual only differed from the heterosexual in terms of sexual object choice, yet it repudiated the therapeutic consequences of psychoanalytic thinking.

Despite its complexities, *Against the Law* must be seen on a simple level as a distinctly modern 'coming out' narrative. It was perhaps the first book ever published in Britain by a male homosexual who openly used his name, who offered a frank story of his life and who argued forcefully for rights for other men like himself. Wildeblood did all these things. Afterwards he told the Wolfenden Committee, 'I am certainly very much happier now that I do not have any need to conceal'.[56] Such stories are abundant today; they were not in the 1950s. But it was in the 1950s that the writing of narratives like Wildeblood's became increasingly possible, a development, as Carolyn Steedman argues, related to a new valorisation of the self after the war. *Against the Law* was part of that project. It was a work that contributed to the making of a respectable homosexual identity out of a confluence of competing discourses that circulated in Britain during the decade after the end of the Second World War. Just as the Kinsey Reports heralded 'an accelerating reflexivity on the level of ordinary, everyday sexual practices', so must Peter Wildeblood's autobiography be seen in terms of the contribution it made to distinctly modern forms of selfhood.[57]

In an earlier age Wildeblood might have fled to France, as Wilde had done. Or he might have escaped into the greenwood, as had Maurice and Alec in E.M. Forster's 1914 novel, *Maurice*. But as Forster noted in 1960, in the terminal note to his then still unpublished novel, two world wars demanded and bequeathed new forms of state regimentation, which the public services adopted and extended, resulting in a patrolled and built over island in which there was no place left to escape.[58] In such a context, Wildeblood believed that his best option was to 'come out' and take his case to the public. This course of action is perhaps only possible after escape into the greenwood becomes impractical and once a category of homosexual selfhood has emerged into which one can 'come out', a category to which Wildeblood contributed in the process of narrating his own life.

Forster claimed in his terminal note that he had believed, optimistically, that knowledge would lead to understanding. By 1960, however, his faith appeared to have waned. Wildeblood, by contrast, remained optimistic, displaying a liberal commitment to the power of reason that was ubiquitous in Britain in the 1950s. That decade witnessed the consolidation of the therapeutic state, based on the belief that experts, with their 'modern knowledge', could assist in the eradication of any number of social maladies. But if the post-war language of the experts — especially that of psychiatry — influenced government policy in unprecedented ways, it also influenced those who sought to articulate and defend new forms of selfhood. Constituted at the intersection of competing knowledge systems, Wildeblood attempted to use the best of 'modern knowledge' to make sense of his own life and to argue for reform of what he took to be antiquated laws. He offered that knowledge to thousands of others so they might do likewise.

8. The Labour Party: Modernisation and the Politics of Restraint

Martin Francis

On 4 July 1948, the eve of the inauguration of the National Health Service, Aneurin Bevan recalled at Belle Vue in Manchester his sufferings in the South Wales coalfields of the 1920s. Part of his speech has become the stuff of political legend:

> In my early life I had to live on the earnings of an elder sister and was told to emigrate. That is why no amount of cajolery and no attempt at ethical or social seduction can eradicate from my heart a deep burning hatred for the Tory Party that inflicted those bitter experiences. So far as I am concerned they are lower than vermin.

Such invective from the Minister of Health was nothing new, but this time he appeared to have gone too far. Churchill christened Bevan the 'Minister of Disease', accused him of 'morbid hatred' and suggested that it might be appropriate when launching the new medical service to ensure 'that a person who so obviously needs psychiatrical [sic] attention should be among the first of its patients'. Within the Labour Party, too many were quick to suggest that Bevan's outburst reflected a lack of judgment and self-discipline, which was dangerously inappropriate for one holding high office.[1] He had broken recognised codes of political behaviour, the continued existence of which was vital to prevent public life falling into anarchy and contempt. This small, though notorious incident might seem unworthy of further attention. But historians would be advised to dwell a while here before continuing. For the tenets of civility which

Bevan had transgressed were not universal and timeless, but were, like all codes which have been created and promoted in an attempt to regulate behaviour, historically specific and contingent. Norms of expression and restraint in politics vary and can offer insights into the changing emotional conventions of political discourse.

What made Bevan's splenetic outburst reprehensible was that in the immediate post-war decades restraint and self-discipline were presented as vital ingredients of Labour's project of modernity. Labour sought to recast both the economy and society along lines that were rational and functional; to replace private economic chaos with public economic order. A new meritocratic polity would be created. Those wishing to increase the efficiency of the nation would be freed from the shackles of a capitalist system of ownership that was cast as both monopolistic and irrational. The socialist commonwealth would embody rational and enlightened progress, in sharp contrast to the policies of the Conservatives, the latter represented by Harold Laski as the 'enemies of reason', or by *Tribune* as the 'astrologers of a dead tradition'.[2] But the construction of a new rational order and the spurning of obscurantism required serious, sober and ordered behaviour from Britain's political leaders. In the late 1940s and early 1950s emotional control and restraint became a critical motif in Labour's self-presentation. Self-discipline was considered a vital requirement for effective public service and displays of unfettered emotion in politics were regarded as inappropriate.

The intensity of controversy and critical comment generated by Bevan's 'vermin' speech was a telling reminder that unregulated genres of political discourse were no longer acceptable. This imperative was partly dictated by Labour's desire to demonstrate to both the Tories and to the public (especially the middle classes) that they were fit to govern, but it was also part of a much broader agenda. Self-discipline was prioritised because it was perceived as vital to the complex task of social and economic reconstruction. An emphasis on restraint matched contemporary codes of manliness, at a time when masculinity seemed to be under threat from a blurring of gender roles and the increased visibility of homosexuality. Uncontrolled emotion also transgressed a conception of British (or at least English) national identity which was rooted in self-restraint. Labour politicians made their commitment to self-control manifest in speech, mannerism and dress. However, the pursuit of a modern rational order based on balance and proportion in speech and behaviour (what George Mosse has termed the 'golden mean') was neither unproblematic nor uncontested. [3] The Labour Party had been created to defend and celebrate the interests and values of male manual labour, and it therefore often proved difficult to privilege what were essentially middle-class modes of restraint and rationality against modes of working-class emotionality. This tension became focused on the issue of what will be termed here 'authenticity'. Labour was only able to commit itself to modernity after serious negotiation with the party's 'ancestral voices'. Moreover, the extension of affluence from the mid-1950s revealed that Labour's emphasis on self-discipline was out of step with the rest of the population, and that personal restraint, far from being an emblem of modernity, was archaic and redundant in a world which prioritised personal choice. So while personal restraint was central to Labour's project of modernity through to the mid-1950s, it was less germane to the modernity of the late-1950s consumer society.

This emphasis on emotional control was not unique to the Labour Party. While Labour sought to present its opponents (especially Churchill) as suffering from a distinct lack of self-discipline, post-war Conservatives too were keen to promote moderation and restraint. [4] The tension between Tory restraint and authenticity left one leader (Macmillan) appearing superficial and frivolous and led another (Eden) to suffer a complete mental and physical breakdown.[5] The Labour Party in the 1945 to 1964 period is therefore only one of a number of possible sites on which the complex interplay between emotional restraint and the changing definition of modernity can be explored. This investigation is confined to male politicians and does not treat the issue of potential differences between masculine and feminine conceptions of either restraint or modernity. This is not to deny that the signifiers of self-restraint were critically gendered. For the figures discussed below, self-control in politics was valued as a masculine virtue, contrasted with the ill-disciplined nature of both the feminine and the non-heterosexual male other. Labour's modernity was highly self-conscious, contrasting its post-war restraint with earlier forms of political discourse (especially those associated with the struggles of the 1930s), which had privileged a more elemental emotionality. However, Labour was in fact adopting and refashioning a set of pre-existing scripts of self-control, notably Victorian constructions of the restrained middle-class male persona. That Labour's post-war restraint had connotations of moral earnestness is not surprising, given that the party's project of modernity had a definite nineteenth-century heritage, operating in 'a framework for public action they had inherited from the Victorians'.[6]

The Function of Restraint

Restraint in politics was in part a reflection of a growing emphasis among twentieth-century psychologists on the necessity for increased emotional self-control. By the 1940s academic studies on both sides of the Atlantic were in agreement that unrestrained anger was 'a sign of trouble, not a healthy emotion'. The Second World War had made emotional control particularly pertinent, with the carnage of the battlefield and the horrors of the Holocaust offering dire warnings of how destructive human aggression could be, if not properly restrained.[7] The belief that the war had been prompted by the mesmerising demagogy of Hitler and Mussolini made violent rhetoric increasingly unacceptable. Significantly, during the faction-fighting of the 1950s, prominent Labour leaders compared Bevan to a variety of Fascist demagogues. Gaitskell told Crossman that there were 'extraordinary parallels between Nye and Adolf Hitler', while Douglas Jay presented Bevanite delegates to the 1952 party conference as whipped up into 'the type of frenzy which Hitler and Goebbels excited'.[8] Bevan's vituperative speech to the Parliamentary Labour Party (PLP) after his resignation in 1951 encouraged both Hugh Dalton and Chuter Ede to compare the former minister's behaviour to that of Oswald Mosley.[9] Restraint was vital for the successful transition from war to peace. The need to reintegrate servicemen into civilian life made the domestication of aggression imperative at the end of hostilities. The military had a vested interest in fostering and enhancing male aggression, even at the cost of a profound misogyny and violence (sublimated or enacted) against women.[10] This instinct would have to be defused if men were to bolster, rather than tear down, the companionate family which was seen as the bedrock of social reconstruction after the war. Contemporary marriage guidance manuals stressed the need to manage anger, condemning conflict both between husbands and wives, and between men in the corporate and service economies.

Following the Second World War, restraint was also highly valued because of increasing concern about adolescent crime, which were widespread. The Archbishop of Canterbury and the Minister of Education both made statements on the subject in 1949, the former's comments being particularly alarmist.[11] British cinema in the period shared this preoccupation with young offenders (both male and female) in dramas such as *Brighton Rock* (1947), *The Boys in Brown* (1949), *The Blue Lamp* (1950) and *Good Time Girl* (1948).[12] Social psychologists like John Bowlby placed the blame on wartime evacuation, asserting that the separation of children from their parents had encouraged anti-social neuroses which were becoming frighteningly manifest in the teenage years.[13] But there was also a belief that adults needed to set a proper example of emotional control to young people. Significantly, an anti-Labour cartoon which appeared not long after the 'vermin' speech, portrayed Bevan, and those two other promoters of perceived partisan invective, Hugh Dalton and Emmanuel Shinwell, as members of a teenage street gang, wearing casual garb and carrying clubs.[14]

The monumental task of economic and social reconstruction after 1945 stipulated quiet efficiency rather than anti-social aggression or gaudy showiness. The rebuilding of Britain required a disciplined and purposeful workforce. Those who failed to appreciate the serious task at hand — the feckless, the work shy, the plutocratic 'parasite', the black marketeer and the 'good time girl' — received short shrift. The British post-war production drive saluted both the restrained dignity of manual workers and the expertise embodied in the disinterested professional manager or technician.[15] Labour placed a high value on the technocratic expert, who was presented as impartial, responsible and discreet, as well as on the cool rationalism of the scientist. In the early 1960s, Harold Wilson linked Labour with scientific and rational modernity and condemned the Conservatives as 'a group of obsolete Edwardians'.[16] However, the equation of socialism with science was already a theme of Labour rhetoric in the late 1940s.

Herbert Morrison took steps to develop 'this country into a truly scientif-ically-minded modern nation', while Stafford Cripps insisted that the scientist 'be looked upon as a valuable and equal co-operator in every phase of the solution of our problems of living'.[17] Labour's enthusiasm for both planning and science implicitly reinforced the party's preference for ratio-nalism and order in personal behaviour.

The identification of Labour with rational technocracy was helpfully underscored by the presence in the Attlee government of figures such as Gaitskell and Wilson, who had served as temporary civil servants in wartime Whitehall. Wilson in the late 1940s was the very model of the restrained and competent administrator. He was thorough and well briefed but, as his old friend Arthur Brown remarked, 'he did not emanate any burning passion. What he communicated was ... how to run a committee system and how to get things sorted out.' Another observer suggested he was 'too well versed in economical and civil service work to rant and rave like a soap-box journal-ist'. As Wilson's biographer has stated, 'He was not glamorous, but glamour was not the style of the 1940s. He stood for unpretentious youth, well-trained efficiency and modernity.'[18] These stolid qualities commanded awe and respect among contemporaries. Christopher Mayhew, meeting Wilson for the first time since Oxford, recorded: 'Six years work with Beveridge and his [Wilson's] various ministries have made him superhuman. I watched his bulging cranium with anxiety as he talked'.[19]

Expert knowledge provided guidance for human conduct at a time when, despite the strong religious beliefs of many senior Labour figures, society was becoming increasingly acknowledged as secular. Worn down by the stresses of being Morrison's Parliamentary Private Secretary, Mayhew sought relief from 'irrational feelings of anxiety and guilt'. Despite the intervention of Lord Longford, he remained unpersuaded of the possible salvation offered by religion and chose instead to follow the suggestion of Evan Durbin to see a psychiatrist. While a session with a Freudian analyst (who attributed Mayhew's agonising over making speeches to infant bedwetting) was not a success, Mayhew did not lose his faith in secular expertise and it was with the help of a psychotherapist that he finally recovered his 'mental balance'.[20] Labour's faith in reason and dispassion-ate expertise necessitated a downplaying of the tradition of romantic protest which the party had inherited from Carlyle, Ruskin and Morris. In the late 1950s the Campaign for Nuclear Disarmament (CND) argued that the Bomb represented the elevation of the expert and the triumph of technology at the expense of ordinary people. CND preached a gospel of moral absolutism and was willing to 'give credence to routes of truth beyond or apart from the rational'.[21] But in so doing, the disarmers set themselves against a Labour hierarchy which privileged the expert and the rational. The codes of restraint ensured that the building of socialism, while still deeply concerned with questions of ethics as much as economics, necessitated more than a commitment of faith.[22]

The demands of economic recovery and social reconstruction provided the overriding rationale for the insistence on the solemn and phlegmatic persona of the technocrat. However, no less significant, albeit less explicitly articulated, was the assumption that self-restraint among male politicians was necessary for the preservation of a separate sense of masculine identity in the aftermath of the blurring of gender roles promoted by the Second World War. Emotional control had long been a key facet of normative masculinity. Prior to the eighteenth century, men were relatively free to rage when the mood took them, and temper was seen as an acceptable form of manliness.[23] But post-Enlightenment bourgeois society required a 'quiet strength' which did not conflict with virtues such as fair play, harmony and order. The dominant tropes of masculinity in the nineteenth century sought to reconcile order and movement: virility was prized, but only if it was harnessed by harmony and proportion. In Britain the evangelical tradition lauded a combination of public activism and self-control, while private schools and imperial service cultivated a notion of heroism based on moral imperatives rather than physical endowment. By the early twentieth century, normative masculinity placed great weight on controlling the passions. By contrast, various countertypes — women, homosexuals, Jews, people of colour — were construed as being restless and formless, lacking control, order or direction. Despite the contribution of femininity to the domestication of inter-war politics, as late as the 1940s, Labour politicians could be found projecting the realm of the 'feminine' as closer to nature than that of the 'masculine'.[24] The former was perceived as only incompletely subject to rational controls.[25] The prominent Bevanite,

Ian Mikardo, held female members of the National Executive Committee largely responsible for the leadership's intolerant and aggressive response to dissent:

> It so happened that in those years we had on the Executive a number of people who were dedicated haters in the gold-medal class. All of them except one were women — Alice Horan, Jean Mann, Alice Bacon, Bessie Braddock and the undisputed world heavyweight champion hater Edith Summerskill. The only male fit to take the ring with these amazons was Jim Matthews, an NUGMW official.[26]

While the politics of restraint prioritised a domesticated discourse, 'domestication' in the immediate post-war years was often held to be more readily compatible with masculine than with feminine modes of behaviour. Such ambiguities were perhaps the inevitable consequences of a party, committed to the representation of the working class, embracing the styles and practices of an essentially middle-class conception of normative masculinity.

Self-discipline not only differentiated normative masculinity from a feminine other, but also distinguished it from non-heterosexual conceptions of manliness. Various experts who gave testimony before the Wolfenden Committee, 1954–7, accepted that the apparent post-war increase in 'sexual deviancy' was a result of insufficient self-restraint. Frank Powell, a metropolitan magistrate, told Wolfenden that 'there is such a thing in life as self-control, and I do not see why that should not be exercised ... most crime is caused ... by uncontrolled natural instincts'.[27] The serious-minded technocrat lionised by Labour was implicitly counterpoised to the dominant construction of the homosexual in the early 1950s as superficial, frivolous, idle and effeminate. The new technocratic and meritocratic élite also upheld the virtues of a dignified and masculine virility, in contrast to the pre-war Conservative establishment which was viewed as insipid, effete and unmanly.[28]

Self-restraint figured in contemporary discussions of national identity as well. In 1955 the sociologist Geoffrey Gorer asserted that in England 'the control of aggression ... has gone to such remarkable lengths that you hardly ever see a fight in a bar'. For Gorer, 'this orderliness and gentleness, this absence of overt aggression' constituted one of the basic dynamics of English character. The English were shy and moderate in their pursuit of personal pleasure (Gorer of course was writing before the arrival of late-1950s affluence) and liable to self-deprecation. Gorer insisted that the English did not lack the potential for aggression, but that it was 'very severely controlled, so that it rarely appears in overt or public behaviour'.[29]

Gorer's correlation between emotional control and national identity had been crystallised by cultural developments during the war. Antonia Lant has argued that wartime British feature films and magazines adopted an aesthetic of restraint, in which American-style glamour and artificiality was renounced in favour of simplicity and realism. Films such as *The Gentle Sex* (1943) and *Brief Encounter* (1945) signalled their national cinematic identity by implicitly contrasting their deglamourised female characters with ordinary lives, as against the extravagant appearance of Hollywood heroines. A repudiation of spectacle and display was therefore central to dominant conceptions of Britishness in the 1940s.[30] Thus if self-restraint was pivotal to articulations of national identity, then it might be a further factor in explaining why transgressions of moderation like the 'vermin' speech were looked upon with such displeasure. Significantly Morrison said of Bevan, 'I am doubtful how well he knew the British temperament'.[32] Others sought to excuse Bevan's behaviour on the grounds that he was Welsh and was therefore not constrained by the norm of 'potentially strong aggression under very strong control', which Gorer insisted characterised *English* national identity. Tony Benn believed Gaitskell's promotion to the Treasury in 1951 had deeply hurt 'Nye's Celtic pride', while Douglas Jay felt Bevan's resignation speech proved 'that the Celt is sometimes as unable to understand the Anglo-Saxon as the Anglo-Saxon to understand the Celt'.[33] After a shouting match across the cabinet table in 1946, Dalton, who possessed some (well-diluted) Glamorgan ancestry, passed Bevan a note saying: 'As half a real Welshman to a real half Welshman, we must allow for these poor Saxons' lack of understanding of our high-spirited natures'.[34]

Yet most contemporaries were less concerned to explore the possibility of differing conceptions of Britishness, within the sub-nations of the United Kingdom, than they were to convince themselves that restraint clearly distinguished British politics from the undomesticated genres of political discourse to be found in the United States. Across the Atlantic, the continued resilience of the myth of the frontier and its associated codes of toughness made the utilisation in political rhetoric of the language of unreconstructed machismo appear less archaic.[34] The refined aristocrat Lord Halifax, British Ambassador to Washington between 1940 and 1946, had been horrified at the violent antipathy directed towards both Roosevelt and Truman by their Republican opponents.[35] The raw edge of partisan debate in the United States was further sharpened by the domestic politics of the Cold War. Anti-Communism proved to be a major barrier to the complete domestication of American politics before the mid-1950s, as the violent and vituperative language of the McCarthy era was to demonstrate all too clearly. It was not until Eisenhower's relaxed consensual style finally eclipsed McCarthyite hysteria in the mid-1950s that the expression of American political emotion became more circumscribed.[36] Self-control in politics offered a means of differentiating British public life from a transatlantic other, at a time when fears of American cultural annexation were increasingly to the fore as a result of the decline in Britain's world power status. It was not surprising that Michael Foot chose to reply to Gaitskell's infamous attack on the Labour left at Stalybridge in 1952 by claiming that the former Chancellor's paranoid assertions were indistinguishable from the rhetoric of the American anti-Communist 'witch hunts', and he doubted that 'Senator McCarthy himself had ever attempted a ... more despicable smear'.[37]

The Manifestations of Self-Control

The politics of restraint within the Labour Party were more than a debate about political style and language. The issues were embedded through the actual speech, mannerisms and dress codes of its major social actors. Despite Labour's enthusiasm for the language of technocratic experts to assert their 'modern' credentials, party leaders continued to treasure moderation and simplicity in speech. Morrison felt it 'desirable that the party leaders should try to develop a style of speech and exposition which is characteristic of the thinking of the general run of British people ... simple, clear, sincere, direct and calculated to convince'. One of Bevan's failings, Morrison insisted, was his 'desire to be highly intellectual and a master of strange words'.[38] Tony Benn was also critical of Bevan's 'characteristic philosophical waffling, full of phrases like "in the problem of succession of power we are the contemporary culprits from an evolving imperialist trans-mutation"'.[40] Douglas Jay explained Gaitskell's triumph over Bevan in the 1955 leadership contest in terms of their differing rhetorical styles:

> Gaitskell shared with Stafford Cripps one rare quality which was immensely valued by the solid core of Labour MPs. By calculated lucidity and unadorned rational argument, he in the end produced a more *emotional* conviction than rhetoric could achieve. Bevan's most splendid speeches entertained, impressed, even enthused. But when one inquired of his hearers next day what he had said they were often not at all sure. And they were even less sure what he might say next.[41]

The perceived link between overly ornamental language and lack of control was registered in Gaitskell's dismissal of guild socialism. This genre of socialism, Gaitskell claimed, was not merely 'anti-rational and emotional', but was 'expressed often in extravagant and abusive language'.[42] Unadorned language was perceived as suitably 'British'. Hugh Dalton attacked Tony Crosland's *The Future of Socialism* (1956) for overly pretentious language and 'Teutonic-American-Sociological-Psycho-Analytico-Pathologico' jargon.[43] The world of politics paralleled contemporary academic developments, with 'ordinary language philosophy' seeking to repudiate metaphysical abstraction.[44] It should not be assumed however that the correlation between 'plain English' and self-control was altogether unproblematic. Edith Summerskill criticised her male colleagues for their overblown and flamboyant rhetoric and ventured that simplicity of speech might be a distinctly feminine virtue:

> A woman speaker rarely burns much midnight oil on inventing aphorisms or flights of oratory; her biological structure may have something to do with this approach to speech-making. Nature has planned her primarily on strictly utilitarian lines and her functional

sense rejects the superfluous ... [44]

In the domain of speech at least, the elision of restraint and normative masculinity did not pass entirely uncontested.

The repudiation of extravagance and the preference for understatement were extended from speech to gesture. Body language was expected to project self-reliant authority through economy of movement. Powerful gestures were to be kept to a minimum, used only for emphasis, and not at all if the speaker wished to suggest calm.[45] Bevan was criticised not merely for lack of moderation in speech, but also for lack of composure in his body language. In 1952 Dalton described the left-wing rebel as 'sweating with hatred'.[46] During Bevan's resignation speech, Benn observed that he 'swung on his feet, facing this way and that and his outstretched arm sawed the air'.[47] The *Manchester Guardian*'s correspondent also noted Bevan's 'variety of gesture', raising his 'quivering index-finger above his head', clawing 'the air towards him with an open palm' and pausing 'to pass his hand through his unruly forelock'.[48] At the subsequent PLP meeting Benn recorded that Bevan 'shook with rage and screamed, shaking and pointing and pivoting his body back and forth on his heels. His hair came down, his eyes blazed.' This spectacle was contrasted with the restrained speech and comportment of Harold Wilson, who had also resigned from the cabinet over the 1951 budget.[49]

The ethic of restraint was also evident in male dress codes in the period immediately after 1945. In the nineteenth century bourgeois men adopted stiff, austere, ascetic (and usually black) clothing, to distinguish their serious sense of moral purpose from aristocratic frivolity.[50] In the 1890s some socialists adopted bohemian and 'artistic' dress to signify their rejection of bourgeois conventions.[51] But in the twentieth century Labour politicians had embraced the conventional man's suit, accepting both working-class traditions of respectability and proving Baudrillard's dictum that black, white and grey clothes provide a paradigm of dignity, control and morality.[52] As Ruth Rubinstein has written, 'the attire of modern power holders, the sombre suit ... denotes holding back personal feelings, or self-restraint, and focusing energy on achieving organisational goals, or goal-directed behaviour'.[53] Moreover, the suit had a powerful democratic connotation, with its collective representation of the twentieth-century 'everyman'. This did not mean that all politicians wore the same conservative grey suit, devoid of ornament, nor that Labour figures had no desire to express their individualism through dress. Aneurin Bevan rejected the basic functional Co-op suit, worn by many of his proletarian colleagues, in favour of the sartorial charms of Savile Row, while Tom Williams retained the pre-war high winged collar.[54] However, this was not an age in which politicians set fashions, in contrast to the inter-war years when the public had emulated Anthony Eden's choice of soft felt hats.

Generally, the sombre suit was seen as a reassuring reflection of self-control and authority. Restraint in dress reflected immunity from distraction, and so the preference was for clothing which was unprovocative in colour and thick and stiff. An inconspicuous appearance was deemed a necessary standard for those seeking to demonstrate seriousness and devotion to duty. When, as Minister of Housing, Macmillan visited the flood damage at Lynmouth in Devon in 1952, he was criticised for extravagance in both speech (he declared the havoc reminded him of the trenches of the First World War) and dress (he was wearing a rustic cloth cap).[55] Restraint in clothing in the late 1940s differentiated the serious male authority figure from the anti-social black marketeers, the 'spivs', with their flashy whip-striped suits, check sports-coats, flannels and tendency to 'flamboyance in public places'.[56] By the early 1950s anxieties had shifted to the 'teddy boy', whose dandified clothes were represented as an indicator of criminal deviancy.[57] Conformity in dress also dramatised normative masculinity in an era when it was widely believed that homosexuals could be mapped by their extravagant mannerisms or flamboyant clothing.[58] Tailors advised their salesmen to avoid 'dangerous' items such as loud colours or 'sporty' attire.[59] Moreover, as the controversy generated by the 'New Look' in women's fashions in 1947 demonstrated, at a time of austerity and economic stringency many deemed it 'unpatriotic' to engage in needless frivolity. Self-restraint in speech, gesture and dress reflected the moral earnestness necessary for the building of Labour's New Jerusalem.

That politicians articulated the prerogatives of restraint through their speech, mannerism and dress can be seen in the public persona of Clement Attlee, who remained leader of the Labour Party until 1955. If self-control

among politicians were a vital precondition for economic and social reconstruction, for the preservation of dominant conceptions of masculinity and
for the promotion of British national identity, the unassuming and reserved
premier personified this post-war type. Ellen Wilkinson declared in 1946:
'In politics now glamour has definitely passed. The fashion, as the war ends,
is all for the quiet, competent, efficient man of affairs who gets on with his
job with the minimum of fuss and limelight. Into this new era Mr Attlee
fits perfectly.'[60] Attlee had no time for either loquacity or over-emotionalism, and his terse style as both speaker and writer was legendary. Even his
tennis playing was described as 'steady and unpretentious'.[61] Such restraint
was not achieved without effort. An American author remarked on what
few other observers noticed about the premier, that when 'speaking about
the poor, he twines his fingers until his knuckles show white. If he did not
control himself, he might lose balance. And it would never do for an *English*
statesman to lose balance, of course.'[62]

Attlee's self-discipline signified moral courage and disinterested devotion
to duty. Despite the obvious echoes of the codes of manliness promoted in
the imperial heyday of late-Victorian Britain (and he was a product of the
Haileybury of the 1890s), Attlee offered an essentially sedate archetype of
masculinity, appropriate to a more domesticated age.[63] René Krauss
observed that Attlee was:

> an excellent bridge player, altogether a model husband and a tender
> father. He is the favourite companion of his four children ... He is
> perfectly happy when, with his pipe drawing well, he can revel in a bit
> of carpentry. His three daughters used to keep rabbits as pets. He
> knocked together a new hutch, thoroughly enjoying the sawing and
> hammering.[64]

Being domesticated however did not make Attlee any less manly. The
solidity of his masculinity was implicitly contrasted with the weakness of
his predecessor as Labour leader, the effete and highly strung Ramsay
MacDonald, who played 'Hamish the Hart' and reputedly indulged in
'girlish' party games with aristocratic hostesses.

Both Attlee's shyness and his sober and inconspicuous attire marked him as the paradigm of the English character delineated by Gorer. An American writer described him thus:

> He wears well-worn, well-cut suits, a soft collar and a soft felt hat ...
> If you met him on a railway train, you would guess him to be both
> intelligent and kindly ... You would probably not ... have any talk with
> him. He is shy. Moreover, he would, almost certainly, be absorbed in
> papers or a book. If you met him out of England, you would not have
> an instant's doubt about his being an Englishman.[65]

His essential 'Englishness' was also indicated by his economy in speech and print. Dalton remarked on the characteristic understatement of Attlee's memoirs that: 'only an English statesman could have written such a book'. Douglas Jay, praising Attlee's preference for common sense, concluded: 'If ever there was a wholly English character, it was Attlee' .[66] When contemporaries contrasted Attlee's restraint with Bevan's wrathful tantrums they were not just contrasting two very different personal temperaments or two different political styles. They were reaffirming the dominant conventions of emotional control, which were central to Labour's project of modernity, and which were also seen as essential to the preservation of traditional gender hierarchies and definitions of national identity.

The Challenges of Authenticity and Affluence

The problem was that while the dominant code of the age was restraint, many politicians yearned for what might best be termed 'authenticity'. Many feared that there was now insufficient passion, protest and righteous indignation in Labour politics. Some of the older generation attributed this development to the increased presence in the PLP after 1945 of the professional middle classes. Jim Griffiths lamented the passing of the old proletarian Labour Party, with its 'old "cloth-cap" MPs ... those horny-handed sons of toil'. He was distressed that 'the "cloth cap" is giving way ... to the "cap and gown". The [post-war] Labour benches ... are rich in academic talent, but those of the thirties were richer in the character moulded in life's struggles.'[69] The death of Ernest Bevin in 1951 was symbolic; the passing of a man whose elemental, visceral and sprawling style and genuine plebeian origins (he was one of the few Labour leaders to possess hands scarred by manual work) had guaranteed the representation of working-class 'authenticity' at the highest levels of the party. At the level of political debate, senior Labour figures (at least before Suez) complained about the lack of manichean issues such as mass unemployment or Fascism which had exercised them before the war. Kenneth Younger told Dalton in 1954 that for the younger generation 'the emotions' and 'the moral indignation that used to find a natural vent at home' were now redirected towards colonial and racial issues abroad. Dalton, who thought this was a poor substitute, condemned the 1955 general election as demure. He recalled how times had changed since he 'first went to Bishop Auckland as prospective candidate in 1928, and met leading members of the party, they were nearly all unemployed miners, shabby and hungry. Last month they were in evening dress ... yes including some miners, at the Civic Dinner.'[69]

The younger generation was no less concerned about authenticity. In 1962 Douglas Jay argued that Labour should welcome, rather than bemoan, the fact that because of modern technology, fewer and fewer routine tasks would have to be performed by manual labour: 'We do not wish man always to labour underground to get fuel, or dig in fields with his own hands ... or heave molten plates of metal about the floor'.[71] But other middle-class socialists were more ambivalent, pursuing modernity, but still prizing the dignity of honest proletarian toil. In the late 1920s Gaitskell had rejected the frivolity of the Bowra Group at Oxford in favour of the authenticity of the Nottinghamshire miners, among whom he worked as a Workers' Educational Association tutor, while in the 1950s he was keen to socialise with his working-class constituents in South Leeds.[70] Tony Crosland spent his summer holiday in 1959 working on a Grimsby trawler, while Tony Benn cheered himself in 1960 singing hymns and lubricating comradeship with beer at the Boilermaker's annual party.[71] In 1954 Bevan famously condemned those Labour leaders who behaved like a 'desiccated calculating machine', refused to be 'swayed by indignation', and who 'talk about a dying child in the same way as ... about the pieces inside an internal combustion engine'.[72] This critique of the 'calm and objective accents' in which

Labour's vision of socialism was now being presented has often been identified as a specific assault on Hugh Gaitskell.[73] If so, this was ironic, since Gaitskell himself found emotional control increasingly difficult during the later 1950s. Gaitskell placed great faith in the power of reason, enthusing over logical positivism at Oxford and commending his friend Evan Durbin for his 'pursuit of truth ... through the patient and unswerving application of logical thought'.[74] In his diary Gaitskell criticised the over-emotionalism of figures as diverse as Bevan, Griffiths and Shinwell. Following the Defence Minister at a rally in 1951, he was irritated that members of the crowd 'were so drunk by the emotional nonsense that Shinwell had talked that it was impossible to make them think at all'.[75] However, Gaitskell's commitment to social justice owed as much to moral indignation as to cold reason and, during the Suez affair in 1956, he found it increasingly difficult to contain his anger at Eden's actions. Indeed, by the end of the crisis the press were taking great delight in presenting Bevan as the measured statesman and Gaitskell as the over-emotional hysteric.[76]

The most serious challenge to the language of restraint in the world of politics was to come from the restoration in the late 1950s of a consumer society which had been placed in suspended animation by the priorities of wartime and post-war economic recovery. The shift from austerity to affluence meant the return of a culture which was 'at odds with competitive, rationalised production'. Modernity was now defined not in terms of rationality and restraint, but in terms of immediacy, impact and sensation.[77] Britain in the late 1950s seemed to be undergoing the same cultural shift that Warren Susman had detected in the United States at the turn of the century, as 'character' (duty, work, morality, integrity, manhood) gave way to 'personality' (getting ahead in a corporate society, the prioritising of attractiveness and fascination).[78] The new sensibility foregrounded self-indulgence and self-fulfilment rather than self-discipline. Affluence promoted strongly defined cultural discourses which were in competition with the dominant political codes of all the major parties. Many commentators have noted that Labour was slow to recognise this change, often finding the culture of consumption and its associated hedonism distasteful. The puritanical strictures of the Webbs and traditions of working-class moralism remained remarkably resilient during this period.[79] In the early 1950s the notion of restraint had helped yoke Labour's vision of modernity to a clear sense of national purpose. By the late 1950s this association proved much more difficult since the modernity of affluence took America as its cultural reference point.

The transition from Attlee to Gaitskell in 1955 undoubtedly helped Labour's attempt to accommodate itself to this new environment. Gaitskell had long identified the United States with modernity and was impressed with its meritocratic and competitive vision of a classless society. Gaitskell's leading supporters, Tony Crosland and Roy Jenkins, tried to transcend the competition between the spheres of the formally political and the cultural. Gaitskell, while he rejected crass materialism, appreciated the cultural importance of the renewed emphasis on private pleasure. The 'Hampstead Set', with their love of nightclubs, dancing, jazz and parties were keen to keep up with the younger generation. There was less moral earnestness in high places in the party than there had been a decade earlier.[80] Gaitskell believed that Macmillan's decision to wear a white fur hat on a visit to Moscow was a typical 'stunt' which betrayed the premier's superficiality. Yet in a portrait completed by Judy Cassab in 1957 the Labour leader appeared keen to project an image of informality. He was painted wearing a green sports jacket without either exaggerated padding of the shoulders or the conventionally formal waistcoat.[81] However, there were limits to Gaitskell's embrace of the new age. While privately sympathetic to Crosland and Jenkins' culturalist project for Labour, he was concerned that it might not find sufficient favour with the electorate. If television was indeed 'the most symbolic issue of 1950s modernity', then it should be remembered that as late as 1958 the Labour leader did not possess a television set.[82] Despite the polished election broadcasts produced by the party in 1959, it was only under Harold Wilson that the party leadership fully entered the televisual age. Indeed, in the aftermath of the 1959 general election some Labour activists and candidates felt that the 'slickness' of the broadcasts had compromised the party's authenticity.[83]

How far Labour had unshackled an emphasis on emotional control from its conception of modernity by the time it returned to power in 1964 is uncertain. In that year the American sociologist Edward Shils condemned British society for a 'constriction of spirit', the fostering of a national character 'frowning on enthusiasm, distrusting spontaneity and regarding soundness and steadiness as the highest of human virtues'. Such cultural norms, Shils argued, had helped preserve unjust social hierarchies, the 'puritanical suppression of feeling and imagination' contributing to 'a restraint on aspiration'. His hope was that Labour could help correct this lack of vigour and promote a 'conception of new possibilities of life'.[84] Wilson, however, proved an ambiguous leader for this particular crusade. His complex persona reflected the difficulties of reconciling political and cultural norms in the age of affluence. He had certainly loosened up since his days at the Board of Trade, and now exhibited a taste for populism and a 'common touch' which he had seriously lacked in the late 1940s.[85] However, his defeat of George Brown in the 1963 leadership contest was an obvious victory for the virtues of self-discipline, his opponent possessing an all too obvious indiscipline, excitability, recklessness and lack of inhibition. Brown's fatal weakness was his drinking, but contemporaries believed this merely aggravated a wider lack of emotional control; in the words of his biographer, he 'could become intoxicated as much through his feelings as from drink'.[86] Moreover, despite the use of the term 'white heat', Wilson's 1963 conference speech projected a cool, technocratic vision of socialism, and he possessed a puritanical streak which differentiated him from his predecessor.[87] The changes and the continuities in Wilson's public persona between 1945 and 1964 suggest that the centrality of self-restraint to both the world of politics and to Labour's conception of modernity had been diminished by the affluent society, but that it had not entirely vanished. By the early 1960s, the politics of restraint had begun to appear as an earlier version of modern political discourse and selfhood, but it was certainly not yet redundant or irrelevant. The Labour Party's struggle with emotional control reflects on a microcosmic scale Britain's tortured relationship with modernity, or (more accurately) with a number of different modernities. Modernity has proved fluid, unstable and unfixed, or in the words of Alan O'Shea: 'modernity is not one discourse, but the site of intersection of several, which do not sit easily together'.[88]

9. 'New Conservatism'?
The Industrial Charter,
Modernity and the Reconstruction of British Conservatism after the War

Harriet Jones

The idea of modernity is central to Conservative Party autobiography during the years following the 1945 electoral defeat. The party's leading policy makers quite consciously undertook a project while in opposition that aimed to remodel the organisation, membership, policies and style of the party in order to distance itself from its unpopular pre-war image and to bring Conservatism into closer harmony with the aspirations and preoccupations of the mass of British voters. This project was claimed to have resulted in a 'new Conservatism'. Indeed, 'new Conservatism' became an important narrative strand in post-war historiography and is still to some extent embedded in popular understanding of the party in the 1945-64 period. As John Ramsden has pointed out, 'the years between defeat in 1945 and the return to power in 1951 have acquired a legendary significance in the party's history'.[1] The narrative of 'new Conservatism' has been portrayed most vividly in the memoirs of party leaders. By the 1970s such accounts had firmly established the story of post-war reform and modernisation. For example, in The Art of the Possible (1971), Lord Butler wrote:

> The overwhelming electoral defeat of 1945 shook the Conservative Party out of its lethargy and impelled it to re-think its philosophy and re-form its ranks with a thoroughness unmatched for a century ... [T]he Conservatives, when thrown into opposition, were provided with a healthy opportunity and a compelling motive for bringing both their policies and their characteristic modes of expression up to date.[2]

In *Tides of Fortune* (1969), Harold Macmillan similarly depicted his role as that of the radical outsider battling against reactionary thinking:

> My purpose was ... to emphasise the need for a thorough 're-think-ing' of policy. Only a genuine process of modernisation and democratisation would enable us to face the problems of the day, and to seek the support of the electorate in due course with any hope of success ... [W]e needed a party ... which could comprise all that was common to those who reject Socialism but wanted progress.[3]

Macmillan went on to assert that 'in the years that were to follow, a new Conservative Party was to be created, spiritually attuned to the life of the post-war world and the new society'.[4]

'New Conservatism' was the party's response to the new political envi-ronment of the 1940s. The party had undoubtedly come to be associated negatively with pre-war economic and social policies by 1945 to the extent that a vote for Labour was a vote for reconstruction and change. The party's leadership clearly recognised that this association had to be broken before Conservatism could recover its former position. This transformation was undertaken largely through the language and style of policy presen-tation. The turning point came in 1947 with the publication of *The Industrial Charter*, the first and most significant policy publication of the opposition period. A great deal of effort went into the drafting of the *Charter*, and it marks the beginning of a new language of Conservatism in post-war Britain. The *Charter* was significant, not because it marked a departure in the policies or ideology of the party, but because it associated Conservatism with progress, prosperity and the new language of civic culture in Britain which had emerged from 1942.

Little else was new in the 'new Conservatism' of these years. The Conservative Party largely failed in its attempt to broaden and democ-ratise its organisation, for example, a point which has long been accepted by historians of the party. Images of democratisation of the party's struc-ture and membership were carefully and deliberately cultivated under the Chairmanship of Lord Woolton. In particular, the leadership sought to associate the party with youth and a wider class basis of support. Woolton's memoirs and party propaganda in the period suggest that there was a groundswell of popular support for the right, but this image was largely manufactured by the leadership.[5] A large proportion of the party's income was spent fostering this impression. At one point in 1948 Woolton was employing 246 missioners to recruit new members door-to-door. This unsurprisingly resulted in impressive membership figures by the end of the 1940s, but it hardly implies a spontaneous outburst of popular support for Conservatism, especially as membership figures once more declined after 1951.[6] The Young Conservative organisation was launched at the end of the war and by mid-1948 there were over 2,000 branches with approximately 150,000 members. But the Young Conservative movement, however large it might have been, functioned largely as a social meeting ground rather than a political movement.[7] The Maxwell-Fyfe Report (1949) was heavily promoted as a means to democratise the composition of MPs and constituency leaders, who were overwhelmingly upper and upper-middle class.[8] But the social composition of candidates and constituency leaders remained broadly similar to the pre-war period. In 1945 48 per cent of Conservative MPs came from the professions and 27 per cent from business backgrounds. In 1964 those percentages were virtually identical. The percentage of Conservative MPs who had attended public schools was 76 per cent in 1945 and 75 per cent in 1964.[9] In organisational terms therefore, the historians of the party have viewed the claim to 'new Conservatism' with a considerable degree of scepticism.

In terms of policy, on the other hand, there has been a guarded acceptance of the view that the party did transform itself markedly after 1945. The pivotal moment is generally regarded to have come with the publication of *The Industrial Charter* in 1947. Curiously little critical literature has appeared to alter the view that the *Charter* represented a significant shift in the party's thinking. It is generally represented as marking the accommodation of Conservatism to the idea of the mixed economy and the welfare state. But close examination of the origins and text of the Charter demonstrate that here, too, there was little change or radicalism in the content of policy. Co-partnership schemes in industry had long been discussed and debated within the party and were mentioned in *The Worker's Charter*, the section of *The Industrial Charter* that was published as a separate and final part of the general policy statement. But the proposals contained within *The Worker's Charter* were only ever meant to be taken up voluntarily and, in any event, were never pursued by the party in government after 1951.

The *Charter* has often been described as 'left wing', heavily influenced by men like Macmillan, who had become reconciled to a mixed economy before 1939. This is misleading, for it was in fact the liberal free-marketeers who showed the keenest interest in its development. By the beginning of 1946 nationalisation was seen as the most urgent point of difference with the Attlee administration, taking precedence over all other areas of policy. The Industrial Policy Committee (IPC), which produced the *Charter*, originated in the desire to launch a defence of the market and its ability to arbitrate fairly between capital and labour without the intervention of the state. Thus, for example, it was Oliver Lyttelton who was responsible for the early work done on co-partnership from the end of 1945.[10] His paper, 'The Worker and Industry', was the first to be considered by the IPC when it began to meet in the autumn of 1946.[11] Lyttleton called for a series of measures to break down the current atmosphere of distrust in industrial relations, including joint consultation, contracts of service, profit sharing, employee shareholding, promotion by merit, industrial training schemes and incentives in wage structures. Moreover, co-partnership was not a new idea. The party's Research Department (CRD) had in fact originally taken an interest in such schemes at the end of the 1920s, and it was from this previous research and thinking that Lyttelton drew his ideas. There was a general consensus amongst post-war Conservative leaders from disparate wings of the party that co-partnership or corporatist strategies represented the modern form of industrial relations policy.

The Worker's Charter proposals must be viewed through a Cold War lens. Free enterprise in Britain had certainly been shaken by the experiences of 'war communism' and the public focus on reconstruction from 1942. But from the spring of 1946 the context of these domestic debates rapidly altered as the containment of Communism in Europe became the new priority. This was viewed as not only an external threat but also a fight against domestic subversion. Anthony Eden justified the IPC's work to the sceptical backbenchers of the 1922 Committee in October 1946 by stressing that 'Shinwell and Bevan are drawing an iron curtain over the future prospects of important industries'.[12] This interest in co-partnership in the immediate post-war years was widespread throughout western Europe, where political movements of the centre-right were attempting to devise policies with cross-class appeal that could deliver high production rates in the private sector and so challenge the threat of socialist intervention. There is some evidence to suggest that there was correspondence with European Christian Democrats and Conservatives over the *Charter*, and that it was both influenced by and an influence upon political developments on the Continent.[13]

The British Conservative Party was certainly aware of developments in other European countries and paid attention to practices which could be adapted to British needs.[14] But the *British Worker's Charter* was not radical, especially when compared with *Mitbestimmung* in West Germany. First, while joint consultation was considered desirable in Britain, worker directors on boards of management were firmly rejected; nowhere is there any indication that anyone in the Conservative Party was willing to go that far. Second, the proposals were to be voluntary rather than compulsory. Few voices in the party advocated the compulsory introduction of co-partnership, and this was reinforced as it became clear that there was widespread resistance to the idea among Conservative industrialists. British Conservative interest in co-partnership schemes was considerable in the 1940s but dwindled after 1951 when the threat of further nationalisation had receded. Co-partnership was effective because it seemed progressive; but it was a tactic in the temporary struggle against nationalisation, and as such it was as important to the right as to the left. Men like Lord Cranborne and Oliver Lyttelton were arguing that it was essential for private industry to demonstrate a sense of responsibility for the 'common interest ... of capital, management and workers and an overhaul and redeclaration of the rights and duties of each' — the old conception of 'sides must be broken down'.[15] It was only by moving in this direction that private industry could be saved, and it was considered vital that such a process should begin immediately.

The modernisation of Conservative industrial policy in the post-war period cannot, therefore, be located in the substance of policy, which carried forward ideas that had similarly featured in pre-war debates within the party. What did change, as Butler intimated in his memoirs, quoted above, was the party's 'characteristic modes of expression'. In other words, it is in questions of language and presentation that the actual modernisation of right-of-centre politics in Britain after the war can be identified.

The first and most important exercise in the construction of this modernised language of Conservatism was focused on industrial policy, and this is what makes *The Industrial Charter* a text of such lasting significance. The Industrial Policy Committee (IPC), which wrote it, spent little time debating the content of the party's industrial policy but it spent months considering how industrial policy should be described, presented and promoted.

The Industrial Charter was meticulously drafted, because it was ultimately through language and image that the party hoped to make an impression on the public mind. Butler told the members of the IPC after the first two meetings: 'we should, by the simplicity of our language and the directness of our appeal, be able to reach the heart and minds of the working population, who are at present in some doubt whether the panacea "Nationalisation" has sufficient regard for their own interests.'[16] The emphasis was placed on persuading 'ordinary' citizens that Conservatism stood for the rights of the individual set against the impersonal demands of the state. During the war, Labour had won the initiative in policy, in part by characterising pre-war Conservative economic and social policy as inefficient, unjust and disengaged. Labour was able to contrast images of pre-war depression and unemployment with wartime collectivism, full employment and industrial production. *The Industrial Charter* overturned that formula, and it is this accomplishment that makes the text so interesting. In this new discourse, heavily influenced by early Cold War rhetoric, socialism at home was depicted as inefficient and dogmatic. It was contrasted with Conservative freedom, efficiency and modernisation. Now it was not the Conservatives who were backward-looking; rather, it was the Conservatives who held out the promise of a prosperous future. While this approach would be refined in subsequent publications, *The Industrial Charter* represents a watershed because it was the point of transition between a discourse of reconstruction and a new discourse of the Cold War in early post-war British history.

Contemporary Labour policies were variously described in the *Charter* as 'the imposition of a rigid straitjacket of doctrinaire political theory', as exacerbating 'class war', as 'extravagant and unprincipled', or as 'meddlesome interference', 'sapping dangerously the independent character of the people'. The Conservatives were offering, by contrast, 'to give the people, not orders, but opportunity', to provide 'equality of opportunity and incentive to win a variety of rewards', to create 'a partnership between the government, Industry and the Individual', to 'plan for abundance' and to develop 'a modern technique for maintaining employment'. In short, the Conservatives promised 'to humanise, not to nationalise'.[17] Descriptions of Conservative attitudes are peppered heavily with words like confidence, freedom, enterprise, responsibility, nation, opportunity, incentive, justice, rewards, fair, prosperity, abundance, efficiency, modern, modernisation, partnership, consultation, co-operation, partnership. These are offset by descriptions of Labour which employ words like controls, restrictions, crisis, stifle, scarcity, snooping, queues, burdens, totalitarian, inefficient, bureaucratic. The language of the *Charter* flipped the political rhetoric that had dominated the 1945 campaign; now it was the Conservatives who embraced the future while Labour addressed old problems rather than the needs of a modern society. The Conservatives considered the needs of the whole nation while Labour represented narrow class interest. The following extract, taken from the introduction to the pamphlet, gives a flavour of the text:

[T]he Government totally misconceive wherein lies the greatness of a free and resourceful nation. They imagine that the men and women who fought and worked together in the war can now be exhorted, controlled and regimented into producing goods, building houses and rendering services in time of peace .... The Conservative policy is the opposite: to give the people, not orders, but opportunity ... the Socialists have carried their passion for equality to lengths which have stifled man's will to do the best of which he is capable. The desire for increased rewards, whether it be expressed in terms of the profit motive or higher wages, animates the great bulk of mankind. We hold that there should be healthy rewards for work done. We condemn excessive profits and shall propose methods to curb monopolies and unfair privileges ...

We offer to all ranks of industry both a task to fulfil and the reward for doing it well.

178 Moments of Modernity

To the worker we offer a new charter giving assurance of steady employment, incentive to test his ability to the utmost, and status as an individual personality.

To the consumer we offer the ultimate restoration of freedom of choice, the prospect of a better standard of living and protection from restrictive practices.

To the owner and shareholder we offer confidence in the future and a share in Britain's revived prosperity.

To the manager we offer encouragement to raise the efficiency of his industry to the highest pitch, and a personal incentive to become a highly trained man and to reap a greater reward for greater responsibility.

To the individual trader we offer fair competition, greater elasticity, and less wastefulness from the operation of controls; in short a fair reward for initiative, effort, and personal service.

Let the whole nation go forward under the inspiration of these ideas to the immediate work which lies ahead. It is hard work. Let each of us feel a personal responsibility for our part in it and for the resurgence of our national greatness.[18]

Of particular relevance is the repeated stress placed on the status of the individual in relation to society and the state. The *Charter* argued that socialist rationalism allowed no possibility for the fulfilment of individual ability but rather exhorts, controls and regiments. Conservatism was offering, by contrast, the opportunity for individual achievement in a free society. The recognition of individual status had always played a central role in Conservative philosophy, but here that notion was extended and contrasted with the austerity and controls introduced during the war and continued after 1945. The *Charter* described the role of the state in terms of its ability to enhance and extend the personality of the individual: the worker was promised 'status as an individual personality', the consumer was offered 'restoration of freedom of choice', the manager was encouraged to take 'greater responsibility'. The nation thus became the sum of its individual citizens. The 'resurgence of our national greatness' depended upon the extent to which each individual was enabled to fulfil his or her own ability. In this way, the text of the *Charter* endowed the individual with a renewed sense of responsibility and sense of purpose that would be extended in the party's policies after 1948, stressing the abandonment of controls and the introduction of incentives in welfare and taxation policy. In this sense, the *Charter* provides a fascinating example of the expanded role of the self, discussed by Anthony Giddens and highlighted in the introduction to this volume.

The promotion of the *Charter* was treated as seriously as its drafting had been. When details of the publication timetable were discussed in the Spring of 1947, the Committee became increasingly concerned that its proposals should secure the unequivocal endorsement of Churchill. Any inkling of half-heartedness 'would have most harmful effects' within the party and among undecided voters.[19] The party's endorsement of the *Charter* at the 1947 Party Conference was carefully stage-managed and was virtually unanimous, despite significant pockets of resistance. As we shall see, public reaction to the *Charter* was broadly favourable, although public opinion surveys and correspondence suggested a large degree of public scepticism over the extent to which it could be taken seriously as the true intention of the leadership.[20]

While endorsement of the *Charter* was certainly manipulated by the party organisation in order to ensure overwhelming approval, there is little evidence of widespread resistance to the *Charter* within the party. Predictably, the arch-reactionary, tired and emotional Sir Waldron Smithers, backbench member for Orpington, wrote a wild and rambling attack, citing scripture in his condemnation of this compromise with Communism.[21] More importantly, the research department of the Progress Trust submitted a memorandum on the *Charter* to the CRD in July.[22] The Trust disagreed with the Charter's endorsement of the Coalition White Paper on Employment on the grounds that full employment was incompatible with a truly democratic society. It wanted to see a more explicit endorsement of free enterprise, a more explicit statement that controls would be temporary, a less conciliatory line towards the trade unions and a more aggressive endorsement of denationalisation.[23] On the whole, however, correspondence within the party concerning the *Charter* was supportive. Indeed, the task of publicising the *Charter* appears to have led to considerable co-operation between the party and Aims of Industry (the lobby group of industrialists founded in 1942 to promote free enterprise after the war), which went on to promote a high-profile campaign against further nationalisation. This confirms the extent to which the *Charter* was viewed within the party as a defence of free enterprise rather than a compromise with socialism.

While the *Charter* was met with approval within the party, the relationship between 'new Conservatism' and the popular perceptions of the electorate was far less satisfactory, highlighting the extent to which the modernising process had been imposed from above. Indeed, this effort and activity made little impact on British society and popular culture. In spite of efforts to sell the new language of Conservatism to the public, politics in Britain continued to be separated from the experiences of ordinary citizens. As Steven Fielding, Peter Thompson and Nick Tiratsoo have argued in their study of the Labour Party and popular politics during this period, there are considerable problems with the idea that the late 1940s represented a high-point of active electoral and civic participation.[24]

Mass Observation (MO) was commissioned by Central Office in April to gauge public reaction to the *Charter*.[25] There are certainly problems with the MO survey and risks in drawing conclusions from it. But its findings, published at the beginning of September 1947, were taken seriously by Central Office and must have been disappointing to Conservative strategists. The MO report stressed first of all the difficulty of finding enough people who were interested in party politics: 'a very large number of people know little about party politics and care little', it argued, claiming that 68 per cent of those questioned said they could think of nothing in Conservative Party policy of which they either approved or disapproved. The report also stressed a growing level of cynicism with party politics in general, concluding that 'any effort at all to obtain interest in a particular political party or policy is immediately confronted with a solid wall of disinterest and disbelief in at least a third of the people of this country'.[26] Mass Observation also believed that the format of a political pamphlet was a particularly ineffective method of disseminating information and that any pamphlet published by any party would be met with widespread apathy, indifference and scepticism. Over 80 per cent of the whole sample, when presented with copies of The *Industrial Charter* and recent pamphlets from the other parties, admitted that they had never seen nor heard of any of them. There appeared to be 'extreme confusion on any subject even remotely concerned with party politics'.[27] Indeed, when respondents were given copies of the abridged version of *The Worker's Charter* with the word 'Conservative' blacked out, about one person in eight of the whole sample (an even higher proportion amongst middle-class respondents) believed it to be the work of the Communist Party. Broadly speaking, there was a general belief that *The Worker's Charter* was left-wing in origin, either Labour or Communist.

A majority of Mass Observation's respondents could not identify any differences between the Conservative and Labour Parties. Among those who did, working-class respondents and Labour voters gave answers along the lines that the Conservatives were for the rich and Labour for the workers. About 10 per cent of middle-class respondents and Conservative voters also distinguished the parties as representing different classes, but some 20 per cent simply stated vaguely that the parties were 'different' without further elaboration. Many respondents in all categories gave non-political or personal explanations for the differences. A fifty-five-year-old charwoman, for example, replied that 'The Labour [sic] are out for themselves and don't care about the people, but the Conservatives are wonderful, Mr Churchill should be sitting on the throne of Heaven'.[28] When asked specifically about industrial policy, the picture grew even more confused. Less than one per cent of the whole sample gave answers that suggested any detailed acquaintance with current policy, or even gave an indication that they knew what industrial policy was. On the other hand, when asked more specific questions, it did seem to be clear in most people's minds that the Conservatives were for free enterprise and against government controls and nationalisation. Thus there was overwhelming evidence to suggest widespread public apathy and confusion about political issues in general. This was a problem that challenged Labour policy-makers to the same extent that it did the Conservatives.[29] Michael Fraser, at the Conservative Research Department, remarked upon reading this section of the report that 'one might almost be excused for coming to the conclusion that Mass Observation is some subversive Fascist or Communist organisation formed with the object of undermining confidence in the democratic way of life!' More seriously, he pointed out that political apathy and cynicism were hardly new developments in British politics and that the increasing participation of the young (particularly through the Young Conservatives) contradicted the idea that apathy was widespread. At the same time, the party took seriously the problem of political ignorance.[30]

When participants in the survey were asked to comment on specific points raised by the *Charter*, and shown extracts of the document on which to comment, several points emerged. There was broad support, even amongst unskilled workers, for the small trader and for Commonwealth preference. The Mass Observation research also revealed that there was vehement disagreement over the issue of ending controls and rationing, although most middle-class respondents were in favour of this policy. Even amongst this group, however, there was broad recognition that a reduction in controls would be followed by a rise in prices. Michael Fraser remarked after reading this section of the report that it 'is not merely that there is a consumer fear of a consequent rise in prices. In various occupations producers and distributors have now become accustomed to controls and their operation and they have found out how to use them to their own advantage.' Controls had become a 'useful new form of restrictive practice' and there was a 'great new vested interest' in their maintenance.[31] The idea of a worker's charter attracted very little interest compared to the position of the small trader or controls; the idea appeared 'to be new to most people and rather outside normal thought'.[32] While the idea of profit-sharing appealed to the majority of both working-class and middle-class respondents, only a minority believed such schemes to be possible or practical. This note of scepticism was not confined to profit-sharing; the report stressed that there was a stream of doubt surrounding many of the Conservative proposals. As a thirty-five-year-old baker who voted Labour commented, 'I don't know what to think. It's all right on the outside but it's the inside that counts. I just don't trust them that's all.' Among middle-class respondents, while 47 per cent were favourably impressed by *The Worker's Charter*, a further 47 per cent reacted to it cynically. Mass Observation also found the public understanding of what Conservatism stood for ran well behind current policy thinking. For example, Conservative respondents individually approved of the trade unions to a far greater extent than they believed their party approved of them officially; less than one per cent answered that the party officially approved of trade unions. This again reinforced the conclusion that most respondents believed *The Worker's Charter* to be left-wing: four times as many Labour voters approved of it as Conservative voters. It was hardly surprising in the circumstances that Mass Observation stated that 'it is difficult not to come to the conclusion that to most people, Conservatives included, a Conservative Industrial Policy is not yet in any way a living idea'.[33]

It is one thing to develop a new political language and another to disseminate it. The Mass Observation survey clearly pointed to a need for further propaganda before 'new Conservatism' could be identified and understood by the general public. Those within the CRD felt that the message needed repetition and reinforcing in a popular medium.[34] David Stelling, the Conservative commentator asked to draft 'a new and even more popular version' of the *Charter*, told Clarke in November that 'I have tried to avoid the old clichés and slogans that cut no ice, and have aimed at the language of the cinema'.[35] There were also attempts to promote the *Charter* through a strip cartoon. In addition, the advertising firm of Mather and Crowther was called in to discuss the production of flip charts which could be taken directly on to the shop floor for meetings with workers.[36]

In order to counteract the cynicism surrounding the implementation of *The Worker's Charter*, it was suggested as early as June that it might be useful to publicise a list of industrialists who had already implemented innovative industrial relations programmes.[37] In March 1948 a large meeting took place between members of the Conservative Central Office, its Research Department and Aims of Industry (the industrialists' lobby group) to discuss means of co-operation between the two organisations. The research departments agreed to share information, while Aims undertook to compile a list of firms which might consent to be quoted in connection with propaganda on the *Charter's* implementation.[38] Aims of Industry was interested at this time in advertising schemes in the United States to promote free enterprise — as was evident from the subsequent 'Mr Cube' campaign.[39] There was already considerable overlap between the Aims leadership and the Conservative Party, but from this point co-operation took off further, both through regular formal meetings and personal contacts. As a non-party lobby group, Aims was able to promote a more aggressive stance than the party was able to sponsor at this time. But there is evidence that the Aims campaign was conducted with the full co-operation and encouragement of the party. Joint research on firms implementing the *Charter*, for example, was eventually published by Aims under the title *The Industrial Charter Works* in 1949. As one of Woolton's aides explained to James Hutchison (a backbench member of the IPC): 'You will appreciate, I am sure, that this is a document which could not be produced by us officially owing to the danger of it being construed as a boost for certain individual industrial firms in particular, and in general as an advertisement for "big" business. We shall, however, ensure a wide distribution of this pamphlet through our organisation.'[40]

The extent to which *The Industrial Charter* had any real impact on subsequent Conservative legislation is debateable. Of course, the Churchill government did reduce and then abolish controls, reduce taxation and public expenditure in explicit areas such as food subsidies, embark upon a limited degree of denationalisation, and maintain a 'high and stable level' of employment. At the same time, however, there was no progress after 1951 on the implementation of a code of conduct for industry, as espoused in *The Worker's Charter*. The unions and employers were unwilling to arrive at such a point voluntarily, and the party was unwilling to impose industrial co-partnership schemes through legislation.[41] After the Ministry of Labour submitted its proposals for a code of conduct for industry to the National Joint Advisory Council in February 1953, there was little further progress. This state of affairs was rather embarrassing for the party. As one prospective candidate inquired of the CRD: 'I am constantly being asked in the Local Press and elsewhere — "What has happened to the Tory Election promise to institute a Workers' Charter?" Would you be good enough to let me know what the answer is?'[42] When the government cautiously raised co-partnership in industry again in 1954, it met with no enthusiasm from either side of industry.[43] There quite simply did not appear to be any votes in co-partnership, and *The Worker's Charter* was allowed to die a lingering death.

This failure to implement specific proposals in the Charter should come as no surprise and does not detract from the importance of the text in the post-war history of the party. Its specific proposals, as argued previously, were not particularly significant. The conciliatory language of the Charter, on the other hand, was scrupulously adhered to after 1947. The Conservatives, both in opposition and in office, continued to placate the labour movement. This position had a strategic objective. As early as 1949, David Clarke explained to Central Office that 'We are seeking in fact to edge the Trade Unions more and more into a middle position where they will gradually become neutral in politics'.[44] The party believed that it could sell its policies to the labour movement. The Cold War provided a powerful discourse that could be employed in domestic policy debates. Cold War themes were easily married to the party's stress on free enterprise and a reduced role for the state. These policies, in turn, were increasingly discussed in terms of individual incentive, opportunity and freedom:

> In the fully socialised states on the other side of the Iron Curtain the right to strike has been withdrawn, and the Trade Unions have virtually disappeared altogether. I read recently that in Russia the legal maximum of six months imprisonment for being absent from work for one day is considered now too lenient — and the worker has now no Trade Union to appeal to on such an occasion ... We ask all those who believe in the proper industrial functioning of Trade Unionism for the protection and advancement of their members, who wish to see this process continue, to join us, the party that believes in the system of free enterprise, the system which has given us and America the highest standard of living for all the workers ever achieved in the history of man, and the system which alone can preserve Trade Unionism as we know it in this country.[45]

This basis for a Conservative appeal to the worker was only deepened as economic growth and full employment continued over the following decade.

From the early months of opposition in 1945, the Conservative leadership had recognised the central importance of reconstructing its image as the party of One Nation. The development of industrial policy was thought crucial to the success of this objective and was thus the first and most trumpeted plank of policy development after the war. The *Industrial Charter* proposed a co-operative, efficient and modern, free and private sector model for industrial relations. Grounded in a language which stressed individual freedom, it was intended to provide a non-socialist alternative for workers in the new Britain. Conservative industrial policy from that time remained cautious and conciliatory, focused on the importance of selling its alternative model to the skilled worker. The atmosphere of economic crisis which dominated Churchill's early months back in power made that objective even more imperative; the caution with which that government approached policy alternatives such as the aborted ROBOT scheme of 1952, or cuts in the social services, can be largely explained by the priority accorded to the maintenance of class unity in the event of another war, or economic collapse. That early sense of urgency was dispelled after March 1953. Economic and international stability from that time enabled successive Conservative governments to proceed with a series of economic and social reforms while delivering a rising standard of living to most consumers.

The most innovative suggestions of *The Industrial Charter* were never implemented by the Conservatives, who had promoted their proposals with such urgency from 1947. The *Charter* did not represent a tangible break with past policy, although the acceptance of government's responsibility to maintain a 'high and stable' level of employment, together with the willingness to tolerate a limited mixed economy, did represent a partial compromise with Keynesian economic theory. The importance of *The Industrial Charter* lay rather in its proclamation of an alternative vision of the future, of the way that Conservatism would shape modern society. Conceived, written and promoted during the onset of the Cold War, it should be understood in terms of the sense of urgency that surrounded the Conservative reconstruction of policy in light not only of the defeat in 1945, but also in terms of the broader developments in the position of British Conservatism in relation to private capital during this period. While its proposals were never implemented, the *Charter* was influential in a textual and a linguistic sense. As an influential text, it was particularly effective in overturning the political language of the mid-1940s, which promoted socialism and nationalisation as efficient, modern and just, as judged against pre-war Conservative policies which were associated with unemployment at home and appeasement abroad. The *Charter* can thus be identified as a pivotal moment in which the language of the party began to promote a 'new Conservative' image which identified private enterprise, with a limited role for the state in the management of economic policy and social welfare, as 'free', 'efficient', 'fair' and 'modern' when set against a socialist model that was 'stifling', 'meddlesome', 'wasteful' and promoted a class-based view of society that was both reactionary and narrow. This linguistic development reflected the early history of the Cold War period and the transformation of the Soviet Union from ally to enemy in the public mind. It also reflected growing frustration with continued rationing and controls. As Britain entered the post-war era, the Conservative Party incorporated these developments in its own language and approach. In particular, the language of post-war Conservatism came to stress the importance of individual fulfilment and opportunity.

This new language was carried forward in Conservative rhetoric and propaganda on many fronts during the 1950s. As with industrial policy, however, policy modernisation in other fields contained important elements of continuity, but repackaged in the language of new Conservatism. The phrase 'property-owning democracy' was first used after the war by Anthony Eden at the Blackpool Conference of 1946 (although its origins date to the 1920s).[46] Initially conceived in the context of co-partnership and employee shareholding, the idea of property-owning democracy was soon extended to housing policy. In 1950 the party famously promised that private enterprise would enable the housing industry to produce 300,000 houses a year and that home ownership would be extended under a future Conservative government. That target was achieved and surpassed by 1954, providing a basis for the less popular reform of rent control and the reduction of the public housing sector in the second half of the decade. The election campaigns of 1950 and 1951 were run on the general theme of 'setting the people free', which married Cold War rhetoric to the Conservative objectives of reducing levels of direct taxation and stimulating individual incentive. Economic liberalisation after 1951 was presented wholly in this manner. In education, the party defended tripartism in secondary schools by arguing that different types of schools would be better suited to the individual achievements of each child. Albeit subject to underinvestment and fiscal stringency, education provision was expanded and developed by Conservative governments after 1951 and promoted as the centrepiece of an 'Opportunity State'. Across the range of policy-making, the Conservative governments of the 1950s pursued an agenda that coupled traditional objectives with a new language and basis of appeal.

The idea of a 'new Conservatism' in Britain after the war was promoted in party literature, propaganda and in political autobiography. 'New Conservatism' has become a significant narrative strand in post-war historiography. It has long been viewed with a degree of scepticism in academic historiography, largely because the party's modernisation project clearly failed on a number of levels. The organisational changes associated particularly with Lord Woolton's chairmanship of the party were successful in so far as they repaired the disruption to party structures experienced during the war and restored the efficient operation of the party's management. But reorganisation and reform failed to broaden and democratise the composition of the party, or to achieve anything resembling a mass popular Conservative movement. Policy-making innovations succeeded in reunifying a party that had become fragmented and demoralised by electoral defeat in 1945. But the record of the 1951-64 Conservative governments has typically been described in terms of missed opportunities and thirteen wasted years.

'New Conservatism' was accompanied neither by a new basis of popular support nor a radical new policy agenda because it was almost entirely a linguistic phenomenon imposed from above. The new language of Conservative politics succeeded in marrying the principles of Conservatism to the emerging discourse of the Cold War by associating the party with the idea of freedom, prosperity, broad property ownership and democracy. This is illustrated with particular clarity in the case of *The Industrial Charter*, which as the first exercise in post-war policy-making can be understood as a pivotal moment in the transition between the era of reconstruction and the era of the Cold War in domestic British politics. Its significance resides in the successful modernisation of the language of centre/right discourse so quickly following the trauma of 1945. From 1947, modern Conservatism provided a convincing non-Socialist alternative vision of post-war Britain to the electorate that associated the party's traditional defence of free enterprise and social responsibility with a new stress on individual freedom and achievement. In this sense the party succeeded in constructing a 'modern' framework for policy debate that would ensure the continued importance and relevance of Conservatism in post-war British politics.

10. Reveries of Race: The Closing of the Imperial Moment

Bill Schwarz

It is difficult to think of England other than as an old country. The official rhetorics of the nation systematically play upon ancestral themes, evoking ancient verities possessed, uniquely, by the English. This would seem especially true of the 1950s when, it might appear, those most committed to the historic nation, and habituated to its colonial customs, were confronted by a new generation whose delight in an Americanised mass culture afforded English youth little inclination to reflect on the virtues of national affiliation. By the end of the decade the codes of colonial England gave every indication of slipping quietly into the nation's collective memory. As the imaginative literature of the period attests, the empire signalled not the future but the past.

Revolt against the national past occurred in many different registers. The new cosmopolitanism, for example, shaped by the changing consumption patterns of the 1950s, was powerfully etched in an important image from the period: the young conquistadors of the emergent subcultures disporting themselves along the high streets and shopping parades of the dullest urban ethnoscapes, exulting in their refusal to conform to those around them. These subcultures were in part driven by the desire to appropriate and internalise national and ethnic identities which were far removed from the orthodoxies of England. As Dick Hebdige has shown with characteristic flair, young white men and women, while ambling back and forth along their mean streets, could project themselves as something quite other — as American, Italian or even black, evidence of the extraordinary symbolic capacities of ethnic identification. Hebdige has argued that, within the inner life of these symbolic forms, a 'phantom' history of race and ethnicity was played out, at the very moment when the diversification of Britain's ethnic composition was about to change.[1] Such a reading projects, on the one hand, old England and on the other the mobile subjects of a new modernity — 'missionaries of movement and disorder' — free from the inhibitions of the ancestral nation.[2]

There is some truth in this depiction of cultural polarisation. And yet nations, and the ethnicities allied to them, are also peculiarly modern manifestations of collective identity. Eric Hobsbawm has written that the 'basic characteristic of the modern nation and everything connected with it is its modernity'. In a slightly different vein, Benedict Anderson has insisted that nations are modern in part because of the narrative forms in which they are inscribed.[3] What makes nations modern is not the content of their discursive field, which may invariably hark back to the archaic, but the way that this discursive field itself is put together: in this, as Anderson suggests, the public media are decisive.

What is true of nations applies equally to the structures of ethnic belonging. The process of becoming modern can turn on the telling of old stories, the fabrications of memory serving to compensate for the dislocations of modernisation. The compulsive inventiveness of these stories is as significant as their mythic details: content and form are indivisibly one, the oxymoron of a conservative modernity signifying an important historical truth. More specifically, the imperative to think ethnically can be a consequence of the social forces of modernisation.[4] The intensity of identifications with white Englishness in the 1950s and 1960s suggests that new cultures were being formed as a result of this process, the ancestral idioms notwithstanding.

This is one paradox. Another is that the practice of appropriating the attributes of ethnic others was not simply confined to the self-consciously modern partisans of subcultural subversion. It is too easy to think of Englishness as a self-enclosed category, magically reproducing a civilisation of never-ending insularity. Despite appearances, England has never been insular; notwithstanding the relentless affirmations of the purity of the island-race, English ethnicities have been irredeemably fictive, amalgamated and wayward. As much as anything, this is the unintended legacy of empire. Just as nations may, on occasion, look like pre-modern relics and yet be constitutive of modernity, so ethnicity, despite protestations to the contrary, may essentially be hybrid.

Central to my argument is the fact that even the palpably conservative or racist manifestations of ethnic belonging in the 1950s and 1960s may have a more dynamic and complex history than they are conventionally accorded. Despite appearances, they were neither simply recidivist nor in any simple sense only domestic. They were, in their own way, modern. They represented an active reworking of older forms of ethnic identity and marked a particular response to a new set of social circumstances — not least to the closure of Britain's colonial epoch. And they were informed by a broad repertoire of colonial experiences. To put this in a different register, they were shaped by memories of empire in which the legacies of actually existing England played only a part. Learning about race was pre-eminently a matter of the frontier. The frontiers of the empire, in their various forms, created the syntax for a particular style of domestic Englishness. This was as true for the period of decolonisation as for earlier more manifestly imperial moments. That 'the fact of whiteness' had to be asserted at such volume, and so insistently, indicated the depth of the transformations underway. The axis of the national culture itself had turned; to be white at the beginning of the 1950s was a different matter from being white twenty years later.

Throughout the 1950s and 1960s sections of the English population came to imagine themselves living in a 'white man's country'.[5] The power of this perception lay in its symbolic not its empirical truth; it voiced a fantasy of England becoming its imagined past again. What previously might have been assumed about the ethnic configuration of the nation now required to be spoken. Yet to think in such terms — to employ the rhetoric of a 'white man's country' — was to revive an older imperial vocabulary, which had been common at the turn of the century as a means of describing the real frontier societies on the edge of the empire. To think in these terms was to believe that the frontier — between the white English and their black others — had truly come home, the primal colonial encounter now relocated onto the domestic domain itself.

How the empire was imagined and remembered in the 1950s, in popular life as well as in the official institutions of society, is a problem of genuine complexity. There indeed was much forgetting when a new generation was born that could only remember the empire at one remove, by way of other people's memories. But the channels of memory did not completely run dry, nor have they since. The legacy of empire is still too deeply imbricated in the nation and in its ethnic longings. Memories of empire during the 1950s seeped into the wider dramatisations of ethnicity which were stirred by the onset of black immigration, one displacement triggering the next. Part of my purpose here is to begin to map these memories. The kind of maps we need resist conventional representation as stubbornly as any song-line. One thing though is sure: we cannot tell the story with only the map of England spread before us.

Jan Christian Smuts

These are abstract formulations which need an empirical focus. My detailed argument examines the figure of Jan Christian Smuts, the Prime Minister of South Africa and hero of the empire. Smuts died in 1950 and there followed much debate in Britain about how best he should be commemorated. This discussion, indicating how he was both remembered and (by implication) forgotten, provides an initial way into the post-war drama of empire. For a British generation born around the turn of the century, Smuts would have been an entirely familiar figure, more visible than any other colonial statesman, and more prominent than many domestic politicians. It is revealing that a man so central to the self-definition of the English and to the conception of their civilisation could so quickly slip from view.

Smuts, born into a Boer family in 1870, was sufficiently anglophile that he chose to study at Cambridge University, an unusual move for a native Afrikaans speaker. In the Anglo-South African War (or Boer War) of 1899-1901, however, he was incensed by the free-booting capitalist adventurism of the leading British imperialists — Rhodes, Milner and Chamberlain — and in consequence unhesitatingly supported the Boers, his own patrimony, against the British. In his determination to destroy the British Empire he was driven to advocate guerrilla warfare in India, forcing the metropolis to fight on every front. Yet in the face of defeat he believed that a single option presented itself: accommodation to the British in the hope that the authentic traditions of English liberalism would, before too long, prevail over the mercenary opportunism of Milner and his kind. The moment at which this reconciliation occurred assumed mythic resonance in Smuts' subsequent recountings of his life, winning him to the cause of English civilisation. When the Liberals were returned to power in 1906 Smuts was quick to visit the new Prime Minister, Henry Campbell-Bannerman: 'I used no set arguments, but simply spoke to him as man-to-man and appealed only to the human aspect, which I felt would weigh deeply with him'.[6] As Smuts was fond of explaining, the spirit of liberality ran so true in Campbell-Bannerman that he was immediately impressed by the virtue of Smuts' pleading and declared at once the new administration's intention to offer self-government to the vanquished South African colonies.

Smuts became the principal advocate in South Africa of maintaining his nation's links with the British crown and, whenever the opportunity arose, promoting the cause of English civilisation. The British empire, he believed, had come to an end the evening he talked with Campbell-Bannerman: the rapacious polity, which could heroise Rhodes or Milner, had of its own accord transmuted into a freedom-loving confederation of autonomous nations, held together only by shared respect for the common historic values of England. To argue in these terms was at the same time to distance himself from the intransigent elements within Afrikaner nationalism; in its place Smuts favoured a fusion of the Dutch and British into a newly vibrant colonial nationalism, founded on the shared affiliations of whiteness. Smuts' first political speech dilated on the need to ensure 'the consolidation of the white race'.[7] Fully conscious of his role as a nation-maker (with the founding fathers of the United States, and Lincoln too, at the back of his mind), Smuts played a critical role in the creation of the Union of South Africa in 1910. He was later to be Prime Minister, between 1919 and 1924, and again between 1939 and 1948, while serving as deputy Prime Minister in the coalition years, between 1933 and 1939. Even excusing filial hyperbole, one can accept the basis of his son's claim, made shortly after the death of his father: 'There is, in fact, very little in South Africa that did not spring from his fertile brain'.[8]

There were many in South Africa who abhorred Smuts. He created legions of political enemies. A multitude of others loathed him personally. Nor did he make any attempt to disguise his attraction for the larger imperial stage, which his detractors perceived (with justice) to carry with it a commensurate disregard for what Smuts saw as the provincialism of his own nation. 'Here in England my work has been much approved by high and low', he wrote in 1929 in a typically gloomy mood to his wife back home: 'only in my own country this belittling occurs and what the cause or motive is I fail to see. It is a funny world — enough to disgust one.'[9] The attraction of the metropolis proved compelling for Smuts. He loved the inheritors of Quaker radicalism. He loved the imperial men who walked the corridors of power. He loved being lauded by all and sundry: the men who stood in awe of his intellect and — this austere, unerotic man — the women who fell for him. The public representatives of metropolitan England, Tory and Labour, imperialist and radical, created Smuts in their own image. 'The most considerable person in Greater Britain', was the verdict of A.G. Gardiner in 1916, a view emanating from the heart of the New Liberalism. A year later C.P. Scott of the *Manchester Guardian* believed him to be 'perhaps the most popular man in the country'.[10] He became the civilised incarnation of the imperial frontier, statesman and philosopher, the fount of wisdom on every conceivable matter of significance.

In March 1917 Smuts arrived in London to attend the first Imperial Conference. His reputation as the military leader of the South African forces in East Africa had preceded him and he was compared to Caesar, Cromwell and Napoleon. The following month Lloyd George persuaded him to join the war cabinet (notwithstanding his lack of representation at Westminster), a post he held for some eighteen months. During this time he was honoured as an exceptional public man. An intimate of his even had Smuts claiming that the King had requested him to remain in Britain so that he could become Prime Minister.[11]

In September 1939 Smuts led the campaign inside South Africa to persuade first the cabinet, and then Parliament, to abandon neutrality — and a potential alliance with the Axis powers — and to support the Allies. Becoming Prime Minister once more as a result, he again moved close to the power-centres of the imperial state, an influence redoubled when his old friend Churchill assumed office in May 1940. From South Africa he broadcast on the BBC to Britain, rivalling Churchill and Priestley in popularity, and he himself tuned in every night to hear the BBC reports from Daventry. In his own way he became something of an unlikely star of the new media, becoming 'a particular hero of the cinema newsreels'.[12] Penguin devoted one of its early paperbacks to his biography.[13] In 1941 the King bestowed on him the rank of Field Marshal. Returning to London

again in October 1942 he addressed both houses of Parliament. The intro-
ductory speech was given by Lloyd George, the thanks by Churchill, while
the assembled worthies, in characteristically schoolboy fashion, offered a
spirited rendition of: 'For he's a jolly good fellow'. Fifteen million people
in Britain listened to Smuts' speech on the BBC; Pathé, Movietone and
Gaumont newsreels all covered it at length.[14] Leo Amery, witnessing the
speech from the Royal Gallery, exulted in the wisdom of this 'prophet of
Empire', while Chips Channon — diarist, socialite and lofty cynic —
initially finding the speech 'so bromidic' that he was convinced it must have
been drafted by Eden, was later completely charmed by the South African
and came to hold him in high esteem.[15] Even George Orwell, far distant
from conservative political allegiances, could at this time quite unselfcon-
sciously maintain of Smuts that: 'Few modern statesmen are more
respected in Britain'.[16]

In the immediate post-war years he was a commanding personality at the
inauguration of the United Nations, drafting the Preamble to the new
organisation's founding document. He was one of the speakers to launch the
BBC's Third Programme, taking the opportunity to reflect on the inherent
liberality of the new Commonwealth which had arisen, he suggested, as a
direct consequence of the bankruptcy of British imperialism during and
after the Boer War.[17] When Stanley Baldwin died, Smuts was chosen to
replace him as Chancellor of Cambridge University. During the royal tour
of South Africa in February 1947 he had the time of his life, ubiquitous in
the newsreel and television reports, performing his many official duties
with all the pomp he could muster, but also — when the occasion allowed
— happy to fool around both for the cameras and for the delight of his
guests. With his defeat by the National Party in 1948, his following in
Britain became yet more intense, as the new government in South Africa
became increasingly hostile to all things British.

In British political life, Smuts represented himself and was perceived as
an authentically *imperial* statesman who carried within him a vision of the
whole empire, unimpeded by mere national interest. This was a more
complex and ambivalent politics than it might first appear to be. Smuts was
proud of his own colonial nationalism and never for a moment forgot that
he himself was a founding father of the new nation of South Africa. For
all his love of the metropolis, he was neither English nor British, but South

African — indeed, one of the first South Africans. Those at the centre were right to see him as a man of the frontier. Owing to the particular exigencies of the national composition of the new South Africa (in which from 1910 white British and white Dutch learned to organise an alliance in order to maintain supremacy over the black population) Smuts had long appreciated the importance of subsuming national allegiances to the larger requirements of race. All his life he was unequivocally a white supremacist. More particularly, he was drawn to the particular encodings of white authority which were manifest in the British Empire. At the core of these idealised projections of white civilisation lay the fictions of England. As an article of faith Smuts believed that these were not the exclusive preserve of the metropolis. Here lay his wager with history, for he came to be convinced that other nations would claim for themselves the values, cultures and customs which the British called their own.

To think in this way did not involve for Smuts a denial of colonial nationalism in favour of the nationalism of the metropolis. Englishness, without the centring of England, can properly be understood in Smuts' case as an *ethnic* structuring in which individual nations represented local variants of the larger entity, or in the vocabulary of the day, local patriotisms. Kith and kin, the mother country, the Commonwealth, the crown — these and cognate terms all alluded to those expansive affiliations, manifest in the peculiarly providential history of the English. Sometimes these attributes were described as British, sometimes as English; but whichever term was invoked the purpose of their incantation was to insist on their universal applicability. The values nurtured in a single national history could be dispersed universally, the particular transformed into the general. Just as Walter Scott made Scotland (in Smuts' eyes) 'a possession for the whole human race', so the empire — 'the greatest actual political achievement of time' — universalised the ethnic codes of its core nations.[18] Smuts, colonial and former enemy of the empire, came to inhabit this inheritance with the supreme confidence of one who had undergone a conversion of Pauline intensity, learning to speak its mysteries with greater fluency than accredited nationals whose mother-tongue it was. Like generations of Scots and Welsh before him, he was pulled into a field-force of English *ethnicity*, reviving it as no domestic could. With him the moral truth of the frontier, in all its force, came home.[19]

If, in the colonies, whiteness determined the structures of inclusion and exclusion, within the culture of metropolitan Britain it was largely unspoken. It was signified powerfully enough — in the symbol of the crown, in the providence of the English, in the daily habits of a freedom-loving people — but it worked silently, through many displacements. Smuts, however, was born into a culture in which the divide between black and white was spoken about incessantly: he lived his life as a white man in a way that Churchill, for example, was not required to do. As he knew the black man, he knew better what it was to be white. In consequence, Smuts became one of those who assumed a strategic position in creating for the domestic political élite a way of articulating race which conformed to the codes of English ethnicity, reorganising them in the process. To give this greater specification, in an age of universal political rights, Smuts struggled to reconcile his faith in the supremacy of white civilisation with a genuine regard for liberty and democracy. He persevered in his attempt to provide democratic justification for his own belief in the immutability of racial difference. On his death in 1950, he bequeathed to the British a discourse on race which could be recuperated by post-war domestic politicians when called upon to have something intelligent or acceptable to say on the issues of empire and immigration. The legacy of an instinctive supremacism or racial superiority became transmuted into matters of culture, civilisation and disposition. Whether it was in tempering the enthusiasm of black nationalist leaders, or justifying white landladies' refusal to let rooms to black applicants on account of the other tenants, a way of articulating racial superiority emerged which appeared to confirm the essential liberality of the English. In this sense Smuts functioned, for the British, as a philosopher of race.

Many people in Britain, especially those who shaped public opinion, read his writings or heard him lecture. Many more gained an image of him through the wireless and the newsreel. By the end of his life, even those who had never read a word he had written would have known of him. They would have known that he stood against South Africa's National Party and thus against the injustices of apartheid. And they would have known too (for they were told it often enough) that he represented 'the best' of England's destiny overseas, equally firm in his determination to hold back the vague menace which the idea of Africa itself continued to signify in the post-war world. Audiences watching him in the cinemas may have been impressed or bored to tears; they may have cheered or booed. But in his persona these complex histories were condensed.

Memorialising and Forgetting Empire

When Smuts died on 11 September 1950, Lord Samuel broadcast a tribute on the Home Service, while BBC television announced the passing of 'one of the greatest and best-loved statesmen' of South Africa.[20] Further tributes came from Attlee, Churchill and the King, which were all duly reported in *The Times* the next day.[21] In the House of Commons on 13 September Attlee spoke again about his faith in Smuts: most remarkable, he argued, was Smuts' 'intense belief in all that we call the British view of life'.[22]

In South Africa the Nationalist government offered a state funeral, which the family refused. In its place a full-scale military funeral was held in Pretoria, which received due coverage in the British press and the news-reels, as did the activities of the civic day set aside to honour his memory the following June. Collections for a memorial fund in South Africa had been initiated even before the funeral occurred, though Smuts' widow made it clear that she wished for a 'live' memorial rather than a statue, obelisk or plaque.

But the private wishes of colonial widows, however esteemed their husbands, appeared to have carried little influence on the decisions of the public men in London. From October, the matter of a suitable statue of Smuts in the capital became a periodic issue. In June 1951 Attlee finally proposed to Parliament that there should be such a statue, and in this he was supported by Churchill and by the leader of the Liberals, Clement Davies. 'It is right', Davies suggested, 'that future generations, here in London, should see in the form of a statue the man whom we were privileged to know, and to see again the strong features, the perfectly shaped head and the virile bearing of this man, who was an inspiration to his fellow men throughout the whole of his long and varied career.'[23]

By July 1952 there appeared the first indication that a statue to Smuts might prove contentious. Eirene White, the Labour MP and daughter of Thomas Jones, a close friend of Smuts, had this to say to members of the memorial committee:

I would draw the attention of the Committee to the fact that we have citizens in other countries of the Commonwealth who may, perhaps, have rather less reason for gratitude to the late Field Marshal ... he did not always show in his domestic career the magnanimity which he displayed towards his former military opponents in this country. In dealing with Africans and with the coloured peoples and with those people in the Union of South Africa whose origins were in the Asian countries of the Commonwealth, his actions sometimes left something to be desired. I think it would be unfortunate if, in choosing a site, we chose one which might be considered not quite appropriate by some of our fellow citizens of the Commonwealth. I say this because there have been some suggestions in the Press that this monument might be placed in Parliament Square. There may be some members of the Commonwealth who would find it extremely incongruous to have a statue of Field Marshal Smuts placed in immediate proximity to that of Abraham Lincoln.[24]

Such doubts provoked a predictably outraged reaction from the Tory MP for Surrey East, Charles Doughty, who argued that 'Field Marshal Smuts was one of the greatest members of the British Empire that has ever lived'.[25] However, the questions exercising other members of the committee were barely to do with Smuts at all; they were principally aesthetic. Tom Driberg, for example, a seasoned critic of British colonialism, agreed with Eirene White, but felt more impelled to press his own case for commissioning a young sculptor who would produce a work of genuine interest. This was a view echoed by Marcus Lipton, the MP for Brixton, who declared himself 'not concerned with the merits or demerits' of Smuts, but wanted something striking to emerge as a memorial: 'If the Minister were to say that two or three monuments are to be removed to make room for a better one in memory of Field Marshall Smuts, then I should be more inclined to support the Motion now before the House'.[26] The tyros of modernity warmed to their theme. Malcolm Bullock, representing Crosby but residing in Middlefield, Great Shelford near Cambridge, was convinced that 'London possessed some of the worst statues in the world' and decried 'the old hack sculptors who go round not only London but the provinces as well'.[27]

If it had not been for the intransigence of Doughty, business may well have concluded with a constitutional majority solemnly voting for the new iconoclasm. However, when another member, Charles Pannell, eventually endorsed White's views, a colossal rumpus broke out between Doughty and the chairman, on the one hand, and the Labour representatives on the other. Doughty had recently made himself notorious for his wild attacks on Fenner Brockway and on Brockway's attempts to persuade Parliament to outlaw the colour bar. In this context, and with tempers rising, the connection between Smuts and segregation was at last made explicit. These ructions notwithstanding, none of the members saw fit to oppose the statue of Smuts: they agreed it should proceed, *nem. con.*

The memorial committee, chaired by Smuts' old friend and erstwhile high commissioner in Pretoria, Lord Harlech, went about its business slowly. It was only in December 1955 that the Minister of Works, Nigel Birch, first publicly announced both the location and the sculptor. The location was indeed to be Parliament Square — due in part, perhaps, to the interest which Churchill had been taking in its redesign. Smuts was to be placed in the heart of the square, alongside Palmerston, Derby, Disraeli and Peel; the traffic would separate him from Lincoln (and Canning), who were positioned in an outer orbit, thus protecting the susceptibilities of Eirene White's colonials.

The choice of sculptor, Jacob Epstein, was even more complex. He was hardly youthful, as Driberg would have been quick to aver. Indeed, he was barely younger than Churchill or Smuts. And there is reason enough to think that, by the 1950s, he was tolerably close to the cliché of the 'old hack', ready to take any commission that came his way. But he did once boast a reputation as an aesthetic heretic. This was a heresy which had had its roots in an appropriation of black Africa or, as Anthony Blunt had described it in the *Spectator* in 1935, Epstein revived European art 'by an infusion of dark blood'.[28] Epstein was indeed an artist who had been transformed by the aesthetics of the black Atlantic. But at the same time, and certainly by the 1950s, he had become a kind of archetype of a conservative modernity: the émigré who reconstructs the forms of the national culture but who simultaneously subscribes to its deepest reflexes.

Epstein regretted the Smuts assignment. He was required to consult with the Ministry of Works and with the Royal Fine Art Commission and he also needed approval, in the early stages, from Attlee too. The minutiae of the details of Smuts' military uniform generated a number of controversies with the various authorities concerned. By March 1956, when the project should have been completed and unveiled, the plinth was still nowhere to be seen. After many postponements, on 17 July 1956 Patrick Buchan-Hepburn, the Minister of Works, finally announced in Parliament that the statue would be unveiled on 7 November by Churchill, as a memorial to 'a great enemy of racial discrimination'.[29] The mishaps, however, were not yet over. A week before the ceremony, a controversy blew up over the correct spelling of Smuts' middle name. By the day itself Churchill had pulled out on grounds of poor health — though his wife was of the opinion that he was ready for an excuse not to do it.[30] And, in a rather different order of events, the constant delays meant that the unveiling coincided with the domestic climax of the Suez crisis.

At dawn on 6 November, the Anglo-French seaborne forces landed at Port Said, prepared to take control of the entire canal zone. The British cabinet met at 9.45 a.m. The Chancellor of the Exchequer, Harold Macmillan, had been on the telephone to Washington before the meeting took place, anxious about the run on the pound. The pressure on the Prime Minister, Anthony Eden, intensified. Eisenhower, facing imminent re-election, was furious, as were all the leading American politicians. It also became clear that the British cabinet was backsliding. The ceasefire was agreed. If there was a single day which marked the collapse of Britain's imperial ambitions, 6 November 1956 must be regarded as the most convincing contender.

On 7 November, as Smuts was officially resurrected in Parliament Square, Eden was trying to contain the damage in a series of desperate telephone conversations with Eisenhower. The urgency of the Suez crisis made Smuts' unveiling a forlorn occasion. Eden was absent, as was the entire cabinet. A tiny cluster of guests witnessed the event. Churchill had excused himself, though his brief words were read out. The official unveiling was conducted by W.S. Morrison, the speaker of the House of Commons, who (perhaps also with Smuts' views on Goethe and Whitman in mind) informed those assembled that the last thing Smuts had said to him was this: 'Morrison, it is a great thing to be a man — a great thing'.[31]

The band of the Irish Guards played while pedestrians got on with their business, with little more than a cursory glance at the ritual being played out.

In the six years of procrastination in getting the monument constructed, from his death in 1950 to the unveiling of 1956, Smuts slipped out of the defining rhythms of popular memory. For those who knew him, and for a particular generation of imperial men, memories of him remained invincible. But for the majority who did not know him, and for new generations, his image became progressively weaker. There was, of course, an inevitability about this process, which was nothing more than the inevitability of mortality and of the creation of new generational cultures, which in the 1950s were particularly marked. Yet there was another dynamic at work. By 1956 it was becoming increasingly awkward to project unadorned, heroic epics of imperial life. All the theatrical apparatuses were in place for the commemoration of Smuts as the personification of the monumental history of empire. All, that is, bar the living principal actors. The statue, the military band, the enormous Union Jack draping the bronze figure: the stage was set. In place of the politicians were their wives and daughters: Lady Churchill, Clarissa Eden, the daughter of Smuts. The monumentalisation of Smuts, and of the empire he represented, turned out to be an empty affair. It was an elegy not only for Smuts but for the British Empire itself. By 1956, in the larger national culture, Smuts had become a hollow man, his effigy in bronze signifying — Epstein's aspirations notwithstanding — 'gesture without motion'. Nor was this simply a consequence of the immediate political emergency. It suggests the presence of a larger historical fracture and the coming of a generation which could be forgetful about empire.

Especially telling was the Movietone newsreel of the Smuts unveiling. In the mid-1950s newsreels were still a singularly powerful means by which the domestic population came to know about national and foreign events. In 1956 only some fifteen per cent of the adult population watched television, while in the region of a thousand million cinema tickets were sold annually. The newsreel at this time claimed its role as sovereign medium of the topical, a genre which was neither quite news nor quite entertainment. Even so, the development of the newsreel genre proved an uneven process, for there were occasions when light-hearted topicality was not appropriate. After all, this was still the time when cinema programmes closed with the national anthem.

Movietone allocated the Smuts unveiling just twenty seconds. The shots were conventional and quite without visual interest; they were accompanied by elevated funeral music in deference to a public man departed. The voice-over, tempered and respectful, could have come straight out of the pages of *The Times*. This was news, with the nation tightly demarcated and determinedly straight-faced. After the Smuts item came a longer feature on the cycle and motor-show at Earl's Court, which was altogether more fluent: in thirty-four seconds it conveyed wonderment at the spectacle of the modern and pride in the inventiveness of the British, while its narrative worked by topical allusion (the wealth of the *arrivistes*, Sir Bernard and Lady Docker; threats of petrol shortages), humour, irony and pun. The divide between the new consumerism and the old imperialism could not have been more striking. This in turn was followed by news from Hungary (cynicism of the Kremlin bosses) and finally by Suez, represented as 'our boys' bringing restraint and civilisation to the near East.

This is micro-history with a vengeance, marking the onset of a media epoch in which cognitive structures became attuned to programme flows composed of twenty- or thirty-second segments. The monumental narratives that in earlier decades had seemed the natural mode for representing imperial Britain no longer carried the same authority. It is not that they entirely disappeared (witness the statecraft of Churchill's funeral), nor is it the case that such media-driven forms had not been active in the organisation of national, popular cultures in previous periods. Rather, it has more to do with a cultural diversification and the shifting imperatives of cultural authority, the axis turning sharply — in an age of mass culture — to the popular. The ability institutionally to hold in place official or monumental public narratives, with a central, fixed referent, diminished as these stories became more complex to manage. To put this in a metaphorical idiom, the cultural authority of the (imaginary) Home Service citizen, located in a very particular national and imperial history, was confronted by an unprecedented array of competing public possibilities. In such a culture the monumental memory of Smuts had limited popular reach.

Remembering Race: The Dynamics of Conservative Modernity

There is reason to suppose that in the second half of the 1950s formal allegiances to imperial Britain slackened, unhinged, at least in part, by the effects of new American consumer cultures. But this, and the dichotomy which followed from it, was only part of the story. Equally critical was the dynamic of displacement, in which the symbolic transactions of a declining colonial order migrated to emergent cultural formations and transmuted in the process, disporting themselves as if they had entirely broken free from the histories in which they had been formed. Ethnic identities themselves, driven by memories of the national past, could be played out in the new arenas of mass culture, signifying a conservative modernity. Dick Hebdige hinted at this himself when he suggested that subcultural styles and their associated musics became scenarios in which a 'phantom' history of race could be re-enacted, the older properties of imperial memories taking on a new life in the interstices of consumer culture. Memories of empire did not disappear the moment decolonisation occurred in a neat symmetrical *coup de grace*; they continued to be located in the national culture but were reactivated in a new, manifestly more modern, symbolic environment. The repositioning of British culture at the end of the 1950s around new electronic media produced not a new amnesia or forgetfulness (as some theorists suggest), rather its reverse: new resources and new archives for remembering.

Many guardians of colonial civilisation believed the advent of American-driven consumer culture brought with it barbarism. This was a perception which was often racially overdetermined. If earlier in the century intimations of 'dark blood' had been received through the forms of high modernism, by 1956 the medium of rhythm and blues, or in its more commodified form, rock 'n' roll, was moving to the centre of popular culture. While the resurrection of Smuts in Parliament Square testified to a culture determined to uphold the essentials of white civilisation, through more subterranean channels some versions of the black experience did indeed break into the cultures of white England — heavily mediated, perhaps, and with unknown consequences, but present nonetheless. In May 1956 *Melody Maker* reported the views of Asa Carter, of Alabama's

Citizens' Council, that rock music was no more than the means of 'pulling down the white man to the level of the negro It is part of a plot to undermine the morals of the youth of our nation. It is sexualistic, unmoralistic, and the best way to bring people of both races together.' This, patently, was an extreme view, formed in the particular history of the American South. But in Britain cognate ideas were heard in more modulated registers: from politicians (Marcus Lipton, agnostic about Smuts, held no such equivocation about the dangers of rock music), in the popular press, from the BBC, from religious groups, in *Melody Maker* itself.[32] With only a degree of irony, Margery Perham, in her Reith lectures of 1961, put it like this: 'Africa knew how to use the syncopated magic of the drum to summon ecstasy. Even unconsciousness. And perhaps, in the abandonment of our youth to this spell, she inflicts a subtle revenge!'[33] While the final preparations for Smuts' statue were in train, exuberant crowds 'ranted and raved' outside the Gaumont cinemas in Dagenham, Leyton and Stratford, in East London, fired up simply by seeing *Rock Around the Clock*.[34] For those anxious about such developments, it seemed as if white civilisation were endangered from within, confronted not by visible antagonists from outside but by invisible forces deep within the culture of the metropolis itself.

Yet to pose a simple polarisation between the old colonial cadres, in the suburbs of Purley and Camberley, representative of the past, and the subcultural insurrectionists in Dagenham or Leyton, representative of the future, is to miss much. For the masquerades of ethnic identification, white or black, old or new, were forged in a dynamic in which contending psychic investments in an imagined homeland were intense. For white Britons who suddenly believed themselves to be on the frontier, the inherited, formal monumental narratives of empire were, perhaps, anachronistic. But the deeper syntax bequeathed by the cultures of colonialism — in which the white man and the racial frontier figured powerfully — produced a symbolic repertoire in which white ethnicities could be imagined anew. A culture in Britain in the 1950s and the 1960s, which witnessed a dramatic reinvention of the idea of the white man, was indebted to something deeper than John Ford movies.

In early September 1958 a number of white youths embarked upon a night of 'nigger hunting', as they later described it in court. Unable to get into their local rugby club in Notting Hill they drove to a pub in

Bloemfontein Road in Acton. It was the General Smuts. Not too much should be made of such coincidences. But it is the case that as Britain divided in the 1950s and 1960s around a politics of ethnicity, South Africa became one means by which domestic, white Britons could live out their own ethnic dramas. In this, the formal politics of decolonisation generally played only an oblique part.[35] For the majority, Smuts was largely forgotten. But his high-minded defence of segregation, his faith in white civilisation, his dedicated insistence on holding the frontier — these convictions could be heard long after Smuts and other tribunes of empire had passed from public memory. In part, Smuts bequeathed to a new generation of public leaders a *politics* of race, with its appointed language and philosophy, which could, when pressed, represent itself as a democratic politics. In part too, the populist reimagining of what it was to be *white* owed much to the unconscious presence of a received colonial syntax. The frontier ceased to be the stuff of fiction and came to be relocated at the end of the street, palpable and present. Through a complex process of symbolic displacement, the neighbourhood became imagined as a colonial frontier. Even when the rhetoric drew from putatively ancestral verities, the context was entirely modern. The new home may have been stocked with all the accoutrements of consumer culture, but it could still be deemed to exist on the vertiginous edge of the nation. The intoxicating figure of the white man was strangely dislocated from the processes of modernisation; he was formed by them but wedded in the imagination to an invented past. And this was a past in which England and its larger empire played a defining role.

Lofty praise for the moral virtue of Jan Christian Smuts, as the personification of enlightenment in racial politics and as the embodiment of the British way, was indicative of a political culture whose own memory had been formed deep in the history of colonialism. This was a collective memory in which amnesia could be organised. In 1956 a statue was erected in memory of Smuts, the man identified by W.E.B. DuBois as 'the greatest protagonist of the white race'.[36] But in the process other memories were obliterated. If one visits the site today one can just about make out a faint inscription on the stonework where the figure of Smuts now stands:

> From 1865 to 1950 there stood on this site the memorial fountain in
> memory of Sir Thomas Fowell Buxton Bart MP and others in

commemoration of the emancipation of the slaves under the British flag in 1834. The memorial now stands in the Victoria Tower Gardens.

Six years after the statue was unveiled Nelson Mandela was on a clandestine visit to London. Like previous generations of political activists he took time out for tourism, walking around Westminster with his friend and comrade, Oliver Tambo. They saw the statue of Smuts. 'Oliver and I joked that perhaps some day there would be a statue of us in its stead.'[37] Nearly, but not quite.

11. New Towns for Old: The Fate of the Town Centre

Peter Mandler

For those pundits and journalists bent on portraying Britain as 'an old country', its economy constrained and its culture warped by nostalgia for a lost rural idyll, the fate of the town centre in the two decades after 1945 poses peculiar problems. These decades were, of course, years of unparalleled modernisation in town and country across Europe, years in which the physical face of the Continent was transformed by the spread of the automobile, the tower block, the office block and the concrete civic centre. Yet even in this context of transformation, Britain stands out as unusually enthusiastic about the exchange of 'new towns for old', a slogan which pointed not only to the construction of genuinely 'new towns' on greenfield sites but also to the razing of 'old towns' and the erection of modern ones in their place.[1]

The story — a complex and absorbing one that deserves a book-length treatment — in fact reveals not one but several aspects of British modernity in the immediate post-war years. In the brief treatment that follows, two elements will be emphasised. First, the planning system installed after the war by the Attlee governments — sometimes cited as evidence of the romantic, paternalist tendencies of the British élite — will be considered in its intentions and initial ambitions for town centres. The British planning system was fully consonant with developments elsewhere in Europe which were seen, at the time, as the cutting-edge of modernity, the modernity of the experts and 'informed' opinion seeking to reconstruct a Europe founded on its glorious past but setting course for an equitable, democratic and high-technology future. Second, the actual development of town centres in the 1950s and early 1960s will be surveyed, a process in which the national planning regime played a surprisingly limited and steadily diminishing role. New commercial and political forces were, instead, dominant. These reveal the modernity not of the expert but of the voter, the consumer, the worker. While still roughly consonant with pan-European trends, this modernity manifested itself earlier and more fully in Britain than elsewhere, comparatively untrammelled by the planners' vision, revealing a Britain where consumer democracy and economic modernisation — far from being restrained by timidity and bureaucratic nannying — were the masters.

The 1940s: A Golden Age of Town Planning?

Analyses of post-war urban development still tend to lay all the blame for its failures (and what little credit is owing for its successes) at the door of the planners — the authors of the planning regime instituted during and immediately after the war — and their henchmen, the architects. The planning regime is routinely described as monist, functionalist, paternalist, super-rationalist and authoritarian; the values it embodies are held to be the 'traditional' values of the British intelligentsia — a passion for neatness and order, a horror of democracy, a contempt for the vigour of modern urban life. Guided by these values, it is said, planners sought to mould a healthy, satisfied and subservient citizenry by physical means, without consent (much less participation) and thus without consideration for the democracy's true needs and desires.[2] So convenient is this scapegoat that it has been seized upon both by pro-growth critics of 1960s vintage (such as Peter Hall), who blame it for delivering an insufficiently modernised city, and by limits-to-growth critics of the post-1960s era (such as Alison Ravetz), who blame it for the 'clean-sweep' policies of the 1960s with their contempt for the historic core and the familiar townscape.[3] Most such treatments — being planning histories rather than integrated histories of urban development — devote the bulk of their attention to the genesis and spirit of the planning regime in the immediate post-war years and treat the subsequent rapid turn of events — abortive implementation, transformation, dismantling — as epiphenomenal.

Yet it could be argued that, even in its short-lived 'golden age', the British planning regime was no more utopian or authoritarian than its equivalents elsewhere in Europe. The feature of the British system which most struck contemporaries as novel and futuristic was its national scope, at least on paper. Labour nationalised development rights and values in land and thus won theoretical control over land use on a national scale; it also controlled by license all building activity and the location of industry. With these tools, central government proposed to redistribute employment and population from city centres in general, and from the south-east especially, confining urban sprawl around old centres with green belts and authorising new development in neglected areas and purpose-built new towns. These policies were accompanied by a rhetoric that was both élitist and utopian, implying that the entire country could be redesigned scientifically and professionally by architects and planners. This impression *or* implication was reinforced by the neat land-use maps that accompanied early advisory plans, with their concentric circles of population densities, neat packets of segregated uses and geometric traffic grids.

Much of the planners' utopian rhetoric, however, stemmed not from strength but from weakness. In 1945, Britain was well behind its chief Continental rivals in practical experience of physical planning. It had a reputation for leadership in the field, gained from the reputations of visionaries such as Ebenezer Howard and Patrick Geddes; but these visions were realised only in controlled experiments such as Port Sunlight or Hampstead Garden Suburb. In many places on the Continent, by contrast, planning was less adventurous but better established in the mainstream of political and civic life, not so much through the agency of central government as through the efforts of urban patriciates with greater autonomy, a stronger sense of continuity and identity and closer ties to the technical professions than in Britain.[4] The wartime consensus around social reform and nationalisation seemed to British planners a golden opportunity to overcome this historic weakness. They sought to benefit from the vogue for centralised social and economic planning generated in wartime by the Beveridge Report and encouraged the public to draw an analogy between the 'planning' of social insurance or the organisation of industry and the 'planning' of the built environment. Such an analogy would enable town planners to acquire sweeping powers at central-government level that they had never been able to secure locally. The nationalisation of development rights, for instance, was a blunt instrument aimed at securing for British planners the powers of development control that many Continental planners had built up piecemeal before the war by means of building codes, zoning, density controls, historic-buildings protections and compulsory purchase powers. After the war, Continental planners continued to develop these traditional tools. They had no choice: the revulsion from authoritarian government felt in most Nazi-occupied countries after the war put national planning in bad odour and forbade the employment of Britain's starry-eyed planning rhetoric, while the reversion to traditional means of local regulation was not only permitted but even celebrated.[5] Yet it is far from clear that the new centralised system conferred any lasting advantages upon British town planning. The analogy with social and economic planning was false and vulnerable to exposure: town planners lacked the political clout wielded by advocates of the welfare state or the nationalisation of industry. Their fundamental political weaknesses remained, but were obscured for a time by the dazzling rhetoric and the conceptual sweep of the national planning system.

Beneath the legislative rhetoric, British planners' practical ambitions for their cities did not differ all that much from those of their Continental counterparts. All European planners since the 1930s had been operating on the expectation of slow economic growth, slow population growth, slow traffic growth. Their job was to steer this incremental development gently along more functional and healthy channels. Their development plans were simple and static because that was a fairly realistic picture of the European city in the first half of the twentieth century. This is why Patrick Abercrombie's London plans can be described as both utopian (in scope) and conservative (in design). The same could as easily be said of the pre-war and post-war plans for Paris, Amsterdam or Cologne, also cities in which development had to be blended with large historic cores. In Britain, as on the Continent, the real visionary planning was largely confined to badly bombed cities and new towns. Far too many generalisations about national planning traditions have been based on a few oddball cases like Coventry or Rotterdam.

While the post-war planning system did mark a sharp break from historic British practice, and appeared to stand equally sharply from the broader European pattern, this had as much to do with the weakness of the British planning tradition as its strength. In reality British planners were moving after 1945 into a position similar to that held before the war by Continental

Even the more radical city-centre restructurings of the early 1950s, such as the famous shopping mall at Coventry, were planned on a domestic scale with softened 'modernistic' features. Illustration provided courtesy of the Architectural Review

planners. Only in one respect does the British national planning system stand out as fundamentally distinctive: the green-belt policy of containing conurbations, especially London. The Danes imitated the containment policy as early as 1949 in their Regulation of Built-Up Areas Act; city planners throughout Northern Europe tried to adapt it to local conditions by the insertion of 'green wedges' into their plans, wedges which did not contain cities but directed their growth along radial lines, as in Amsterdam, Copenhagen, Kiel and Cologne.[6] These planners did not have the national or even regional system necessary to preserve proper green belts, and containment was the one part of the British national system that was preserved (even reinforced) throughout the post-war decades. However, the social and cultural significance of Britain's green-belt policy has been subject to widely differing interpretations. Contemporaries in the 1950s were convinced that it was a sign of foresighted modernism, guiding development along balanced and healthy lines and allowing for functional differentiation between town and country.[7] In the rapid-growth 1960s, the green belt became a hated symbol of rural nostalgia throttling the vital city.[8] More recently, it has been persuasively argued that green belts were supported as much by cities keen to preserve their population densities and rateable values as by counties keen to stave off overspill.[9] In any case, planning ideology clearly played only a limited, dependent role. The simplest explanation for Britain's green-belt policy might be the country's unique extent of urbanisation. England was in 1945 the most crowded country in Europe, and, apart from Singapore and Hong Kong, the most crowded in the world. The Netherlands, another crowded country, also came the closest to adopting the British system of urban containment.[10]

Similarities between British and Continental thoughts on planning appear greater still when we dip below the national level and look at individual city plans. Here British planners again had theoretically utopian powers, conveyed by central government, to control private development and to acquire land for grandiose public works. But in explaining their intentions to the wartime and post-war public, planners often went out of their way to reassure people that these powers would not be used to make a 'clean sweep' of the familiar, human-scale townscape where it had survived. Of course, the opportunities provided by bomb damage and the solution of the compensation problem would be used to tidy up past messes, provide modern housing and shopping facilities and so on. But in contrast to the rhetoric about national planning, the rhetoric applied to local planning was decidedly upbeat about preserving the familiar, historic fabric and feel of towns. Thus the *Architectural Review*, in a special reconstruction issue in 1941, predicted that:

> each locality will naturally express itself in its own way and in relation to its traditional background. It is reasonable and natural that people should want the places they are familiar with to retain their distinctive character ... Mature development, both topographically and architecturally, allows this to happen ... The stereotyped Brave New World that people sometimes fear is in the minds of those who visualise future reconstruction on a scientific basis, would only come about as a result of academic planning from outside on the Fascist rather than the democratic model.[11]

The planning ministry's 1947 handbook on *The Redevelopment of Central Areas* persisted in this view. It recommended retention of the 'existing main street pattern', improving and opening up the old system rather than replacing it with a new one, with new building to be designed in careful relation to the old. The early advisory plans for post-war redevelopment generally embodied this philosophy, notably in Thomas Sharp's sensitive schemes for cathedral towns.[12] As doctrinaire modernists have always complained, this 'very English concern for the familiar' — in fact, not peculiarly English at all — affected even the designs for the new towns and for badly blitzed centres like Coventry, Plymouth, Exeter and Bristol, which, while not rebuilt on the old pattern, were still planned on a 'domestic scale' in vernacular English interpretations of modern styles. In this they resembled the new towns with their 'bowls of flowers and shrubby roundabouts and patterned paving and utility brick or Portland stone façades'.[13]

The equation between 'democratic planning' and 'the familiar' or the locally distinctive parallels Continental trends closely. In France and Germany blitzed centres were often rebuilt in cheap, modern interpretations of 'regional' styles. Monumental modernism was very much out of favour because of its associations with the monumental classicism of the dictators. Traditional street patterns were retained but replanned so as to accommodate somewhat higher levels of traffic and retail floor-space without affecting elevations and the familiar feel of the town.[14] A few badly damaged centres were replanned on a 'clean-sweep' basis, but Rotterdam and Hamburg are no more typical of post-war town planning on the Continent than Coventry and Southampton are of the British experience. The only genuinely utopian 'clean sweep' of an historic town centre occurred in Stockholm, where the historic street pattern dating to 1644 was superseded by eighteen-storey office buildings punctuating new open spaces.[15]

Despite appearances, therefore, the British planning system was neither exceptionally utopian in its national scale (as many contemporaries thought) nor exceptionally conservative in its design principles (as historians often imply). Its unusual national machinery would not necessarily have produced unusual modern developments in town centres, even if — and these are big ifs — central government had provided the funds and local authorities had agreed to such plans. In the early 1950s, Britain, like other European countries, appeared to be on the path towards the gentle modernisation of its city centres, accommodating modern traffic, commercial and office-space requirements while retaining familiar street-patterns, traditional and sometimes regional styles of architecture and a 'feel' for townscape that planners and ordinary citizens were thought to share. The real divergence between Britain and the Continent occurred not in the planning ideology of these immediate post-war years, but rather in the actual developments of the mid-to-late 1950s. In this period a quite different vision of modernity emerged and imprinted itself on the British town centre, a vision to which planners responded but which was not their own creature.

After 1951: Planning in Retreat

The wonderful British planning system, which so many contemporaries envied and so many scholars have since cursed, was in fact largely dismantled or nullified after 1951.[16] The breakthrough that planners thought they had made in the 1940s proved less than decisive. Deep-seated British traditions of *laissez-faire* were to a great extent restored. The Tory governments after 1951 privatised development values, gradually restoring development rights to landowners, and merged the national planning ministry back into the local government ministry from whence it had sprung; they ended the building license system, again restoring freedom of action to landowners, and loosened controls over the location of industry. Green belts were retained but the new towns programme was scaled back drastically. Planning powers that remained were mostly vested in local authorities, and these were mostly negative: the right to direct private development but only limited ability to undertake major public works.[17] The scaling-back of national planning in a sense only put Britain on a par with most Continental systems, where local authorities had generally held the planning initiative. At the same time, however, this restoration of a level planning-field revealed deeper social and cultural differences between Britain and the Continent that would have a direct impact on the feel of towns from the mid-1950s.

For if British national planners and Continental local planners had similar world-views, British and Continental local authorities did not. Britain's metropolitan intelligentsia frequently complained in the 1950s that whatever civic traditions had been built up in the Victorian period — and these can be overestimated, especially if generalised from exceptional cases such as Birmingham — had long worn thin. One complaint was that in such a highly mobile and changeable culture as Britain's, it had proved impossible to build up for more than a few generations a local intelligentsia that might guide urban planning and design. 'The professional classes as a whole have no roots, no local background', complained the historian W.G. Hoskins in 1956. The explicit contrast was with Germany, where local élites had struck deeper roots and been able to keep their towns 'so beautiful and so compact and unspoiled'. Others spoke of the problem as one of 'civic pride' — the French, the Germans and the Italians had it, the British did not.[18] The public opinion that had organised (or been organised) to defend or reconstruct traditional townscapes on the Continent was not so organised here. Civic beautification societies, long a feature of German culture, were a complete novelty in Britain; the foundation of the Civic Trust in 1957 was a belated attempt to stimulate their formation.[19]

British local authorities instead had their own agenda. They had neither civic élites nor long planning traditions to guide their work. They did have traditions of support for private economic development; before the war, for instance, they had horrified early preservationists by remodelling high streets to accommodate the large multiple shops. Most notoriously,

London's Regent Street was razed to the ground, but authorities elsewhere swept away medieval high streets with equal gusto and less publicity. Compared with what came later, however, these were modest affairs, both in scope and design. In the case of the growing number of Labour author-ities, this commercial agenda was supplemented by the drive to supply housing and social services to deprived groups. Both commercial and housing functions were supported after 1951 by central government policy as a cheaper and more politically expedient alternative to new towns and ambitious public projects in blitzed centres. Local authorities were to leave centre-city projects to private developers and instead, if they so desired, bend their own energies to slum clearance in the dense inner residential rings, with the displaced populations to be rehoused not in new towns but in new (possibly high-rise) urban estates.

Although this latter policy is usually portrayed as a country gentleman's plot to save the country and spoil the city, it was often consistent with Labour councils' own aspirations (and their interpretations of their constituents' desires). While some did try to negotiate for dispersal with neighbouring county councils — Manchester and London, for instance — others — Birmingham, Glasgow, Nottingham — were keen for political and financial reasons to keep trade and population tightly within their own boundaries.[20] For similar reasons of urban politics and economics, many local authorities were happy to throw over the fussy aesthetic controls and organic townscapes of the planners in favour of proposals for centre-city redevelopment advanced by private developers.

The impact of the new *laissez-faire* policies was first felt in London, where the local authorities — the London County Council (LCC) and the City — had been among the most enthusiastic about centre-city planning. Instead, almost immediately after the Tory decontrols of 1954, the full force of private-sector development was felt upon the face of London, over-whelming points of resistance in the local authorities. Anonymous glass and concrete office blocks began to pop up all over London: along the Marylebone Road, along High Holborn, ringing Hyde Park on the east and south, in the heart of the West End on St. Martin's Lane and in St. James's, or replacing a Georgian terrace in Lincoln's Inn Fields. By 1962, the very high blocks over 300 feet were changing not only the streetscape but the skyline of London: the Shell Centre on the South Bank, the Vickers Tower on Millbank, the Hilton Hotel on Park Lane, and in 1963, most notoriously, Centre Point at St. Giles' Circus.[21]

In the wake of Conservative policies of the 1950s, the initiative had passed decisively to the developer, often supported and encouraged by local councils. Where there was demand for office space (as there was, explosively, in London), the developer had almost unlimited call on funds from the City's financial markets. The very largest developments could thus be financed privately, whereas on the Continent similar developments could only be mounted by 'limited-dividend, semipublic or cooperative, and sometimes municipal' enterprises.[22] In London, developers decided where, how and how high building would take place. Despite valiant efforts by the LCC's historic buildings department, the planning department was rarely able to protect the historic fabric or even guide the design of the new developments. As the socialist planning committee chairman later admitted, 'I always had a particular feeling that I mustn't antagonise Big Business'.[23] On the occasions where the local authorities commissioned their own plans — such as Holford's plan for the precincts of St Paul's, jointly implemented by the City and the LCC — developers' pressure forced the architects to skimp on design and to bulk up the floorspace, producing travesties often far from the original conception.[24] And where the LCC did show an inclination to put its foot down, as in its efforts to scale down the Shell Centre and the Park Lane Hilton, it was overruled by central government and the developers were given their head.[25]

London was, of course, a special case. It was always going to be the hotspot of post-war development: the fifteen-year building freeze had pent-up pressures; the wholly unpredicted post-war boom in white-collar employment intensified growth in the nation's financial and commercial centre; developers had unusual power thanks to their links with City financial institutions. Against this, the LCC was also an exceptional local authority. It had started out with first-rate advisory plans (abandoned after 1954) and it possessed a pioneering architects' department which did acclaimed work outside the centre in the design of schools and council housing and also in conserving historic neighbourhoods. But in this case the local authority's ambitions were decisively undermined by central government working in tandem with private capital.

More revealing, perhaps, was the fate of other cities where local authorities were positively delighted to hand over centre-city redevelopment to private interests. Here, rather than in London, we can see 'public opinion' — at least in so far as it was expressed through elected local authorities — embracing comprehensive redevelopment and a vision of modernity startlingly different from that of the 'men of 1947'. The controlled-growth plans and methodical 'tidying up' envisaged by the architects of the 1947 regime had hardly come to anything outside of the blitzed centres and new towns. In the early 1950s there had been little development of any kind outside of these special areas. Most local authorities focused their attention on redeveloping inner-ring housing. Public interest in planning — which had been whipped up only to a certain point by Labour — was manifestly declining.[26] City centres were particularly badly hit by this atmosphere of inertia. By the late 1950s, they were getting very shabby indeed, congested with traffic and rapidly losing whatever amenity value they had retained from the pre-war world. Compared to working-class residential districts, city centres also seemed to have no important political constituency. Office workers were not yet taken seriously as a class and many local authorities had a prejudice against the shopping districts of city centres as catering only to up-scale consumers, in an economy where most working-class shopping was still local.[27] Local authorities were therefore politically free to do whatever they wanted with centres, or whatever they could afford.

When, in the late 1950s, private capital began to search for development sites outside London, it was welcomed with open arms. In most places at first this was an entirely piecemeal affair, as in London but on a smaller scale. Historic street patterns were retained by default but individual out-of-scale buildings were constructed on top of them with little regard for design. Isolated office blocks went up in the centre of Liverpool on cleared sites. In Bristol, a pre-cast concrete garage and office block appeared on Queen Charlotte Street within a hundred yards of an eighteenth-century theatre and a seventeenth-century inn. The effects of piecemeal redevelopment were particularly dramatic in smaller historic towns. In Gloucester, 200 listed buildings were demolished in the 1950s and 1960s, dismembering the medieval core. At Bath, the Georgian core was faithfully preserved but defined so narrowly — only a few hundred yards across — that it was soon dwarfed by high buildings on its edge, including an extraordinarily obtrusive concrete podium with brutal modernist hotel and multi-storey car park hardly a hundred yards from Pulteney Bridge. Historic towns that remained relatively unaffected, such as Norwich, were saved not so much by civic design as by the lack of development pressure.[28]

The slow pace of redevelopment outside the south-east in the 1950s, combined with the piecemeal dismemberment of historic town centres, helps to explain the extraordinary zeal for what was known as 'comprehensive redevelopment' in the early 1960s. The prospects for development outside London began to brighten: the London boom had begun to slacken, demand for new offices and private-sector housing outside London grew, and land prices shot up everywhere. A new consensus was brewing behind a more *dirigiste* version of urban (and, now, also regional) planning. Politicians, developers and planners alike recognised that economic growth could no longer be managed by a piecemeal, private-sector approach; traffic works on a huge scale were called for, but so was centre-city replanning to provide retail and office space. This was a kind of planning aimed not at substituting for but at inviting and facilitating private developers' schemes. Central government began grudgingly to steer development away from London, and urban authorities geared up for a big push. Cities like Liverpool, Newcastle and Leicester *for the first time* set up planning offices separate from the engineer's department. City planners, frustrated for so long, leapt at the chance to undertake large projects and were easily induced into a Faustian bargain with private capital.[29]

The result was an enormous increase in the number of central redevelopment plans of a kind that had been previously conceivable only in blitzed centres. Whereas fifteen such schemes were under consideration at the Ministry of Housing and Local Government in 1959, seventy were on the table in 1963, and by 1965 over 500 schemes were said to be under preparation.[30] These schemes, unlike the plans of the late 1940s, were characterised by gigantism and a belief in the technological quick-fix. Encouraged by local-authority bosses, retailers and developers, the planners abandoned their worthy 1940s language of amenity, aesthetics and control in favour of the exciting 1960s language of growth. Huge tracts of inner-city were to be cleared and rebuilt with retail and office development. Urban motorways were to provide ready vehicular access. In the words of one Conservative broadside, readily endorsed across the political spectrum and by leading planners, it was necessary to embrace with open arms the 'magnetism of the Big City', 'to *re-form* our cities to the demands of modern life', indeed to recognise that the conurbation was the distinctive British contribution to modernity: 'we believe that the social and economic forces which have shaped Britain into a cluster of big cities are the very forces which have established her place in the world'.[31]

There was little sentimentality about historic townscapes that had been decaying since 1940 and in many cases had already been sliced up by piecemeal redevelopment. City centres were to be made 'liveable' not by preserving the familiar (which was deemed grey and boring) but by projecting a vision of modern vitality. Motorways were portrayed as 'an exciting new element to be added as a positive feature to the central area landscape', providing the sense of 'movement' which was thought necessary to keep city centres alive; the old street patterns, derided as 'medieval cart tracks', were to be swept away and replaced by a new pattern planned for the whole of the centre; new building, it was held, could reproduce the 'solidity and strength' of old stone and brick using 'dark aggregate concrete panels'. An urban renaissance around Britain was thought to be in the making.[32]

Private developers were obviously one motive force behind the push for growth in town centres. Planners — who had to abandon most of their design and development principles in order to embrace the new move — were on the whole responding to rather than leading events. Much the same could be said for architects, who are usually credited with far more creative power than they had in reality. What is harder and more controversial to determine is the degree to which social and political forces — the forces of a complex modern democracy — were complicit or even responsible.[33] There seems little doubt that local authorities, lacking strong aesthetic and design commitments of their own and (in the case of Labour authorities) losing faith by the late 1950s in the prospects for a publicly directed urban renewal programme, welcomed the advent of comprehensive redevelopment schemes promoted by private developers. At the top, there was a political consensus behind such schemes.[34] At the grassroots, there was at least little resistance. Recent research has suggested that the considerable democratic pressure exerted upon local councillors for the redevelopment of inner-ring working-class housing must bear as much responsibility for the rash of tower-block constructions in the early 1960s as any arrogant imposition by modern architects or planners. Constituent pressure for

Warwick House

Warwick House is a five-storey office block that was
completed in 1966. Designed by Garbutt, Archibold and
Archibold, it has a dark-blue tile finish. It is now
occupied by the local section of the Land Commission.
It is outside the generally recognized office area, and was
allowed by the Minister on appeal.

Gunner House was designed by R. W. Graydon, A.R.I.B.A.,
group architect to the development company, and is a
six-storey building with shops and restaurant on the
ground floor and offices above. The black slate sawtooth
ground floor and upper gable was designed to retain
views of nearby St. Mary's spire (by Pugin) and to fit
firmly into the character of this blackened stone area.
The curtain walling has blue panels. On one side of the
building is an old pedestrian way within which are the
ruins of the old Gunner Tower.

Gunner House

The first stage of the building by the Norwich Union was
built for the company's own offices. It will be the podium
from which will spring a taller building that will be
erected over the present roadway when this is shortly
re-aligned. The buildings have been designed by
Cartwright, Woollatt and Partners to fit into the stone
character of this part of the City.

Illustrations from Wilfred Burns' manifesto for comprehensive redevelopment, Newcastle:
A Study in Replanning at Newcastle Upon Tyne, *London, Leonard Hill, 1967.*
Even Burns, one of the most sensitive and thoughtful of planners, presided over vast tracts of
anonymous commercial architecture. Note his pride in what he thought were considerable
accommodations to historic traditions (Warwick and Gunner Houses, left), although whatever
concessions to the 'stone character' of Newcastle, represented by the Norwich Union building
(above), would soon be dwarfed by the 'taller building' to be built atop it

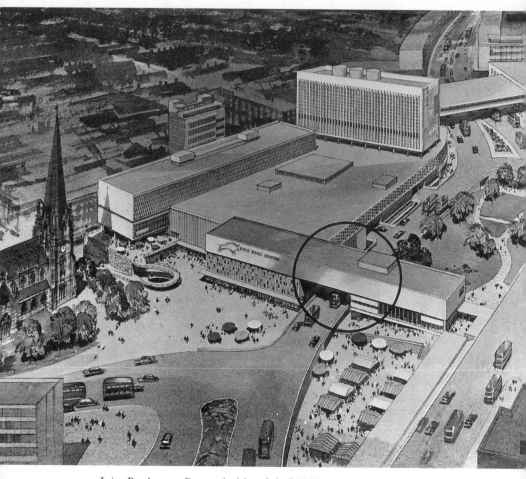

Laing Development Company's vision of the Bull Ring Centre, Birmingham which, as its designers later admitted, betrayed a misplaced confidence in the ability of traffic and humans to interact fruitfully. Indoors, the Bull Ring became the 'Aladdin's cave' of commerce that Birmingham wanted, but the public areas outdoors were first cut back and then rapidly deserted and vandalised.
Photograph: Laing plc

modern rehousing seemed to outweigh by far countervailing sentiment for the preservation and rehabilitation of traditional housing.[35] As for the disposition of historic town centres, there seemed to be hardly any countervailing sentiment at all, thus making local councillors more susceptible to propaganda on behalf of comprehensive redevelopment. It was widely felt that, as the architect and planner Lionel Brett put it in 1960, 'smart typists and skilled young workers will not put up with Victorian by-law streets much longer'.[36] This feeling encouraged civic leaders, who had been wary of the planners' visions of the 1940s and dubious about the popularity of any planning issue beyond housing, to put themselves at the head of crusades for comprehensive redevelopment a decade later: witness the high profile of the City Engineer Sir Herbert Manzoni in Birmingham; the visionary leadership of Newcastle Council's T. Dan Smith; the cross-party impact of the redevelopment campaigns in the *Daily Post* and *Echo* in Liverpool. Responsibility for comprehensive redevelopment spread far beyond the planners' and the architects' camps.

It follows that responsibility for the failure of comprehensive redevelopment must also be spread more widely, for few would doubt that it was a failure. Even at the time, Newcastle's planner Wilfred Burns, while plugging comprehensive redevelopment as the wave of the future, granted that its aesthetic (as opposed to commercial) impact was 'almost catastrophic'.[37] Across Britain a repetition of London's late 1950s disasters was played out on a grander scale, as provincial schemes were both more comprehensive and less professional (owing to the shortcomings of planners and developers alike) than in the capital. Early redevelopments at Middlesbrough, Burton-on-Trent and Derby were commercial as well as aesthetic catastrophes. Others led to clearances but no rebuilding, as the promised funds failed to materialise. Others were successful financially but in few other ways, as at Euston and St Paul's in London, or in central Newcastle or the Bull Ring in Birmingham.

Many schemes were never executed because civic feeling began quickly to turn against them, for the hegemony of the comprehensive development area, like the hegemony of the tower block with which it coincided, was intense but short, a matter of a few years in the early 1960s.[38] Jack Cotton's grandiose scheme for Piccadilly Circus was blocked as early as 1959, and this led to protests against redevelopment in Bloomsbury and Covent

Garden in the 1960s. The ambitious Lion Yard scheme for central Cambridge was abandoned in 1960, and later the alternative Petty Cury scheme was substantially slimmed down. Oxford's proposed relief road through Christ Church Meadow was abandoned in 1967.[39] By this point, revulsion against comprehensive redevelopment had become almost general, though it did not translate into national policy until development pressures collapsed in the mid-1970s.[40]

Britain's turn against urban modernisation in the 1970s seems to have been more fearful and convulsive than the similar but milder turn experienced by its Continental neighbours at the same time. A wave of 'heritage' consciousness led to the self-diagnosis in the 1980s of some *damnosa hereditas*, an enslavement to the past and a fear of modernity suddenly discerned at the heart of the national character that marked the British off from other Europeans. But the full picture of post-war development tells almost the opposite story. While its planning thought and practice did not depart notably from wider European patterns in the 1940s, Britain did diverge from the European norm in the 1950s by abandoning key elements of its planning regime and permitting unfettered private development in its town and city centres. Consumer sovereignty in a free economy, rather than the 'plan' of local élites or national political consensus, was the guiding force. In conditions of slow growth, this policy had only piecemeal effects at first but it further lowered the already low opinion held by urban authorities, and probably by urban populations, of their historic centres. When economic growth picked up in the late 1950s and early 1960s, as it did throughout Western Europe, British centres were exposed to far more dramatic modernisation than elsewhere.

Continental cities did not, of course, always cope with these growth pressures more successfully than their British counterparts, but they had a wider range of alternative responses. Most notoriously, just at the time that London was abandoning its height restrictions, Paris was sticking to them with remarkable perseverance and channelling growth to the outer ring.[41] But more generally, civic traditions — among élites but also in public opinion mobilised behind 'reshaping' rather than 'rebuilding'[42] — and a well-integrated local planning apparatus were manifestly better able to control development socially and aesthetically: by building up alternative city centres, as in Milan or Cologne; by raising densities along radial axes, as in

Copenhagen; by resort to 'façadism' as in Amsterdam and many French and German cities. Of the cities with the largest historic cores in Europe — London, Paris, Rome, Amsterdam, Cologne and Brussels — London and Brussels certainly stand out as the cities most disfigured by the growth push of the late 1950s and early 1960s.[43] It is hard not to agree with Alison Ravetz's conclusion that, elsewhere in Europe, 'post-war urban development often seemed richer and more successful than in Britain.'[44]

What do these divergent fates tell us about the 'modernity' of Britain's immediate post-war years? Principally they tell us not to accept too mono-lithic an understanding of 'modernity' and particularly not one which is predicated unthinkingly upon an assumed British 'backwardness'. The plans which emerged after 1945 for the reconstruction of British town centres were 'modern' in the sense that they sought to update towns for a perceived new era with new social and economic needs; they were 'modern', too, in representing the ambitions of an expert cadre of planners and social engineers which for the first time felt it had the tools to remodel society according to a collective plan. Here British modernity was converging upon, not diverging from, Continental experiences. In the course of the 1950s, however, this short-lived convergence was aborted. The modernity of the planners, never firmly seated in as anti-bureaucratic and market-driven a polity as Britain's, was dismantled by conservative governments and a different version of modernity was substituted. This market-driven version was portrayed by government — with some justice — as a response both to a democratic decision against planning and to consumer demand for unfettered housing, transport and industrial development. In practice, however, implementing this alternative, market-driven version meant hand-ing town centres over to developers. As a result, across Britain, more historic townscapes were erased, more anonymous commercial architecture was permitted, and 'modern' architecture and planning were more closely asso-ciated with developers' balance-sheet calculations than with intellectuals' or professionals' principles of design. If today we yearn to live in an 'old coun-try', this may reflect not a horror of modernity deeply rooted in British culture, but rather a predictable revulsion from the peculiar — and pecu-liarly cheap and brutal — vision of modernity inflicted upon Britain, a result of the unexpected consequences of 'consumer sovereignty' as interpreted by the governments of the 1950s and 1960s.

12. 'Here is the Modern World Itself': The Festival of Britain's Representations of the Future

Becky Conekin

The 1951 Festival of Britain was conceived in the immediate post-war period, a period characterised by housing shortages, the continuation and even extension of wartime restrictions and rationing, as well as the initial stages of the dissolution of the British Empire. It was to be both a celebration of Britain's victory in the Second World War and a proclamation of its national recovery. There were eight official, government-funded exhibitions in England, Scotland, Northern Ireland and Wales, twenty-two designated arts festivals and a pleasure garden in Battersea. Eight and a half million people visited the London South Bank exhibition and the BBC aired 2700 festival-related broadcasts. On the local level 2000 cities, towns and villages across the United Kingdom organised and funded a festival event of some kind.

Robert Hewison has recently written that 'the lasting imagery' of much of the South Bank exhibition 'suggests that the Festival of Britain was more forward-looking than it really was .... The modernist architecture was a lightweight framework for yet another exploration of Deep England.'[1] In contrast with Hewison's judgment, this chapter argues that the festival betrayed surprisingly little nostalgia. Instead, it set the broad parameters of a social democratic agenda for modern Britain. The expertise of architects, industrial designers, scientists and town planners was enlisted in this government project to construct representations of the country's future. As well as acting as 'a tonic to the nation', the festival's stated intention was to project 'the belief that Britain will have contributions to make in the future.'[2] These projections stressed progress and modernity, with science and planning evoked as the answers to the question of how to build a better

Britain. Everything from living conditions to culture and from industrial design to farm management was henceforward to be different, especially for those whose limited incomes had restricted their life experiences. The goals of redistributing knowledge and constructing a modern, cultured citizenry were ones which the festival planners shared with many within the post-war Labour Party. As such, the festival can be read simultaneously as a public celebration and a government-sponsored educational event.

When the government approved the final, scaled-down version of the festival in 1947 (the original conception had been an international exhibition to mark the centenary of the Great Exhibition of 1851) the Lord President of the Council, Herbert Morrison, was deemed the appropriate head, earning him the title of 'Lord Festival'.[3] Morrison and his Under-Secretary, Max Nicholson, selected most of the festival committee, including the festival's director, Gerald Barry. Barry was the managing director of the liberal *News Chronicle* and a vocal advocate of the festival.[4] In addition to his unbounded enthusiasm for the project, he was well known to Morrison and a personal friend of Nicholson's — the two of them had worked together on *The Weekend Review*, founded by Barry. Barry was, in Nicholson's words, 'a great impresario'.[5]

Apart from two civil servants, the five remaining members of the executive committee were chosen by Barry and Nicholson in consort, to serve as representatives of the constituent councils of art, science, architecture, industrial design and the British Film Institute (BFI). Most of those selected had particular expertise in their fields, as well as being known entities to Barry. For example, Hugh Casson, who was appointed director of the festival's council for architecture, town planning and building research, claimed that 'as an impecunious architect I'd moonlighted, doing journalism: I used to write "What to do with the cupboard under the stairs" ... and I wrote for Gerald Barry in the *News Chronicle* on the future of architecture and all that sort of stuff.'[6] The director of the Council of Industrial Design (COID), Gordon Russell, represented industrial design, Huw Wheldon the Arts Council and Denis Forman the BFI. Ian Cox, who had worked for the Ministry of Information, was chosen as the festival's director of science and technology.[7]

Adrian Forty has described the festival as 'in part an early experiment in technocracy', with the organisation run by designers, architects and engineers, rather than administrators.[8] The festival planners, like the executive committee, were representatives of the new post-war public sphere, dominated by experts and professionals. And if 'much of the Festival was alarmingly like a private club', this was in part thanks to the expeditious nature of its planning.[9] Hugh Casson said more than once that the festival organisation was indeed 'inbred', but that it had to be so. The organisers were charged with the task of putting on the exhibitions quickly; therefore, it was necessary for all members to share the same objectives unequivocally from the start.[10] Bevis Hillier has explained how the festival planners had learned important lessons in their war work, which had taught them the art of long-term as well as *ad hoc* decision-making. Hillier grants that 'earnest young men with double-breasted suits, brigade ties and pipes, may have made later generations smile or wince', but that their shared experiences allowed them to plan and mount the festival exhibitions on schedule in a very short time.[11]

The planners were overwhelmingly middle-class men of the sort Michael Frayn has described as 'do-gooders; the readers of the *News Chronicle*, the *Guardian*, and the *Observer*; the signers of petitions; the backbone of the BBC'.[12] These philanthropic experts were characteristically entering early middle-age in 1951; many of them had been students in the 1930s. Architectural critic, John Summerson, wrote in October 1951 that the festival architects, for example, were 'the troublesome students of around 1935 ... who at that date, discovered Lloyd Wright, Gropius and Le Corbusier for themselves'.[13] Some of the planners, like the landscape architect, Peter Shepheard, saw the war as an interruption to their careers, whilst others acknowledged that they had actually acquired their expertise in the war, on finding themselves working in the Ministry of Information, often designing camouflage or educational exhibitions.[14] Whatever their perspective, war service followed by austerity meant that most of the festival's architects and planners saw the 1951 Festival as their first real chance to design and build modern structures in Britain.

Scandinavian Modernism and the Festival

Most of the festival's planners were influenced by the Stockholm Exhibition of 1930 and it is hardly surprising to find amongst the 1951 festival's official

The view of the Festival of Britain's South Bank from the entrances.
Photograph by de Burgh Gallery, reproduced courtesy of the Architectural Review, *vol.109,*
1951

Designs inspired by crystal structure diagrams

Below and on the next page are a selection of designs for various products inspired by the investigations of the crystallographer. The scientist's diagrams are indicated by letters and the designs for textiles, china, plastics and so forth, which are based upon them, by numbers.

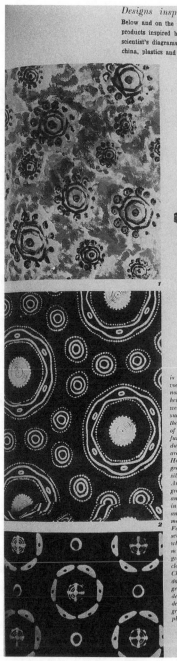

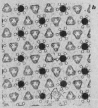

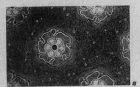

6 & 7, two wallpapers by Robert A. Sevant, for the Festival science exhibition, based on a diagram of the crystal structure of Insulin

Although some of the examples on this and the next page may mark an advance on the previous design standards of the companies concerned, they surely fall a good deal short of what we have come to expect from contemporary industrial design at its best. In one or two the designers seem to have employed the crystallographer's patterns with insufficient thought as to their suitability for the product in question, applying them little changed with an effect the only virtue of which is repetition. There is much to be said for evolving a vocabulary of pattern so long as it is used as a tool, and not as an alternative to creative effort. If the examples here are considered mostly as experiments, they may well mark the first approach to a vocabulary and as such are to be welcomed. It is significant nevertheless that the most successful are those which the imagination of the designer has transformed until they are the furthest removed from their parent diagram. The six products shown in 1–5 are all based on the Haemoglobin diagram a, 1, dress silk designed by Arnold Lever; background in turquoise and pink, design in fuchsia, lemon and black. 2, curtain material for the Festival of Britain science exhibition: white design on a mid-blue background. 3, leather cloth designed by Charles Garnier: dark grey background with design in black, red and white. 4, tie designed by H. Rowland with red background and design in white, straw and black. 5, plate in blue, green and maroon on white designed by Peter Wall, placed on a piece of printed cotton.

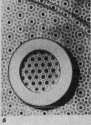

b, 6 has a design in white, canary yellow and black on a chocolate brown ground, and 7, the same colours in the design on a blue-grey

ground. 8, a wallpaper designed by W. J. Odell also based on Insulin but this time on another aspect of it c. The design is in grey-purple, pale lemon and black on a dark green ground. It will be seen in the Regatta restaurant on the South Bank.

records a report on the Stockholm project.[15] Stockholm's modernist, social democratic exhibition was clearly a model. Architectural critic, Reyner Banham, has stated that the semi-official line was that the Festival of Britain was indebted to its Scandinavian predecessor.[16] Both exhibitions marked a departure from the nineteenth-century model of international exhibitions and in many respects the 1951 festival greatly resembled the 1930 Stockholm Exhibition.[17] This was especially true in terms of the way national imagery was married to international pretensions. The organisational structure of both exhibitions was similar, consisting of a small executive committee, a tight-knit staff of experts, and a panel who selected the products to be exhibited.[18] Furthermore, the narrative structure of the 1951 festival seems to have been borrowed from the Scandinavian exhibition. The Swedish project was described by Ludvig Nordström, one of its key planners, as laid out to be an 'amusing and interesting picture-book' with a 'pedagogic purpose'.[19] Likewise, the Festival of Britain was called 'the autobiography of a nation', and visitors were instructed how to go round the South Bank displays, reading them as 'one continuous, interwoven story'.[20] The festival brochures proudly boasted of the originality of this method of display, calling it 'something new in exhibitions'.[21]

One particular chapter or section of the Stockholm exhibition anticipated the 1951 exhibitions. This was the *Svea Rike*, 'a three-storied building topped by a cylindrical rotunda' containing exhibitions designed jointly by the chief of the National Social Welfare Board, a well-known journalist and an architect.[22] The intention of the *Svea Rike* was to 'illustrate how our country has achieved the indisputably high [international] standing that it now occupies within the economic, social and cultural spheres, and what further development possibilities the future might offer'.[23] Its planners declared *Svea Rike* would 'strengthen *'l'énergie nationale'*, and 'stimulate our sometimes sluggish national imagination and without self-arrogance strengthen our self-confidence as a people and a state'.[24] Similar language was used to describe the aim of the Festival of Britain. At the festival's opening ceremony the Archbishop of Canterbury asserted that:

> The chief and governing purpose of the Festival is to declare our belief and trust in the British way of life, not with any boastful self-confidence nor with any aggressive self- advertisement, but with sober

and humble trust that by holding fast to that which is good and reject-
ing from our midst that which is evil we may continue to be a nation
at unity in itself and of service to the world.[25]

In 1951 the reticent British were encouraged to proclaim confidence in their
nation and their way of life, just as the Scandinavians had done in 1930.

Finally, the Stockholm exhibition shared with its 1951 counterpart the
goal of raising 'the taste and cultivation of our entire population'.[26] Both
exhibitions sought to construct new styles of subjectivity in those nationals who attended. Allan Pred has written that the Stockholm planners
aimed, like the Social Democrats, to create a vision of a society 'peopled
by rational, enlightened and socially responsible citizens'. Moreover, the
organisers felt that the Swedish future should include new, functional housing for *all* its citizens.[27] Such a vision of an enlightened citizenry, enjoying
better housing, was also central to the 1951 Festival of Britain.

The Labour Party and the Festival

In line with the goal of constituting a more enlightened citizenry, one
major aim of the festival organisers was to diffuse education, ideas and
tastes, generally the preserve of élites, to the people of Britain. This was
not an exclusively Labour Party agenda, but in the late 1940s and early
1950s it was Labour that was promising nationalisation and common
ownership. For many Labour leaders such egalitarian notions extended in
the direction of a commitment to the diffusion of knowledge. Herbert
Morrison appeared sincere when he asserted that 'the last thing in the world
I would wish would be that this should turn into or was ever contemplated
as a political venture'.[28] However, Hugh Casson, the South Bank exhibition's chief architect, stated that: 'Churchill, like the rest of the Tory Party,
was against the Festival which they (quite rightly) believed was the advanced
guard of socialism'.[29] In addition, a number of prominent members of the
Labour government considered the festival to be an overtly Labour under-
taking, which would contribute to future election success. When Attlee
wrote to Morrison to say that the autumn of 1951 was the best time to call
an election, he explained that this would allow the festival as much time as
possible to amass support for the Labour Party.[30] To this end, Labour

published a special festival magazine, simply called *Festival*, in which the party was accredited both with the success of the festival and with the higher post-war standard of living. In page after page, life under Labour was proclaimed far better than it had been under the Conservatives, especially for ordinary British people.[31]

The Festival's eclectic combinations of education and leisure, didacticism and amusement, arts and pleasure were very much in keeping with the type of Labour Party agenda tabled in the late 1940s and early 1950s. At the 1949 Labour Party conference Morrison declared that: 'Part of our work in politics and in industry must be to improve human nature ... we should set ourselves more than materialistic aims'.[32] The pamphlet *Labour Believes in Britain*, published in the same year asserted: 'Socialism is not bread alone. Material security and sufficiency are not the final goals. They are means to the greater end — the evolution of a people more kindly, intelligent, co-operative, enterprising and rich in culture.'[33] The document insisted that there was a need to stimulate leisure and the arts, as well as arguing for a state-funded holiday council, which would provide cheap holidays for the British people.[34] Martin Francis has asserted that Labour's policy-makers during this period were committed, however modestly, to a version of socialism 'concerned with ... an improvement of the "quality of life" in its widest sense'.[35] The constitutive national projects of the Festival of Britain were very much in keeping with Labour Party policy statements and with the party's social democratic agenda. Diffusing knowledge through popular education, encouraging people to partake in 'culture' in their leisure time, improving their material surroundings, stimulating the arts, broadly fostering an enlightened citizenry 'rich in culture', these were all goals shared by the 1951 festival and the post-war Labour Party.

Agenda for Taste

A strategic site for this new politics of culture was the household. The festival organisers believed that expert knowledge could relay to the British public — as well as to foreign visitors — new, improved ideas about the design of everyday household goods, public buildings, neighbourhoods and homes. Scientific expertise in particular was used to validate this modern agenda for design.

Many of the London festival planners, especially those who were members of the COID or young architects, had as one of their objectives a large-scale change in the tastes of the British public. Their aim was to dispel the fussy, old-fashioned, even 'repellent extravagances of the 1930s', replacing them with simple, clean lines for interior and exterior design and for household objects.[36] These middle-class arbiters of taste hoped that a newly constituted British citizenry would become educated in and eventually embrace 'good design', as defined by the COID and magazines such as *House and Garden*.[37]

The COID was established by the Board of Trade in 1944. The 'upper-class socialists' at the Board of Trade, Hugh Dalton and his successor, Stafford Cripps, were motivated by their commitment to the democratisation of design, as well as by their desire to rejuvenate British manufacturing after the war.[38] The COID stimulated media interest with the 1946 'Britain Can Make It' exhibition, which occupied the entire ground floor of the Victoria and Albert Museum. This exhibition, attended by well over a million people, sought to generate interest among manufacturers and the public in good design, while showing the rest of the world that British industries were producing goods of high quality which could be ordered, even after the exigencies of war.[39] Ironically, 'Britain Can Make It' was renamed 'Britain Can't Have It' by the press, thanks to the fact that most of the articles on display were merely prototypes or for export only.[40] The products were labelled 'now', 'soon' and 'later' — the 'later' label dominated. During the Festival of Britain itself, the COID took overall responsibility for selecting every product in the South Bank exhibition — a total of 10,000 objects in all, used not only in the official displays, but in all aspects of the exhibition, down to the public toilets![41]

The COID's meticulous commitment to good design was shared by another post-war arbiter of taste, the BBC. Programmes such as the *Looking at Things* series, transmitted as part of the BBC schools' broadcasts, worked to a similar cultural agenda. An early instalment aired in September of 1951, asked school listeners *Have You a Seeing Eye?* explaining that:

Designing something means more than just drawing a picture of what it is to look like; it also means thinking about how it is to be made and making sure that it will do its job properly. Not everything you see in the shops has been carefully designed, and the most expensive things are not necessarily the best, nor are the cheapest always the worst ... A 'seeing eye' will help you to distinguish good design from bad, to choose wisely when you go shopping, and to make the best of what you have already ... You can start straight away by looking critically at the things around you — the things you use every day. Look at things in shop windows, although you may not yet be able to buy them.[42]

Such wide-ranging training in 'good design' aimed to educate young people in more aesthetically orientated consumption. The explicit intention was to encourage modernist tastes through the prioritisation of functionality and of high-quality materials.[43]

The Festival of Britain's modernist agenda in design, art and architecture aimed to encourage people of all ages to learn about and, when available, consume well-designed modern artefacts. An official festival brochure entitled *Design in the Festival* (1951), produced by the COID, stated:

There is now no logical reason why well-designed things should not be available to all of us ... They affect our whole outlook, whether we admit it or not; and if we are critical we have to confess that many of them are downright ugly ... one can hardly expect to get a high standard of design unless there is a critical and appreciative public. [44]

The COID's strategy rested on a type of educational popularism which appealed to the rational and cultured citizen. The brochure concluded with the assertion that: 'When consumer knowledge increases still further, the minority of less satisfactory appliances will be reduced to a negligible quantity'.[45] Thus, through the festival's selective exhibition of well-designed goods, the council hoped to continue its re-education of British consumers. By increasing consumer knowledge through the display of objects of a high standard, the COID believed they were encouraging the public to demand modern, well-designed goods when they shopped.[46]

There can be little doubt that the festival helped to shape popular definitions of good and modern design. The term 'Festival style' came to be applied to buildings utilising concrete, aluminium and plate glass, as well as to household furnishings. According to William Feaver, 'the South Bank remained the popularly accepted idea of "modern" for a whole generation'. Other examples of modern design which first appeared at the festival were canework for indoor furniture, blond wood, 'lily-of-the-valley splays' for light bulbs, 'flying staircases' and textiles sporting thorns, spikes and molecular patterns.[47]

In the words of Raphael Samuel, the festival 'was determinedly modernist in bias, substituting, for the moth-eaten and the traditional, vistas of progressive advance: a great looking forward after years of rationing and greyness'.[48] This agenda stretched beyond domestic artefacts to the field of public architecture. Morrison himself described the South Bank site as 'new Britain springing from the battered fabric of the old'.[49] In a London guide, produced in association with the *Architects' Journal* and published in May 1951, the editors asserted that the exhibition was:

> the first full-scale example of modern architecture doing a popular job ... for the very first time in history it is trying to create a still greater thing than architecture, a modern *background*, a twentieth century urban environment. [50]

The South Bank's architects and planners were indeed endeavouring to construct more than just an exhibition, they were attempting to build a vision of a brighter future for Britain — a future that was clean, orderly and modern after the dirt and chaos of the war. In this context, the best-remembered symbol of the festival's modernity was the award-winning vertical feature, the Skylon. Modern engineering meant that the Skylon's almost 300 feet of steel frame clad in louvred aluminium created the illusion that it was floating forty feet above the ground, especially at night when it was lit from the inside. Not only was it modern, it was futuristic and found itself gracing the cover of more than one science fiction magazine. Science fiction author Brian Aldiss wrote, twenty-five years after the event, that 'the South Bank Exhibition was a memorial to the future', and the Skylon was its centrepiece.[51]

A Fusion of Art and Science

Science was central to the modernism of the festival. While the South Bank structures aestheticised the scientific future, the festival also sought to enlist science as the foundation of a new modernist aesthetic. Many of the festival's official exhibitions, from the South Bank to Glasgow, from Belfast to London's East End, were designed to illustrate how science could influence design, architecture and planning.

The festival's executive committee asserted that Britain was uniquely placed in the constellation of post-war powers to mark out a new course for the integration of science and the arts. This co-ordination of the arts and science was envisaged as another British contribution to the contemporary world, alongside all of those already being celebrated in the 1951 London festivities. A festival planning document from 1948 had stated that perhaps 'the greatest single contribution which Britain could make would be to bring Science and the Humanities into step'. It had claimed that neither Russia nor the United States was capable of such coordination. However, Britain could and should coordinate the fine arts with the sciences because a proper balance was essential for the survival of Western Civilisation.[52] Written as it was in the immediate aftermath of the war, this rhetoric reflected a commonly held anxiety about the excesses of science manifested in the recent global conflict — and especially about the role of the atomic Bomb. Britain was in a unique position, the document argued; it was the one country capable of stabilising Cold War hostilities through the reconciliation of art and science.

Such arguments drew on an earlier pedigree. At least since the inter-war years, left-leaning scientists, as well as the Labour Party itself, had been attempting to reconcile 'the two cultures' of art and science. In a Labour Party report on reconstruction after the First World War, the 'greatly increased public provision ... for scientific investigation and original research' was mentioned in the same breath as 'the promotion of music, literature, and fine art, which have been under Capitalism so greatly neglected'.[53] By 1951 the historian of science, Dr Jacob Bronowski, who served as the caption writer for the festival's science exhibition, echoed these themes and suggested that science and culture were not intrinsically opposed. Having himself written a study of William Blake, radio plays and an opera, in addition to his scientific works, he stood characteristically for the integration of the two fields:

> Science and the arts to-day are not as discordant as many people think. The difficulties which we all have as intelligent amateurs in following modern literature and music and painting are not unimportant. They are one sign of the lack of a broad and general language in our culture. The difficulties which we have in understanding the basic ideas of modern science are signs of the same lack.[54]

Bronowski believed that audiences had equal problems in comprehending modern art and modern science. He insisted that both difficulties needed to be addressed by the festival.

The festival pattern group was the quintessential expression of this desire for bridge-building between the arts and science. The group aimed to create a new modernist aesthetic which combined the two fields. Their project attempted to harness science in the pursuit of better British design. Collaborating with the COID, a group of university scientists worked to popularise science by bringing it into ordinary people's homes. The goal was to weave science into the fabric of everyday life by rendering science accessible to everyone. Mark Hartland Thomas, a member of the COID and a distinguished architect who later founded the Modular Society, was the originator of the festival pattern group. Two years before the festival, he had attended a weekend course organised by the Society of Industrial Artists to encourage British designers to broaden their visual archive and draw on new sources of inspiration. One of the papers read at that course was by Professor Kathleen Lonsdale on her own area of expertise, crystallography, a science in which Britain dominated at the time.[55] Lonsdale suggested that some crystal-structure diagrams could provide the bases for original textile designs.

At the same time, a junior colleague of Lonsdale's, Dr Helen Megaw, had begun preparation of an in-house publication for the design research unit. Hartland Thomas wrote immediately to Megaw and discovered that she had produced diagrams which would serve well as patterns for fabric decoration. Upon seeing them, Hartland Thomas decided that the designs should not be limited to textiles. In his capacity as the head of the selection of industrial exhibits at the festival, he convinced twenty-eight manufacturers to join the scheme and use these patterns. The manufacturers represented industries as divergent as plastics and pottery, while the patterns were derived from the molecular structures of compounds such as insulin and haemoglobin.[56] As he wrote at the time:

> I had it in mind that we were at a stage in the history of industrial design when both the public and leading designers have a feeling for more richness in style and decoration, but are somewhat at a loss for inspiration ... these crystal-structure diagrams had the discipline of exact repetitive symmetry; they were above all very pretty and were full of rich variety, yet with a remarkable family likeness; they were essentially modern because the technique that constructed them was quite recent, and yet, like all successful decorations of the past, they derived from nature — although it was nature at a submicroscopic scale not previously revealed.[57]

Hartland Thomas appealed to a classically inspired sense of natural beauty — a beauty of symmetry and repetition. Yet this was now announced as aesthetic; according to Hartland Thomas the new designs would be modern because they were based on atomic structures, only visible as a result of recent developments in science. From the point of view of the festival organisers, crystallography was the perfect science. It was futuristic, yet had its aesthetic origins in the natural world. As such it was perceived as quintessentially British.

Further variations on this scientific aesthetic included Misha Black's upscale Regatta restaurant on the South Bank, decorated with molecular and crystalline motifs on furnishings and tableware and replete with a globule painting by artist John Tunnard.[58] Moreover, the Dome of Discovery, which itself contained a model atomic pile, featured atomic structures and snowflakes in the gallery and dress circle. 'Everything is made of atoms', proclaimed Basil Taylor in the festival's *Official Book*.[59] Yet, science was not only aestheticised in the festival. The exhibitions combined a somewhat fanciful vision of a modernist future with a more or less realistic appreciation of the potential of science to transform everyday life. The official exhibition in Scotland, the exhibition of industrial power in Glasgow, aimed to tell 'the story of man's conquest of "Power" and the part played by Britain in that conquest'.[60] Here, too, science was celebrated, with atomic power portrayed as the triumphant finale to this exhibition designed 'to demonstrate the harnessing of the sources of power on which all industry ultimately depends'.[61] Like most of the London displays, the Glasgow exhibition set out to show British inventiveness and its impact on the world. What dominated in Glasgow were the current products of British heavy engineering.[62]

The exhibition was planned by Alistair Borthwick, who in 1949 had recommended to the festival's Scottish committee that such an exhibition be held in Glasgow. As with the other official festival displays, the Glasgow exhibition told a story. The narrative was divided into eleven essential chapters on topics such as coal, steel, steam, electricity, civil engineering and atomic energy. Professional writers rather than subject experts were engaged to prepare scripts, since it was acknowledged that simply displaying heavy machinery and engineering equipment would not prove sufficiently interesting to most visitors. Basil Spence, the co-ordinating architect, produced a layout plan for an exhibition of 100,000 square feet, presenting the subject matter in two parallel sequences: coal and water — the nation's main sources of power. He was responsible for the design of the first hall, the hall of power, which illustrated this general theme. The hall then led on to more specific displays. The entrance to the hall of coal designed by Hulme Chadwick, for example, featured a symbolic sun created by a 'stroboscopic' flash contained in a perspex sphere. The entrance opened on to the huge relief sculpture of 'God the Creator' by Thomas Whalen.[63] According to the *Glasgow Herald*, this sculpture reworked a Renaissance image, by presenting the 'figure of the God of Nature with right hand outstretched to the recumbent figure of man, pointing out to him the latest possibilities of coal'.[64] The grand finale of the Glasgow exhibition was the hall of the future, containing a spectacular presentation of the new power source — atomic energy.[65]

In the hall of the future, according to the guide-catalogue: 'the visitor walks in the present, looks down on the past, and looks up to the future.'[66] The end point of the display focused on atomic power, claimed as a partly British achievement, thanks to Rutherford's discoveries. The more recent work of British scientists on the atomic bomb was omitted. However, the problematic nature of the new source of power was not entirely glossed over. The catalogue pointed out that the atomic future held out both the possibility of unfathomable positive opportunities and the prospect of utter annihilation, stating:

> The use which has been made of these discoveries and the work which is being based on them today will determine whether we are entering an age of undreamed-of plenty and comfort, or whether we are working out our complete extinction. The scientists have placed a great new source of power in the hands of the engineers, the basic power of the sun. If it is used for peaceful ends, anything is possible.[67]

Such a double-edged appraisal is noteworthy when compared to more popular celebrations of atomic energy in early 1950s Britain. The tone in the festival literature was level and considered, whereas the more prevalent, popular thinking on atomic energy was far less reasoned, presenting it simply as the solution to every kind of modern-day problem.[68]

The solutions to modern problems in agriculture were also perceived to lie in science, according to the official festival exhibition in Northern Ireland — the Ulster farm and factory exhibition. This festival display was held in Belfast and organised jointly by London and Belfast committees. Visited by 156,760 people — twice as many as was originally estimated — the Belfast exhibition's farmhouse and farmyard of the future were juxtaposed with an 1851 farmstead.[69] Here modernity had a clear and direct link to the past. The 1851 exhibit came in the shape of an authentic reconstruction.[70] Its counterpart, the farm of the future, employed new materials and a modern idiom. The buildings were functionally designed as one complete unit, to allow for tending and feeding animals easily in inclement weather. This construction also reduced capital outlay by reducing the number of necessary external walls.[71] The buildings were intended to provide maximum ventilation and light, featuring roofs covered with asbestos units and supported by light steel joists. Concrete floors with good drainage facilities were designed to ensure hygiene in the animal houses and sheds. It was all planned utilising 'building science', as it was termed in the early 1950s. The farmhouse of the future contained features which in

1951 must have seemed very modern indeed, such as a kitchen, living-room and bedroom all on the first floor and all approachable by internal and external stairways, an airy, covered walkway which connected the house to the farm buildings and an uninterrupted view of the farm and fields from both the living-room and the balcony. The living area featured folding, sliding windows leading directly on to the balcony.[72] As Samuel has explained, 'The outside coming in was one of the architectural ideals of the period'.[73] The kitchen boasted fitted cupboards and storage cabinets, along with built-in sinks, just like the latest advertisements for fitted kitchens in the women's and home-design magazines.[74] Overall, the Ulster exhibition's agricultural display combined innovations in hygienic, convenient and affordable farm management, with all the latest modern designs for the home.

'Building science' was the key to the better-known 'live architecture exhibition' built in Poplar in the East End of London. A badly bombed working-class neighbourhood was chosen as the home of a new, modern estate named after local Labour politician, George Lansbury, the architect of early twentieth-century municipal socialism. The Lansbury estate consisted of 'scientifically' built flats and houses, as well as a school, a church and a pedestrianised shopping zone.[75] Science was evoked as the solution to pressing social problems. Not only were the actual residents of the Lansbury estate to benefit from these new features, but so was all of Britain. The estate was the centrepiece of the festival's live architecture exhibition and this meant that the latest British building techniques and planning schemes were on show to all national and foreign visitors. The present and the future of British town planning and responsible architecture — architecture which was committed to enhancing the existing characteristics and character of an area — were displayed for all to see and scrutinise.

As in the Belfast exhibition, the view of the future was clearly linked with the past. Evocations of the frightful history of this 'slum area', as well as a version of the present, littered with 'Jerry-built and pokey dwellings', were on display. These miserable environments were counterpoised by the exhibition's well-planned, 'new urban landscape in which the buildings are growing together as a community'.[76] In short, the problems of the past and present were solved through modern science and planning; the future would be brighter.

One official Festival of Britain guide-catalogue explained how two temporary exhibitions mounted at Poplar elucidated what building research and building science contributed to the new Lansbury estate and to British reconstruction more generally:

> A nearly full-sized model of a part of a house will show the results of bad building, why the house becomes damp, why cold water pipes burst in the winter. Then the pavilion shows how building science tackles the problem of stability, weather resistance, heating, lighting, noise and durability, and finally, how a house should be constructed. The other pavilion contains an exhibition on town planning. It explains in detail the principles upon which the new Lansbury has been designed, and tells the story of Britain's new towns. [77]

The conclusion to the brochure's section on architecture at Poplar proclaimed: 'Here at Poplar then you may catch a glimpse of that future London which is to arise from blitzed ruins and from the slums and chaotic planning of the past'.[78] 'A glimpse of the future' was what this exhibition, like so many of the others in 1951, was planned to provide.

Conclusion

These festival projects and exhibitions reveal their planners' and architects' agendas for bringing about a modern and scientifically assisted version of the future in Britain. The forward-looking representations on show in the summer of 1951 were projected as brighter, better-planned, scientifically researched and more modern than the designs of the past or of the present. However, in addition merely to portraying this new future, the planners were also attempting to alter people's experiences through popular education, in the hope of creating a different world. The festival's exhibitionary complex contained educational and cultural agendas which sought to encourage appreciation of both art and science (often melded together), as well as their incorporation into daily life. From images of the internal structure of a molecule to the latest ideas in farming, the British people were to be the recipients of new, modern knowledge.

Clearly, the festival exhibitions represented only one of many possible ways the post-war British nation could have been imagined. Emphasising an improving, modern future underscored the recovery and renewal of a badly shaken but victorious country — a country which could make a distinctive contribution alongside the superpowers. This collective project of imagining also created a space for an unuttered, yet unmistakable message that the Labour Party, in office since 1945, was the force behind Britain's recovery, as well as its guiding light for the future. A rational and cultured citizenry with greater access to knowledge would be able to evaluate Labour's contribution. Unfortunately for Labour, the general election results in the autumn after the festival revealed that not everyone had heeded the message. For whatever reason, it seems that many found in the Coronation Day celebrations two years later a more reassuring balance of the modern and the quintessentially British.

Notes

Introduction

1. B. Pimlott, *The Queen: A Biography of Elizabeth II*, London, HarperCollins, 1996, p.202.
2. P. Black, *The Mystique of Modern Monarchy: With Special Reference to the British Commonwealth*, London, Watts and Co., 1953; L. Broad, *The A.B.C. Guide to the Coronation*, London, Hutchinson, 1953; H. Marshall, *Coronation Day*, London, Robert Anscom and Co., 1953; Sir C. Petrie, *The Modern British Monarchy*, London, Eyre and Spottiswoode, 1961.
3. Princess Margaret, interview, quoted in Pimlott, *The Queen*, p.193.
4. See H. Hopkins, *The New Look: A Social History of the Forties and Fifties in Britain*, London, Readers Union/Secker and Warburg, 1964, pp.287–8; P. Ziegler, *Crown and People*, London, Collins, 1978, p.97; P. Gordon Walker, 'Crown Divisible', *The Twentieth Century*, vol.CLIII, no.916, June 1953, p.429.
5. See D. Cannadine, 'The British Monarchy c.1820–1977', in E. Hobsbawm and T. Ranger (eds.), *The Invention of Tradition*, Cambridge, Cambridge University Press, 1988, p.133; Pimlott, *The Queen*, p.202.
6. Gordon Walker, 'Crown Divisible', p.405.
7. Hopkins, *The New Look*, p.295.
8. S. Haffner, 'The Renascence of Monarchy', *The Twentieth Century*, vol.CLIII, no.916, June 1953, p.416, our emphasis.
9. M. Sissons and P. French (eds.), *Age of Austerity*, London, Hodder & Stoughton, 1963, p.9. See also Hopkins, *The New Look*.
10. J. Vernon, 'The Mirage of Modernity', *Social History*, vol.22, no.2, May 1997, p.209.
11. S. Beer, *British Politics in the Collectivist Age*, New York, Alfred A. Knopf, 1966, pp.x, 390.
12. D. Roberts, *Victorian Origins of the British Welfare State*, New Haven, Yale University Press, 1960; D. Fraser, *The Evolution of the British Welfare State: A History of Social Policy Since the Industrial Revolution*, London, Macmillan, 1973; P. Addison, *The Road to 1945: British Politics and the Second World War*, London, Jonathan Cape, 1975.
13. See among very many: J. Callaghan, *Time and Chance*, London, Collins, 1987; D. Healey, *The Time of My Life*, London, Michael Joseph, 1989; R. Jenkins, *A Life at the Centre*, London, Pan, 1992; B. Castle, *Fighting All the Way*, London, Macmillan, 1993.
14. P. Hennessy, *Never Again: Britain 1945–51*, London, Jonathan Cape, 1992, pp.453–4.
15. N. Dennis and A.H. Halsey, *English Ethical Socialism: Thomas More to R.H. Tawney*, Oxford,

Oxford University Press, 1988, p.256. The Institute of Contemporary British History has been especially keen to offer a forum for debate on the post-war consensus. See: D. Marquand, 'The Decline of the Post-War Consensus', in A. Gorst and W.S. Lucas (eds.), *Post-War Britain*, London, Pinter, 1989, pp.1–21; D. Kavanagh and P. Morris, *Consensus Politics from Attlee to Major*, second edition, Oxford, Blackwell, 1994 and their 'Controversy: Is the "Postwar Consensus" a Myth?', *Contemporary Record*, vol.2, no.6, 1989, pp.12–15.

16. See especially R.M. Titmuss, *Essays on the 'Welfare State'*, London, George Allen & Unwin, 1958; B. Abel Smith and P. Townsend, *The Poor and the Poorest: A New Analysis of the Ministry of Labour's Family Expenditure Surveys of 1953–54 and 1960*, London, G. Bell and Sons, 1965.

17. This theme is central to several of the essays in the seminal study by V. Bogdanor and R. Skidelsky (eds.), *The Age of Affluence 1951–1964*, London, Macmillan, 1970.

18. See J. Schneer, *Labour's Conscience: The Labour Left 1945–51*, Boston, Unwin Hyman, 1988.

19. See especially B. Campbell, *Wigan Pier Revisited: Poverty and Politics in the Eighties*, London, Virago, 1984.

20. P. Jenkins, *Mrs. Thatcher's Revolution: The Ending of the Socialist Era*, London, Jonathan Cape, 1987, p.54.

21. M. Thatcher, *The Downing Street Years*, London, HarperCollins, 1993.

22. A. Roberts, *Eminent Churchillians*, London, Weidenfeld & Nicolson, 1994, p.3.

23. C. Barnett, *The Lost Victory: British Dreams, British Realities 1945–1950*, London, Macmillan, 1995; also C. Barnett, *The Audit of War: The Illusion and Reality of Britain as a Great Nation*, London, Macmillan, 1986.

24. See Birmingham Feminist History Group, 'Feminism as Femininity in the Nineteen-Fifties', *Feminist Review*, no.3, 1979, pp.48–65; E. Wilson, *Only Halfway to Paradise: Women in Postwar Britain 1945–1968*, London, Tavistock, 1980; D. Riley, *War in the Nursery: Theories of the Child and Mother*, London, Virago, 1983; L. Heron (ed.), *Truth, Dare or Promise: Girls Growing Up in the Fifties*, London, Virago, 1985; C. Steedman, *Landscape for a Good Woman: A Story of Two Lives*, London, Virago, 1986; B. Campbell, *Iron Ladies: Why Do Women Vote Tory?*, London, Virago, 1987.

25. See among very many: S. Hall and T. Jefferson (eds.), *Resistance Through Rituals: Youth Subcultures in Post-War Britain*, London, Hutchinson, 1976; D. Hebdige, *Subculture: The Meaning of Style*, London, Methuen, 1979; R. Hewison, *In Anger: Culture and the Cold War 1945-60*, London, Weidenfeld & Nicolson, 1981; J. Hill, *Sex, Class and Realism: British Cinema 1956-1963*, London, BFI, 1986; S. Laing, *Representations of Working-Class Life 1957–1964*, Basingstoke, Macmillan, 1986; P. Gilroy, *There Ain't No Black in the Union Jack: The Cultural Politics of Race and Nation*, London, Hutchinson, 1987; A. Sinfield, *Literature, Politics and Culture in Postwar Britain*, Oxford, Blackwell, 1989; A. McRobbie, *Feminism and Youth Culture, from Jackie to Just Seventeen*, Basingstoke, Macmillan, 1991; F. Mort, *Cultures of Consumption: Masculinities and Social Space in Late Twentieth-Century Britain*, London, Routledge, 1996.

26. J. Obelkevitch and P. Catterall (eds.), *Understanding Post-War British Society*, London, Routledge, 1994.

27. J. Fyrth (ed.), *Labour's High Noon: The Government and the Economy 1945–51*, London, Lawrence & Wishart, 1993; J. Fyrth (ed.), *Labour's Promised Land? Culture and Society in Labour Britain 1945–51*, London, Lawrence & Wishart, 1995.

28. D. Childs, *Britain Since 1945: A Political History*, third edition, London, Routledge, 1992;

A. Marwick, *British Society Since 1945*, third edition, London, Penguin, 1996.

29. See S. Fielding, P. Thompson and N. Tiratsoo, *'England Arise!' The Labour Party and Popular Politics in 1940s Britain*, Manchester, Manchester University Press, 1995.

30. See N. Tiratsoo, 'Popular Politics, Affluence and the Labour Party in the 1950s', in W.S. Lucas, L. Johnman and A. Gorst (eds.), *Contemporary British History 1931–1961: Politics and the Limits of Policy*, London, Pinter, 1991, pp.44–51; I. Zweiniger-Bargielowska, 'Rationing, Austerity and the Conservative Party After 1945', *Historical Journal*, vol.37, no.1, 1994, pp.173–97; M. Francis, 'Economics and Ethics: The Nature of Labour's Socialism, 1945–1951', *Twentieth-Century British History*, vol.6, no.2, 1995, pp.220–43; J. Lawrence and M. Taylor, 'Introduction', S. Brooke, 'Labour and the "Nation" After 1945', and E.H.H. Green, 'The Conservative Party, the State and the Electorate, 1945–64', in J. Lawrence and M. Taylor (eds.), *Party, State and Society: Electoral Behaviour in Britain Since 1800*, Aldershot, Scolar Press, 1997, pp.153–200; M. Francis and I. Zweiniger-Bargielowska, 'Introduction', S. Brooke, 'The Conservative Party, Immigration and National Identity, 1948–1968', I. Zweiniger-Bargielowska, 'Exploring the Gender Gap: The Conservative Party and the Women's Vote, 1945–1964', in M. Francis and I. Zweiniger-Bargielowska (eds.), *The Conservatives and British Society, 1880–1990*, Cardiff, University of Wales Press, 1996, pp.147–70, 194–223.

31. M. Berman, *All That's Solid Melts Into Air: The Experience of Modernity*, London, Verso, 1983. See also: P. Anderson, 'Modernity and Revolution', *New Left Review*, no.144, March-April 1984, pp.96–113; A. O'Shea, 'English Subjects of Modernity', in M. Nava and A. O'Shea (eds.), *Modern Times: Reflections on a Century of English Modernity*, London, Routledge, 1996, pp.7–37.

32. P. Osborne, 'Modernity is a Qualitative, Not a Chronological Category', *New Left Review*, no.192, 1992, pp.65–84.

33. P. Corrigan and D. Sayer, *The Great Arch: English State Formation as Cultural Revolution*, Oxford, Blackwell, 1985; L. Colley, *Britons: Forging the Nation 1707–1837*, London, Vintage, 1996.

34. H. Perkin, *The Origins of Modern English Society 1780–1880*, London, Routledge, 1972 and *The Rise of Professional Society: England Since 1880*, London, Routledge, 1989.

35. R. Williams, *The Politics of Modernism: Against the New Conformists*, edited and introduced by T. Pinkey, London, Verso, 1989, p.32.

36. A. Giddens, *The Consequences of Modernity*, Cambridge, Polity, 1990 and *Modernity and Self-Identity*, Cambridge, Polity, 1991.

37. P. Mandler and S. Pedersen, 'Introduction: The British Intelligentsia After the Victorians', in P. Mandler and S. Pedersen (eds.), *After The Victorians: Private Conscience and Public Duty in Modern Britain: Essays in Memory of John Clive*, London and New York, Routledge, 1994, pp.1–28; S. Collini, *Public Moralists: Political Thought and Intellectual Life in Britain, 1850–1930*, Oxford, Clarendon Press, 1991.

38. N. Annan, *Our Age*, London, Weidenfeld & Nicolson, 1990, pp.13, 299.

39. See N. Rose, *Governing the Soul: The Shaping of the Private Self*, London, Routledge, 1990; P. Miller and N. Rose (eds.), *The Power of Psychiatry*, Cambridge, Polity, 1986; Riley, *War in the Nursery*; V. Walkerdine and H. Lacey, *Democracy in the Kitchen: Regulating Mothers and Socialising Daughters*, London, Virago, 1989.

40. See among very many: P. Wildeblood, *Against the Law*, London, Weidenfeld & Nicolson, 1955; J. Seabrook, *Mother and Son: An Autobiography*, London, Gollancz, 1979; Heron (ed.), *Truth, Dare or Promise*; Steedman, *Landscape for a Good Woman*.

41. See especially Giddens, *Modernity and Self-Identity*.
42. See G. Spivak, 'Can the Subaltern Speak?: Speculations on Widow Sacrifice', in C. Nelson and L. Grossberg (eds.), *Marxism and the Interpretation of Culture*, Urbana, University of Illinois Press, 1988, pp.271–313.
43. See N. Rose, 'Identity, Genealogy and History', in S. Hall and P. du Gay (eds.), *Questions of Cultural Identity*, London, Sage, 1996, p.131.
44. E. Durbin, quoted in Francis, 'Economics and Ethics', pp.237–8.
45. See especially S.E. Finer, *The Life and Times of Sir Edwin Chadwick*, London, Methuen, 1952; G. Kitson Clark, '"Statesmen in Disguise": Reflections on the History of Neutrality of the Civil Service', *Historical Journal*, vol.II, no.1, 1959, pp.19–40.
46. See for example T. Parsons, *The Social System*, London, Tavistock Publications, 1952; T. Parsons and E.A. Shils, *Towards a General Theory of Action*, Cambridge, Mass., Harvard University Press, 1951; Riley, *War in the Nursery*; Rose, *Governing the Soul*.
47. See D. Riesman, *The Lonely Crowd: A Study of the Changing American Character*, New Haven, Yale University Press, 1951; C.A.R. Crosland, *The Future of Socialism*, London, Jonathan Cape, 1956 and *The Conservative Enemy: A Programme of Radical Reform for the 1960s*, London, Jonathan Cape, 1962.
48. J. Donzelot, *The Policing of Families: Welfare Versus the State*, trans. R. Hurley, London, Hutchinson, 1979.
49. B. Anderson, *Imagined Communities: Reflections on the Origin and Spread of Nationalism*, London and New York, Verso, 1991, p.6. See also E. Hobsbawm, *Nations and Nationalism since 1780: Programme, Myth and Reality*, Cambridge, Cambridge University Press, 1990.
50. Giddens, *Modernity and Self-Identity*, p.21.
51. Z. Bauman, *Legislators and Interpreters: On Modernity, Post-Modernity and Intellectuals*, London, Routledge, 1987, p.111.
52. Osborne, 'Modernity is a Qualitative, Not a Chronological Category', p.75.
53. P. Gilroy, *The Black Atlantic: Modernity and Double Consciousness*, London, Verso, 1993.
54. See A. Pred, *Recognizing European Modernities: A Montage of the Present*, London and New York, Routledge, 1995.
55. See Crosland, *The Future of Socialism*, pp.524–9; *The Conservative Enemy*, pp.237–41; S. Crosland, *Tony Crosland*, London, Coronet, 1983.
56. See the classic study by Richard Hoggart, *The Uses of Literacy*, London, Chatto and Windus, 1957.
57. D. Marquand and A. Seldon (eds.), *The Ideas that Shaped Post-War Britain*, London, Fontana, 1996, p.1.

1. Jazz at the Spirella: Coming of Age in Coventry in the 1950s

I wish to thank the University of Manitoba and the Social Science and Humanities Research Council of Canada for a grant in aid of this research, which is part of a larger project on the Americanisation of popular culture in Britain since the 1890s. This essay is dedicated to the memory of Dud Clews, the original Deaf Rhubarb Blenkinsop, schoolfriend, trumpeter and jazz intimate, killed in a car accident, April 1963.

1. M. Berman, *All That is Solid Melts into Air: The Experience of Modernity*, New York, Verso, 1982, pp.15–36.

2. K. Richardson, *Twentieth Century Coventry*, London, Macmillan, 1972; D.W. Thoms and T. Donnelly, 'Coventry's Industrial Economy, 1880–1980', in B. Lancaster and T. Mason (eds.), *Life and Labour in a Twentieth Century City: The Experience of Coventry*, Coventry, University of Warwick Press, 1985; N. Tiratsoo, *Reconstruction, Affluence and Labour Politics: Coventry, 1945–1960*, London, Routledge, 1990. For culture in inter-war Coventry, see J.B. Priestley, *English Journey*, Harmondsworth, Penguin, 1987, pp.69–76.

3. The city led the country in National Savings, *Coventry Evening Telegraph*, 2 April 1955.

4. For a comparable example from Leicester in the 1930s, see J.F.C. Harrison, *Scholarship Boy: A Personal History of the Mid-Twentieth Century*, London, Rivers Oram Press, 1995, though the Harrisons' house was semi-detached, a social grade higher.

5. Compare the anxieties examined in R. Hoggart, *The Uses of Literacy*, Harmondsworth, Penguin, 1958, pp.291–304, and B. Jackson and D. Marsden, *Education and the Working Class*, Harmondsworth, Penguin, 1966, a study of Huddersfield, another 'boom town'.

6. Thoms and Donnelly, 'Coventry's Economy', pp.27, 45–6.

7. Quote from Arthur Deakin, General Secretary, Transport and General Workers' Union, *Daily Mirror*, 17 July 1953.

8. The standard history of jazz in Britain is J. Godbolt, *A History of Jazz in Britain, 1919–1950*, London, Quartet Books, 1984, and *A History of Jazz in Britain, 1950 to 1970*, London, Quartet Books, 1989. By far the best general (and social) history of jazz for the time is F. Newton, *The Jazz Scene*, Harmondsworth, Penguin, 1961 (alias Eric Hobsbawm, then jazz critic for the *New Statesman*), reprinted under his own name, London, Weidenfeld & Nicolson, 1989. For a suggestive essay on inter-war jazz in Britain, see S. Frith, '"Playing with Real Feeling" — Jazz and Suburbia', in his *Music for Pleasure: Essays in the Sociology of Pop*, Cambridge, Polity Press, 1988, pp.45–63. See also, R. Harris, *Jazz*, Harmondsworth, Penguin, 1953, chapter 12; D. Boulton, *Jazz in Britain*, London, W.H. Allen, 1958; J. Chilton, *Who's Who of British Jazz*, London, Cassell, 1997. The richest primary source is the Oral History of Jazz in Britain held at the National Sound Archive (NSA), consisting of interviews with more than a hundred musicians and other figures in the jazz world. Some similar materials are held at the National Jazz Foundation Archive at Loughton, Essex.

9. *Melody Maker*, 30 May 1953. For data on the jazz public in Britain in the period, see Newton, *Jazz Scene*, pp.271–4.

10. George Webb, NSA interview, 29 October 1986; H. Lyttelton, *I Play As I Please: Memoirs of an Old Etonian Trumpeter*, London, McGibbon and Kee, 1954, pp.123–4, 147; J. Godbolt, *All This and Many a Dog: Memoirs of a Loser/Pessimist*, London, Quartet Books, 1986, pp.4–16 (incorporating and extending *All This and 10 Per Cent*, London, Robert Hale, 1976).

11. Godbolt, *A History of Jazz, 1919–1950*, pp.212–15; Merseysippi Jazz Band (Liverpool), NSA interview, 3 July 1986. For the Mulligan band, see Godbolt, *All This*; P. Oakes, *At The Jazz Band Ball*, London, André Deutsch, 1983. Melly provided his own account of these years in *Owning Up*, Harmondsworth, Penguin, 1970. See also, in his role as cultural critic, S. Melly, *Revolt into Style: The Pop Arts in Britain*, Harmondsworth, Penguin, 1972.

12. Lyttelton, *I Play As I Please*, pp.152–3; 'Blue Heaven in the Basement', *Picture Post*, 10 July 1954.

13. Godbolt, *A History of Jazz, 1919–1950*, chapter 13; J. Fordham, *Jazzman: The Amazing Story of Ronnie Scott and his Club*, London, Kyle Cathie, 1995, provides an excellent

account of the early modernists.

14. Dickie Hawdon, NSA interview, 21 October 1994.

15. For a sardonic typology of traditional and modern uniforms among fans at the end of the 1950s see C. MacInnes, *Absolute Beginners*, Harmondsworth, Penguin, 1986, pp.70–1. For traditionalists' affinities with a parallel contemporary subculture see G. Boyes, *The Imagined Village: Culture, Ideology and the English Folk Revival*, Manchester, Manchester University Press, 1993.

16. Harris, *Jazz*, p.172n.

17. *Melody Maker*, 4 April 1953 and 6 November 1954, the latter headlined 'Fantastic Boom in Jazz Disc Sales'; personal diary, 23 January 1954.

18. Newton, *Jazz Scene*, p.239; Frith, 'Playing With Real Feeling'. For Larkin's own school days see A. Motion, *Philip Larkin: A Writer's Life*, London, Faber, 1993, pp.15–25. In a review of Godbolt, *A History of Jazz*, Larkin recalls his 'vertiginous excitement' at first hearing Fats Waller on Radio Luxembourg as a schoolboy, *Observer*, 12 August 1984. For his jazz criticism, see Larkin, *All What Jazz: A Record Diary*, London, Faber, 1985. Suggestive on the larger context is J. Baxendale, '"Into Another Kind of Life In Which Anything Might Happen": Popular Music and Later Modernity, 1910–1930', *Popular Music*, vol.14, no.2, 1995, pp.137–54.

19. For the 'white Negro' syndrome (a coinage of Norman Mailer), see Frith, 'Playing with Real Feeling', and D. Hebdige, *Subculture: The Meaning of Style*, London, Methuen, 1979, pp.46–59.

20. Diary, 12 March, 14 March 1956. For debates on the quality of British jazz, see Ernest Borneman, anthropologist and critic, *Melody Maker*, 17 January, 31 January, 7 February 1953.

21. The young musicians with whom I regularly played comprised other sixth formers destined for university, grammar school early leavers (a hospital technician and a draughtsman), an art school student, and apprentices in carpentry, engineering and sheet-metal work. The sample approximates to Newton's 1956 profile of the British jazz fan, *Jazz Scene*, pp.271–4. In an excellent piece of sociological field work assisted by Dennis Marsden (see above, n.5), Brian Jackson, *Working Class Community*, London, Routledge, 1968, pp.127–39, identifies a similar constituency with similar satisfactions in a Huddersfield jazz club, c. 1965.

22. For Turner, this was probably a personal default on official masculinity; see his autobiography, *Hot Air, Cool Music*, London, Quartet Books, 1984.

23. Diary, 11 February 1954.

24. R. Baden-Powell, *Scouting for Boys*, London, C. Arthur Pearson, 1947, personal copy inscribed 'From Mummy', pp.134–5, 173. Powell's injunctions became generalised in my memory as 'Treat every girl as you would treat your mother'.

25. On the lack of 'an adolescent apprenticeship in love' for girls as well as boys in single sex schools, see Jackson and Marsden, *Education and the Working Class*, p.152n.

26. Diary, 18 January 1953, 12 April 1953.

27. Cited in M. Jay, *The Dialectical Imagination: A History of the Frankfurt School*, Boston, Little, Brown and Co., 1973, pp.186–7.

28. G. Melly, *Rum, Bum and Concertina*, London, Weidenfeld & Nicolson, 1989, p.58; *Melody Maker*, 15 January 1955.

29. *Momma Don't Allow* was the title of a Free Cinema film on jazz clubs made by Karel Reisz and Tony Richardson in 1956, with soundtrack by the Chris Barber band, see R.

Hewison, *In Anger: Culture and the Cold War 1945–1960*, London, Methuen, 1981, p.153. See also the fictional black American jazz singer, Maria Bethlehem, in MacInnes, *Absolute Beginners*, pp.188–9: 'Maria is big ... She's like a girl, yes, but she's also, in a strange way, just like everybody's Mum', a description perhaps modelled more on Ella Fitzgerald than Bessie Smith.

30. *Spirella Magazine*, June 1955. Spirella opened a model factory in Letchworth, Hertfordshire in the 1920s where it manufactured custom made corsets until closing in 1989 when, as the wags put it, 'the bottom dropped out of the market'. Former corsetières interviewed on radio fantasised about their ideal order — measuring and fitting the Queen. See 'Supporting Cast', BBC Radio 4, 21 August 1995, for which I thank Ruth Richardson. My thanks also to the Garden City Heritage Museum, Letchworth, for access to the extensive company archives of Spirella.
31. For these developments see Melly, *Revolt into Style*.
32. Hewison, *In Anger*, pp.133–4; A. Sinfield, *Literature, Politics and Culture in Postwar Britain*, Berkeley, University of California Press, 1989, pp.159–61, 240, 262–3.
33. I. Davies, *Cultural Studies and Beyond*, London, Routledge, 1995, pp.124–5. See also Hebdige, *Subculture*, p.51.
34. Jazzmen held benefits for defendants in the South African treason trials and refugees from the Hungarian revolution, and played for CND marches. Lyttelton was a some-time vice-president of the Workers Music Association and remains a lifelong socialist. See 'The Trumpet Major', *Observer*, 19 May 1996.
35. For fantasy as psychic management rather than escape see G. Dawson, *Soldier Heroes: British Adventure, Empire and the Imagining of Masculinities*, London, Routledge, 1994, pp.24–6. For the dominant models of masculinity in the 1950s see L. Segal, *Slow Motion: Changing Masculinities, Changing Men*, London, Virago, 1990, pp.1–25. For compa-rable experiences for women, see L. Heron (ed.), *Truth, Dare or Promise: Girls Growing Up in the Fifties*, London, Virago, 1985.

2. State-Sponsored Autobiography

An earlier version of this chapter appeared as 'The Peculiarities of English Autobiography: An Autobiographical Education, 1945–1975', in C. Hammerle (ed.), *Plurality and Individuality: Autobiographical Cultures in Europe*, Vienna, IFK *Internationales Forschungzentrum, Kulturwissenschaften*, Vienna, 1995, pp.86–94. An extended version of the section concern-ing Valerie Avery's *London Morning* will be found in 'Writing the Self: The End of the Scholarship Girl', in J. McGuigan (ed.), *Cultural Methodologies*, London, Sage, 1997, pp.106–25.

1. J. Mullan, 'Feelings and Novels', in R. Porter (ed.), *Rewriting the Self: Histories from the Renaissance to the Present*, London, Routledge, p.131.
2. E. Cox, *Epistolary Bodies: Gender and Genre in the Eighteenth-century Republic of Letters*, Stanford, Stanford University Press, 1996, p.12
3. Ibid., pp.5–29.
4. R. Chartier, *Forms and Meanings: Texts, Performances, and Audiences from Codex to Computer*, Philadelphia, University of Pennsylvania Press, 1995, p.92.
5. L.H. Peterson, *Victorian Autobiography: The Tradition of Self Interpretation*, New Haven, Yale

University Press, 1986.

6. S. Smith and J. Watson (eds.), *Decolonising the Subject: The Politics of Gender in Women's Autobiography*, Minneapolis, University of Minnesota Press, 1992, p.xviii.

7. A. Giddens, *Modernity and Self-Identity: Self and Society in the Late Modern Age*, Cambridge, Polity, 1991, p.53.

8. Ibid., p.76.

9. For a historiography of Protestant selfhoods in relation to writing, and the 1980s insertion of women's writing into it, see M.J. Benknovitz, 'Some Observations on Women's Concept of Self in the Eighteenth Century', in P. Fritz (ed.), *Women in the Eighteenth Century and Other Essays*, Toronto, Hakkert, 1976; P. Delaney, *British Autobiography in the Seventeenth Century*, London, Routledge, 1969; D. Ebner, *Autobiography in Seventeenth-Century England: Theology and the Self*, The Hague, Mouton, 1971; E. Graham et. al., *Her Own Life: Autobiographical Writings by Seventeenth-Century Englishwomen*, London, Routledge, 1989; W. Haller, *The Rise of Puritanism*, New York, Harper, 1958; M.P. Hannay (ed.), *Silent But for the Word: Tudor Women as Patrons, Translators, and Writers of Religious Works*, Ohio, Kent State University Press, 1985; C. Luke, *Pedagogy, Printing and Protestantism: The Discourse on Childhood*, Albany, State University of New York Press, 1989; F. Nussbaum, *The Autobiographical Subject*, Baltimore, Johns Hopkins University Press, 1989; C.S. Pomerleau, 'The Emergence of Women's Autobiography in England', in E.C. Jelinek (ed.), *Women's Autobiography: Essays in Criticism*, Bloomington, Indiana University Press, 1980; O. Watkins, *The Puritan Experience: Studies in Spiritual Autobiography*, London, Routledge, 1972.

10. Central Advisory Committee for Education, *Children and their Primary Schools: A Report of the Central Advisory Committee for Education [The Plowden Report]*, two vols., London, HMSO, 1967.

11. *The Plowden Report*, vol.1, pp.218–19. See also D. Vincent, *Literacy and Popular Culture, 1750–1914*, Cambridge, Cambridge University Press, 1989, pp.89–90.

12. 'What is Good Children's Writing? (A Report on Some Representative Work Sent from Nine Primary Schools in Different Parts of England and Scotland), Part I', *Use of English*, vol.4, no.2, Winter 1952, p.71.

13. 'Creative Writing', *NATE Bulletin, CSE English. An Interim Report*, vol.1, no.3, Autumn 1964, p.31.

14. F. Stevens, 'What is Good Children's Writing? (A Report on Some Representative Work Sent from Nine Primary Schools in Different Parts of England and Scotland), Part II', *Use of English*, vol.4, no.3, Spring 1953, pp.126–32. The term 'creative writing' was first used by the journal *Use of English* in 1962. A secondary modern school head of English described stimulating one of his classes 'to practise a type of creative writing'. What he got from the children on this occasion was poetry. T.A. Thompson, 'Creative Writing in the Modern School', *Use of English*, vol.13, no.3, Spring 1962, pp.187–92.

15. F. Inglis, 'Against Proportional Representation: The Ambitious Heart of English Teaching', *English in Education*, vol.9, no.1, 1975, pp.11–18.

16. G. Thomas, 'The Process of Writing', *English in Education*, vol.6, no.3, Autumn 1973, pp.74–81. Glyn Thomas was head of the English department, Hunstanton Secondary Modern School, Norfolk.

17. 'Twenty-five', *Use of English*, vol.15, no.4, Summer 1964, p.243. See also L.E.W. Smith, 'Creative Writing and Language Awareness', *English in Education*, vol.4, no.1, Spring 1970, p.4.

18. Smith, 'Creative Writing', p.4. L.E.W. Smith was head of English at Millfield School, Somerset. David Holbrook's writings are numerous. Particularly relevant to the current argument are: *Imaginings*, London, Putnam, 1961; *English for Maturity: English in the Secondary School*, Cambridge, Cambridge University Press, 1961; *English for the Rejected: Training Literacy in the Lower Streams of the Secondary School*, Cambridge, Cambridge University Press,1964; *Children's Writing: A Sampler for Students*, Cambridge, Cambridge University Press, 1967; *English for Meaning*, Windsor, NFER, 1979. F.R. Leavis' and Denys Thompson's, *Culture and Environment: The Training of Critical Awareness*, London, Chatto and Windus, 1933, stayed in print and was still being used in some training colleges in the early 1970s.

19. Smith, 'Creative Writing', p.4. For Holbrook's well-known series of laments on the question of class, language and childhood, see note 18.

20. *Culture and Environment* was still in print and in use when Richard Hoggart made what was, by then, a familiar exhortation to English teachers in 1957, to use literature to inoculate their children against mass culture. R. Hoggart, 'Towards a Candyfloss World: 1. Changes in Popular Reading', *Use of English*, vol.8, no.2, Winter 1956, pp.111–17; 'Towards a Candyfloss World: 2. Changes in Popular Reading', *Use of English*, vol.8, no.3, Spring 1957, pp.159–64.

21. D. Dworkin, *Cultural Marxism in Postwar Britain: History, the New Left and the Origins of Cultural Studies*, Durham and London, Duke University Press, 1997, p.116. For the classic account of Scrutiny's influence see F. Mulhern, *The Moment of 'Scrutiny'*, London, Verso, 1979.

22. R. Williams, 'Stocktaking: I. Books for Teaching "Culture and Environment"', *Use of English*, vol.1, no.3, Spring 1950, pp.134–40. Williams wrote here as a staff tutor in adult education, while working for the Oxford University Extra-Mural Delegacy. When Stuart Hall announced the opening of the Birmingham Centre for Contemporary Cultural Studies to primary and secondary school teachers in 1965, he wrote of its proposed services for teachers and of a research project in the planning stage that would be 'directly concerned with the impact of modern forms of communication upon children, especially in the context of the teaching of English' — a research project put on the English teacher's agenda thirty years before, in Leavis' and Thompson's book. S. Hall, 'Centre for Contemporary Cultural Studies', *NATE Bulletin*, vol.2, no.1, Spring 1965, pp.28–9.

23. Dworkin, *Cultural Marxism*, pp.116–24.

24. D. Thompson, 'The Relevance of I.A. Richards', *Use of English*, vol.23, no.1, Autumn 1971, pp.3–13.

25. I.A. Richards, *Practical Criticism*, London, Routledge, 1929, p.351.

26. Thompson, 'The Relevance of I. A. Richards', pp.3–13.

27. D. Thompson, 'Teacher's Debt', in R. Bower, H. Vendler and J. Hollander (eds.), *I.A. Richards: Essays in His Honour*, New York, Oxford University Press, 1973, p.299.

28. University of London, *General Certificate of Education Examination: Regulations and Syllabuses, Summer 1973 and January 1974*, London, University of London, 1971, p.87.

29. University of London, *General Certificate of Education Examinations: Subject Reports, June 1972*, London, University of London, 1972, pp.71–5.

30. University of London, *General Certificate of Education Examination: Subject Reports, June 1984*, London, University of London, 1985, pp.234–42.

31. F.R. Leavis, *Mass Civilisation and Minority Culture*, Cambridge, Minority Press, 1930,

pp.3–5.

32. M. Mathieson, *Preachers of Culture: A Study of English and Its Teachers*, London, George Allen & Unwin, 1975, pp.85–142; C. Baldick, *The Social Mission of English Criticism, 1848–1932*, Oxford, Clarendon Press, 1983, pp.196–234; B. Doyle, *English and Englishness*, London, Routledge, 1989, pp.94–132; J. Dixon, *A Schooling in 'English': Critical Episodes in the Struggle to Shape Literary and Cultural Studies*, Milton Keynes, Open University Press, 1991, pp.79–134, passim.

33. M. Black, 'The Third Realm: An Expository Essay on "Scrutiny"', *Use of English*, vol.16, no.1, Autumn 1964, pp.21–31.

34. From September 1941 it had been published as an ABCA bulletin by the War Office, available only to the three services. Bureau of Current Affairs, *Background Handbooks*, London, Bureau of Current Affairs, 1946; and 1946–61.

35. Recently, attention has been drawn to earlier practices of self-expression and self-narration. Georgie Boyes has discussed the roots of the folk revival in *The Imagined Village: Culture, Ideology and the English Folk Revival*, Manchester, Manchester University Press, 1993 and Ewan McColl described the space provided by the BBC for the narration of every-day lives, from the 1930s onwards, in his autobiography *Journeyman*, London, Sidgwick and Jackson, 1992. See also: D. Morley and K. Worpole, *The Republic of Letters: Working Class Writing and Local Publishing*, London, Comedia, 1983; K. Worpole, *Reading By Numbers: Contemporary Publishing and Popular Fiction*, London, Comedia, 1984; R. Samuel (ed.), *People's History and Socialist Theory*, London, Routledge, 1981, pp.22–48, 50–76; S. Dentith, 'Contemporary Working Class Autobiography: Politics of Form, Politics of Content', *Prose Studies*, vol.8, 1985, pp.60–80; T. Lovell, 'Feminism and the Historians', in *British Feminist Thought: A Reader*, Oxford, Blackwell, 1990, pp.19–67.

36. G. Spivak, 'Can the Subaltern Speak?: Speculations on Widow Sacrifice', in C. Nelson and L. Grossberg (eds.), *Marxism and the Interpretation of Culture*, Urbana, University of Illinois Press, 1988, pp.271–313. Spivak's answer to her interrogative title is a (fairly clear) 'No'.

37. There is some discussion of this pedagogical and political practice in C. Steedman, 'A Weekend with Elektra', *History and Literature*, vol.6, no.1, Spring 1997, pp.17–42.

38. P. Abbs, *Autobiography in Education: An Introduction to the Subjective Discipline of Autobiography and of its Central Place in the Education of Teachers, with a Selection of Passages from a Variety of Autobiographies, Including those Written by Students*, Heinemann, London, 1974, p.22.

39. Ibid., p.12. A typical training college publication is A. C. Hilton (ed.), *Experience Teaches: Contributions from Old Students of Coventry College of Education*, Coventry, Coventry College of Education, 1974.

40. K. Worpole, 'Class of '55', *City Limits*, January/February, 1982, p.39.

41. 'Miss Avery grew up in a drab London street in the years after the war. This book is a sampler of memories, deftly stitched from countless domestic details', *The Times Literary Supplement*, 22 October, 1964, p.965. For traditions of Life's Comedy in music hall, see J.S. Bratton, 'Jenny Hill: Sex and Sexism in Victorian Music Hall', in J.S. Bratton (ed.), *Music Hall: Performance and Style*, Milton Keynes, Open University Press, 1986, pp.92–110.

42. *London Morning* was reissued in the 'Pergamon English Library', 1969 and in the 'Literature for Life Series', Arnold-Wheaton, 1980.

43. E. Austen, 'Writing at Nine Years', *Use of English*, vol.3, no.3, Spring 1952, pp.147–50.

44. D.N. Hubbard, 'The Child and His Writing', *Use of English*, vol.22, no.1, Autumn 1970, pp.50–4. Hubbard lectured at the University of Sheffield Institute of Education.

For expression of the thesis that deprivation of language in childhood is the saddest of poverties see, for example, J.W. Patrick Creber and the National Association for the Teaching of English, *Lost for Words: Language and Educational Failure*, Harmondsworth, Penguin, 1972, pp.72–112, 175–80. For what writing might do see C. Burgess et. al., *Understanding Children Writing*, Harmondsworth, Penguin, 1973, pp.9–68; C. and H. Rosen, *The Language of Primary School Children*, Penguin, Harmondsworth, 1973, pp.85–155. For early understandings of writing's power in a child's life see A.B. Clegg (ed.), *The Excitement of Writing*, London, Chatto and Windus, 1964; Holbrook, *English for the Rejected*.

45. J.H. Walsh, 'Writing about "Experiences"', *Use of English*, vol.16, no.2, Winter 1964, pp.91–103. For a brief history of elementary and primary education in England as a form of compensation for deprivation see C. Steedman, '"The Mother Made Conscious": The History of a Primary School Pedagogy', *History Workshop Journal*, no.20, Autumn 1985, pp.149–63.
46. *The Plowden Report*, vol.1, pp.219–20.
47. Steedman, 'Writing the Self: The End of the Scholarship Girl'. For a plea for a sociology of literary forms see F. Moretti, 'The Soul and the Harpy', in F. Moretti, *Signs Taken for Wonders: Essays in the Sociology of Literary Forms*, London, Verso and New Left Books, 1983, pp.1–41.
48. R.J.W. Selleck, *English Primary Education and the Progressives, 1914–1939*, London, Routledge, 1972; P. Cunningham, *Curriculum Change in the Primary School since 1945: Dissemination of the Progressive Ideal*, Lewes, Falmer Press, 1988.
49. D. Vincent, *Poor Citizens: The State and the Poor in the Twentieth Century*, London, Longman, 1991, p.3.

3. The Commercial Domain: Advertising and the Cultural Management of Demand

1. J.M. Keynes, *The General Theory of Employment, Interest and Money*, San Diego, Harcourt, Brace, Jovanovitch, 1964, pp.107–10.
2. A. Giddens, *Modernity and Self-Identity: Self and Society in the Late Modern Age*, Cambridge, Polity Press, 1991; Z. Bauman, *On Modernity, Post-Modernity and Intellectuals*, Cambridge, Polity Press, 1987.
3. See G. Worswick and P. Ady (eds.), *The British Economy in the Nineteen-Fifties*, Oxford, Clarendon, 1962; B. Alford, *British Economic Performance 1945–75*, Basingstoke, Macmillan,1988; A. Cairncross, *The British Economy since 1945: Economic Policy and Performance*, Oxford, Blackwell, 1992, and his *Years of Recovery: British Economic Policy 1945–51*, London, Methuen, 1985.
4. See C.A.R. Crosland, *The Future of Socialism*, London, Jonathan Cape, 1956; V. Bogdanor and R. Skidelsky (eds.), *The Age of Affluence, 1951–1964*, London, Macmillan, 1970.
5. For the effects of consumption on the post-war working class see J. Goldthorpe, F. Bechhofer, D. Lockwood, J. Platt, *The Affluent Worker: Political Attitudes and Behaviour*, Cambridge, Cambridge University Press, 1968 and *The Affluent Worker in the Class Structure*, Cambridge, Cambridge University Press, 1969. Also P. Willmott and M. Young, *Family and Class in a London Suburb*, London, Routledge, 1960; F. Zweig, *The Worker in an Affluent Society*, London, Heinemann, 1961. For women see Birmingham Feminist

History Group, 'Feminism as Femininity in the Nineteen Fifties', *Feminist Review*, no.3, 1979, pp.48–65; E. Wilson, *Only Half Way to Paradise: Women in Postwar Britain*, London, Tavistock, 1980; C. Steedman, *Landscape for a Good Woman: A Story of Two Lives*, London, Virago, 1985. For youth see M. Abrams, *The Teenage Consumer*, London, London Press Exchange, 1959; S. Hall and T. Jefferson (eds.), *Resistance through Rituals, Youth Subcultures in Post-war Britain*, London, Hutchinson, 1976; D. Hebdige, *Subculture, the Meaning of Style*, London, Methuen, 1979.

6. The most recent global statement about the long-term effects of post-war mass consumption is contained in Eric Hobsbawm's *Age of Extremes: The Short Twentieth Century 1914–1991*, London, Abacus, 1994, chapters 9 and 10.

7. See B. Fine, 'Modernity, Urbanism and Modern Consumption', *Society and Space*, vol.11, 1993, pp.599–601; F. Mort, *Cultures of Consumption: Masculinities and Social Space in late Twentieth-Century Britain*, London, Routledge, 1996, pp.1–12.

8. M. Burton, *Globe Girdling, Being the Impressions of an Amateur Observer*, vol.1, Leeds, Petty and Sons, 1935, p.13.

9. See R. Gosling, 'Gosling on the High Street', Radio Four, 10 July 1992; F. Mort and P.Thompson, 'Retailing, Commercial Culture and Masculinity in 1950s Britain: The Case of Montague Burton, the "Tailor of Taste"', *History Workshop*, no.38, Autumn 1994, pp.106–27.

10. For details of Burton's output and market share see The Monopolies Commission, *United Drapery Stores Ltd. and Montague Burton Ltd: A Report on the Proposed Merger*, Cmnd. 3397, London, HMSO, 1967; K. Honeyman, 'Montague Burton Ltd: The Creators of Well-Dressed Men', in K. Honeyman and J. Chartres (eds.), *Leeds City Business 1893–1993: Essays Marking the Centenary of the Incorporation*, Leeds, privately printed, 1993, pp.186–217.

11. Economist Intelligence Unit, 'Men's Suits', *Retail Business*, vol.4, no.46, December 1961, p.26.

12. See E. Sigsworth, *Montague Burton: The Tailor of Taste*, Manchester, Manchester University Press, 1990, pp.46, 59; Honeyman, 'Montague Burton'.

13. See the Board of Trade, *Working Party Reports on Heavy Clothing*, London, HMSO, 1947, p.9.

14. See '"Pseudo Bespoke by Multiple Shops" and "Cult of Shabbiness" is to Blame for Slump in Business', *Men's Wear*, 10 September 1962, p.7.

15. Quoted in Sigsworth, *Montague Burton*, p.51. See also Burton's, 'Circular Letter to Branch Managers', 1952, Burton's Archives, West Yorkshire Archive Service, Leeds, Box 136.

16. See F.P. Bishop, *The Ethics of Advertising*, London, Robert Hale, 1949, pp.66–7; Institute of Practitioners in Advertising, *Development of the Service Advertising Agency*, Occasional Paper no.2, London, Institute of Practitioners in Advertising, February 1956.

17. Montague Burton, *Manager's Guide*, Leeds, Petty and Sons, 1953, p.55, in Burton's Archives, Box 5.

18. See the plates from Burton's pattern books during this period, *The Trend of Fashion: Exclusive Designs by Burton's* (undated, late 1940s/ early 1950s), Burton's Archives, Box 136.

19. See E. Carter, *How German is She? National Reconstruction and the Consuming Woman in the FRG and West Berlin 1945–60*, Ann Arbor, University of Michigan Press, 1996; S. Piccone Stella, '"Rebels Without a Cause": Male Youth in Italy around 1960', *History Workshop*, no.38, Autumn 1994, pp.157–78.

20. Lt. Colonel A. Wilkinson, 'Reflections on the 4As Convention', Institute of Practitioners

in Advertising, *Institute Information*, vol.3, no.120, June 1956, p.1.

21. Ibid.

22. R. Brandon, *The Truth About Advertising*, London, Chapman and Hall, 1949, pp.vii–ix.

23. Bishop, *The Ethics of Advertising*, p.35.

24. E. Dichter, *The Strategy of Desire*, London, T.V. Boardman and Co., 1960, p.178.

25. Ibid., p.280.

26. D. Thompson, *Voice of Civilization: An Enquiry into Advertising*, London, Frederick Muller, 1943, pp.21–2.

27. Ibid., p.108.

28. Ibid., p.99.

29. J.B. Priestley and J. Hawkes, *Journey Down a Rainbow*, London, Heinemann Cresset, 1955, p.ix.

30. See M. Corden, *A Tax on Advertising?* London, Fabian Society Research Series, no.222, 1961; E. Burton, *The Battle of the Consumer*, London, The Labour Party, 1955.

31. By 1960 there were twelve American-based agencies in London, controlling 30 per cent of aggregate billings. See D. West, 'Multinational Competition in the British Advertising Agency Business, 1936–1987', *Business History Review*, no.62, Autumn 1988, p.474.

32. See especially B. Levin, 'Sir George and the ITV Dragon. Battle Starting Tonight', *Manchester Guardian*, 22 September 1955, p.1; 'Commercial TV — This was the First Night', *Daily Express*, 23 September 1955, p.5.

33. B. Levin, 'ITV Makes its Bow — Polished and on Time', *Manchester Guardian*, 23 September 1955, p.1.

34. J. Hobson, 'The Agency Viewpoint 2', in H. Henry (ed.), *British Television Advertising: The First 30 Years*, London, Century Benham, 1986, p.432.

35. I. Harvey, *The Technique of Persuasion: An Essay in Human Relationships*, London, The Falcon Press, 1951, p.89.

36. Crawford's International, *How to Break into World Markets*, London, W.S. Crawford Ltd., 1965, p.3.

37. See Burton, *Globe Girdling* and *The Middle Path: Talks on Collective Security, Arbitration and Other Aspects of International and Industrial Relations*, London, Petty and Sons, 1943.

38. See Lionel Jacobson's comments in the file marked 'Tip Top Tailors', Burton's Archives, 1957, Box 182.

39. For Anglo-Australian trade relations see J.O. Perkins, *Britain and Australia: Economic Relationships in the 1950s*, Melbourne, Melbourne University Press, 1962; A.F. Madden and W.H. Morris Jones, *Australia and Britain: Studies in a Changing Relationship*, London, Institute of Commonwealth Studies, 1980; G. Whitwell, *Making the Market: The Rise of Consumer Society*, Melbourne, McPhee Gribble, 1989. For Commonwealth preference in British export advertising see 'Seen Advertising Overseas', *Board of Trade Journal*, 1 October 1955, quoted in Institute of Practitioners in Advertising, *Abstract of Information*, London, IPA, May-November 1955, p.363.

40. Giddens, *Modernity and Self-Identity* and *The Transformation of Intimacy: Sexuality, Love and Eroticism in Modern Societies*, Cambridge, Polity Press, 1992.

41. A. Marshall, *Industry and Trade: A Study of Industrial Technique and Business Organisation and Their Influence on the Conditions of Various Classes and Nations*, London, Macmillan, 1927, pp.269–307; A. Pigou, *The Economics of Welfare*, third edition, London, Macmillan, 1929; D. Braithwaite, 'The Economic Effects of Advertisement', *The Economic Journal*, vol.XXXVIII, March 1928, pp.16–37.

42. See K.W. Rothschild, 'A Note on Advertising', *The Economic Journal*, vol.LII, April 1942, pp.112–21; S. Courtauld, 'An Industrialist's Reflections on the Future Relations of Government and Industry', *The Economic Journal*, vol.LII, April 1942, pp.1–17; E.A. Laver, *Advertising and Economic Theory*, London, Oxford University Press, 1947.

43. F.P. Bishop, *The Economics of Advertising*, Chicago, Richard D. Irwin, 1944, p.154.

44. See J. Robinson, 'The Economic Effects of Advertising', *Economica*, new series, vol.IX, August 1942, p.294.

45. Laver, *Advertising and Economic Theory*, pp.14–15.

46. Ibid., p.49.

47. See P. Miller and N. Rose, 'Mobilising the Consumer: Assembling the Subject of Consumption', *Theory Culture and Society*, vol.14, no.1, February 1997, pp.1–36.

48. See IPA, *Subliminal Communication*, London, IPA, July 1958; R. Harris and A. Seldon, *Advertising and the Public*, London, André Deutsch, 1962, pp.180–1.

49. J. Hobson, *The Selection of Advertising Media*, fourth edition, London, Business Publications Ltd., 1961, p.12.

50. For arguments about the importance of the creative artist within the advertising agency see A. Havinden, *Advertising and the Artist*, London, The Studio Publications, 1956; Crawford's International, *How to Break into World Markets*.

51. H. Henry, *Motivation Research and the Television Commercial*, London, ATV, 1961, p.4. See also IPA, *Motivation Research, A Report*, Occasional Paper, no.5, London, IPA, December 1957.

52. Henry, *Motivation Research*, p.5.

53. J. Pearson and G. Turner, *The Persuasion Industry*, London, Eyre and Spottiswoode, 1965, p.42.

54. Ibid., p.79.

55. Ibid., p.149.

56. Ibid., p.163.

57. Hobson, *The Selection of Advertising Media*, p.22.

58. Market Research Society, *Social Class Definition in Market Research*, 1963, quoted in J. Tunstall, *The Advertising Man in London Advertising Agencies*, London, Chapman and Hall, 1964, pp.139–40.

59. D. Riesman, *The Lonely Crowd: A Study of the Changing American Character*, New Haven, Yale University Press, 1951; D. Bell, 'Advertising and the Impact on Society', *The Listener*, 27 December 1956, pp.1069–72; A. Crosland, 'Advertising: Is it Worth It?' *The Listener*, 13 December 1956, pp.976–7.

4. Towards a Modern Labour Market? State Policy and the Transformation of Employment

Research for this paper was funded by the ESRC (Award: R 000 22 1145). The author also wishes to acknowledge the comments of Robert Salais, Nick Tiratsoo, Simon Deakin and Jonathan Zeitlin.

1. S. Deakin, 'The Evolution of the Contract of Employment 1900–1950', in N. Whiteside and R. Salais (eds.), *Governance, Industry and Labour Markets: The Modernising State in the Mid-Twentieth Century*, London, Routledge, 1998, pp.295–323.

2. N. Whiteside, 'The Revolution that Failed: Labour Market Policy in Britain, 1880–1918', *Jahrbuch für Europäische Verwaltungsgeschichte*, no.5, 1993, pp 57–83.

3. N. Whiteside, 'Creating the Welfare State in Britain', *Journal of Social Policy*, vol.25, no.1, 1996, pp.83–103.

4. N. Whiteside and J. Gillespie, 'Deconstructing Unemployment: Developments in Britain in the Interwar Years', *Economic History Review*, vol.XLIV, no.4, 1991, pp.665–82.

5. C. Barnett, *The Lost Victory, British Dreams, British Realities 1945–50*, London, Macmillan, 1995; S.N. Broadberry and N.F.R. Crafts, 'British Economic Policy and Industrial Performance in the Early Postwar Period', unpublished paper, 1995.

6. A. Cairncross, *Years of Recovery, British Economic Policy 1945–51*, London, Methuen, 1986; N. Tiratsoo and J. Tomlinson, *Industrial Efficiency and State Intervention: Labour 1939–51*, London, Routledge, 1993.

7. By 1946, 56 Joint Industrial Councils had been founded or re-established and 175,000 shop stewards were involved in plant-level bargaining, H. Gospel, *Markets, Firms and the Management of Labour in Modern Britain*, Cambridge, Cambridge University Press, 1992, pp.127–9.

8. Cripps, 'Address to Ministers', Autumn 1948, PRO BT 195/20.

9. J. Hinton, *Shop Floor Citizens: Engineering Democracy in 1940s Britain*, Aldershot, Gower, 1994, chapters 8–9.

10. See for example W.A. Brusse and R. Griffiths, 'Cartels and Post-War Reconstruction', paper presented to the Second Congress of the European Association of Historical Economists, Venice, January 1996.

11. N. Tiratsoo and J. Tomlinson, 'Restrictive Practices on the Shop Floor in Britain, 1945–60', *Business History*, vol.36, no.2, 1994, pp.65–84.

12. AACP, 'Summary of Discussion', 26 October 1948, Modern Records Centre [MRC], Warwick, TUC collection MSS. 292 552 31(1).

13. TUC, 'Report of the National Production Advisory Council on Cotton Board's Deconcentration Committee', 30 January 1943, MRC, MSS. 292 557 1. See also 'Report of Cotton Board Committee on Postwar Problems', 1944, Nuffield Archive [NA], C 4/57.

14. *Working Party Report on the Cotton Industry*, London, HMSO, 1946. See also the papers in PRO LAB 8/1250

15. *Daily Dispatch*, 4 December 1946, p.1.

16. TUC document prepared for AACP, March 1949, MRC, MSS.292 552 32(1).

17. This had been anticipated by all major wartime reports. See also North West Division, 'Memorandum' to Ministry of Labour, July 1946, PRO LAB 8/1280.

18. F. Zweig, *Productivity and Trade Unions*, Oxford, Blackwell, 1951, pp.146–7.

19. Evidence for this section is from G. Phillips and N.Whiteside, *Casual Labour*, Oxford, Oxford University Press, 1986, especially chapter 8.

20. Minute, May 1951, PRO LAB 8/1707.

21. In 1933, at the height of the slump, formal worksharing arrangements had been negotiated in: Northumberland, Durham, Yorkshire and in one pit (Blaernavon) in South Wales. Board of Trade Mines Department, 'Memorandum on Worksharing', January 1933, PRO POWE 30/36.

22. W. Ashworth, *The History of the British Coal Industry*, vol.5, Oxford, Oxford University Press, 1986, pp.160–205.

23. Cabinet Committee on Voluntary Absenteeism, 'Report', Spring 1950, PRO COAL

26/171.

24. Official files on absenteeism in the 1940s used in this and the ensuing paragraph include: PRO COAL 26/170–2; PRO POWE 20/79 and 122; PRO CAB 124/706.

25. F. Zweig, *Men in the Pits*, London, Victor Gollancz, 1948, chapter XIV.

26. The records are in PRO T 214.

27. An example is documented in the nurses' pay dispute, 1948–9, when concessions by local authorities effectively forced the Ministry of Health — and the Treasury's — hand. PRO T 214/986.

28. 'Meeting on Sir Cyril Jones' Report on the National Health Service, P.M's room', 21 July 1950, PRO T 214/110.

29. Wage claim by local government officers, PRO T 214/353.

30. Papers in files PRO T 214/1006–7.

31. Minute, October 1951, PRO T 214/1006.

32. J. Cohen, *Minority Report of Working Party on Recruitment and Training of Nurses*, London, HMSO, 1948, Appendix.

33. Nuffield Hospital Trust, *Report on the Work of Nurses in Hospital Wards* (undated, mid-1950s?), MRC, MSS. 229 6 C CO 3 2.

34. The Ministry of Health offered a 12.5 per cent pro rata hourly rate above the Rushcliffe scale (plus free food, laundry and uniform) to all nurses working less than a 30-hour week in February 1947. Campaign papers in MRC, MSS. 229 6 C CO 13 7.

35. Ibid. For the papers of the Cheltenham Conference on the Gloucestershire scheme, introduced in February 1946, which employed part-time mental health nurses on a shift basis.

36. COHSE Papers, MRC, MSS. 229 6 C CO 3 2.

37. C. Webster, *The Health Services Since the War*, vol.1, London, HMSO, 1988, p.300.

5. Limits of Americanisation: The United States Productivity Gospel in Britain

1. J.B. Priestley and J. Hawkes, *Journey Down A Rainbow*, London, Readers Union, 1957, pp.43–4.

2. J.J. Servan-Schreiber's *Le Défi Américain* (published in Britain as *The American Challenge*, translated by Ronald Steel, London, Hamish Hamilton, 1968) was also influential in this context.

3. See M.J. Lee, *Consumer Culture Reborn: The Cultural Politics of Consumption*, New York and London, Routledge, 1993.

4. See S. Ackroyd and D. Lawrenson, 'Manufacturing Decline and the Division of Labour in Britain: The Case of Vehicles', in I. Glover and M. Hughes (eds.), *The Professional Managerial Class: Contemporary British Management in the Pursuer Mode*, Aldershot, Avebury, 1996, pp.171–93; A. Carew, *Labour Under the Marshall Plan: The Politics of Productivity and the Marketing of Management Science*, Manchester, Manchester University Press, 1987; R.R. Locke, *The Collapse of the American Management Mystique*, Oxford, Oxford University Press, 1996.

5. The dimensions of the technical assistance programmes are well described in J. McGlade, 'The Illusion of Consensus: American Business, Cold War Aid and the Recovery of Western Europe, 1948–1958', unpublished PhD dissertation, George

Washington University, 1995.

6. See *Technological Stagnation in Great Britain*, Chicago, Machinery and Allied Products Institute, 1948; E. Johnston, 'How America Can Avoid Socialism', *Fortune*, vol.39, no.2, 1949, pp.116–18.

7. The following paragraphs are based upon information in F.E. Rodgers, 'Report of the United Kingdom Technical Exchange and Section 115-k Program', 6 September 1956, National Archives, Washington, Record Group 469.

8. Ibid. p.49.

9. *A Review of Productivity in the Bronze and Brass Casting Industry*, London, British Productivity Council, 1955, p.7.

10. 'The Value of Studying American Methods', *Engineering*, 30 January 1953, p.138; 'Role of the Business Consultant', *The Statist*, 28 June 1952, p.932; 'Against European Inefficiency', *The Economist*, 4 August 1956, p.414.

11. AACP, *Education for Management*, London, AACP, p.18.

12. The following paragraphs are based on N. Tiratsoo, '"What You Need is a Harvard": The American influence on British Management Education, cir. 1945–1965', in T. Gourvish and N. Tiratsoo (eds.), *Missionaries and Managers: United States Technical Assistance and European Management Education 1945–1960*, Manchester, Manchester University Press, 1998, pp.140–56.

13. This problem persists to the present day. See Commission on Management Research, *Building Partnerships: Enhancing the Quality of Management Research*, Swindon, Economic and Social Research Council, 1994, pp.13–14.

14. E. Sidney, 'Evaluating Management Training', *Industrial Welfare*, vol.38, no.6, p.164; A. Mant, *The Experienced Manager*, London, British Institute of Management, 1969, p.3.

15. R. Heller, 'Britain's Boardroom Anatomy', *Management Today*, September 1970, p.84.

16. T.K. Mullin, 'Folk Management', *The Manager*, August 1965, pp.22–3, 48.

17. 'High Cost of the Human Hand', *The Statist*, 17 June 1950, p.784; W. J. Dimmock, 'Mechanical Handling in Industry and its Effect on Costs', *Mechanical Handling*, vol.38, no.6, 1951, pp.234–9; AACP, *Materials Handling in Industry*, London, AACP, 1950.

18. 'Progress in Materials Handling', *Mechanical Handling*, vol.42, no.11, 1955, p.619.

19. F. R. Ford, 'Some Handling Problems in the Motor Industry', *Mechanical Handling*, vol.45, no.7, 1958, p.487.

20. Department of Industry Committee for Materials Handling Working Party on Materials-Handling Costs, *Materials-Handling Costs: A New Look at Manufacturing*, London, HMSO, 1976, p.4.

21. M. Pritchard, 'Can We Sell Our Way Out of Inflation', *The Manager*, vol.24, no.11, 1956, p.884.

22. R. Lewis and R. Stewart, 'The Men at the Top', *Encounter*, vol.5, no.11, 1958, pp.48–9.

23. V. Mortenson, 'Are Status Symbols Inevitable?', *Industrial Welfare*, vol.64, no.3, 1962, pp.153–4.

24. L. Urwick, *Personnel Management in Perspective*, London, Institute of Personnel Management, 1959, p.14.

25. K. Ashford to T. Evans, enclosed memo, 'The British Motor Corporation', 27 January 1961, PRO LAB10/1627.

26. M. Poole, 'A Back Seat For Personnel', *Personnel Management*, vol.5, no.5, 1973, p.38.

27. D. Davies, *Formal Consultation — In Practice*, London, Industrial Welfare Society, 1962, p.6.

28. W. Durham, 'British Suggestion Schemes', *Industrial Welfare*, vol.62, no.5, 1960, p.275.
29. H. Leavitt, 'On the Export of American Management Education', *Journal of Business*, vol.30, no.3, 1957, p.155.
30. Editorial, *BEAMA Journal*, vol.56, no.156, 1949, p.259.
31. Editorial, *The Engineer*, 2 January 1953, p.2.
32. 'The Cost of Variety', *The Economist*, 29 December 1951, pp.1593–5; see also 'The Way to Simplify', *The Economist*, 5 January 1952, pp.37–8.
33. British Productivity Council, *Better Ways: Nineteen Paths to Higher Productivity*, London, British Productivity Council, 1957, p.34.
34. Quoted in H. Hopkins, *The New Look: A Social History of the Forties and Fifties in Britain*, London, Secker and Warburg, 1964, pp.109–10.
35. H. D. Willcock, 'Public Opinion: Attitudes Towards America and Russia', *Political Quarterly*, vol.19, no.1, 1948, pp.61–2.
36. R. Lowenthall, 'The American "Model"', *The Twentieth Century*, vol.163, no.974, 1958, pp.361–71.
37. G. Turner, *Business in Britain*, Harmondsworth, Penguin, 1971, p.232.
38. This section is based on N. Tiratsoo, 'Standard Motors 1945–55 and the Post-War Malaise of British Management', in Y. Cassis, F. Crouzet and T. Gourvish (eds.), *Management and Business in Britain and France: The Age of the Corporate Economy*, Oxford, Clarendon Press, 1995, pp.88–108.
39. 'How Should a Principal Spend his Time', *The Manager*, vol.19, no.12, 1951, pp.690–1.
40. Quoted in 'Salute to Production Engineers', *Future*, vol.6, no.4, 1951, p.22.
41. D. Granick, *The European Executive*, New York, Doubleday, 1962, p.234.
42. See N. Tiratsoo and J. Tomlinson, *The Conservatives and Industrial Efficiency: Thirteen Wasted Years?* London, Routledge/LSE, 1998.

6. Population Politics in Post-War British Culture

1. M.S. Quine, *Population Politics in Twentieth Century Europe*, London, Routledge, 1996.
2. Sir William Beveridge, 'Population and Unemployment', in R.L. Smyth (ed.), *Essays in the Economics of Socialism and Capitalism; Selected Papers Read to Section F of the British Association for the Advancement of Science, 1886–1932*, London, Duckworth, 1964, p.270. This debate is more fully discussed in P. Thane, 'The Debate on the Declining Birth-Rate in Britain: The "Menace" of an Ageing Population, 1920s–1950s', *Continuity and Change*, vol.5, no.2, 1990, pp.283–305.
3. G.D. Leybourne, 'An Estimate of the Future Population of Great Britain', *Sociological Review*, vol.26, 1934, pp.128–33.
4. B.R. Mitchell, *European Historical Statistics 1750–1970*, abridged edition, London, Macmillan, 1978, p.8.
5. E. Charles, *The Twilight of Parenthood: A Biological Study of the Decline of Population Growth*, London, Watts and Co., 1934; E. Charles, *The Menace of Underpopulation*, London, Watts and Co., 1936.
6. M. Freeden, 'Eugenics and Progressive Thought', *Historical Journal*, vol.22, no.3, 1979, pp.645–71.
7. R.M. Titmuss, *Poverty and Population: A Factual Study of Contemporary Social Waste*, London, Macmillan, 1938, p.53.

8. Thane, 'The Debate on the Declining Birth-Rate', pp.288–9.
9. *Social Insurance and Allied Services*, Report by Sir William Beveridge, Cmd. 6404, London, HMSO, 1942, p.154.
10. Mass Observation, *Britain and her Birth-Rate*, London, John Murray, 1945, pp.21–5.
11. Ibid., pp.206–7.
12. E.M. Hubback, *The Population of Britain*, Harmondsworth, Penguin, 1947, p.246.
13. R.M. Titmuss, 'Pension Systems and Population Change', in Titmuss, *Essays on 'The Welfare State'*, London, George Allen & Unwin, 1958, pp.56–74 (originally published in *Political Quarterly*, vol.26, no.2, 1955).
14. *Report of the Royal Commission on Population*, Cmd. 7695, Parliamentary Papers, 1948–9, vol.19, p.4.
15. Ibid., p.38.
16. Ibid., p.41.
17. Ibid., p.100.
18. Ibid., pp.124–5.
19. Ibid., p.125.
20. Ibid., p.126.
21. Ibid., p.134.
22. Ibid.
23. A. Dummett and A. Nicol, *Subjects, Citizens and Aliens: Nationality and Immigration Law*, London, Weidenfeld & Nicolson, 1990; K. Paul, '"British Subjects" and "British Stock"; Labour's Postwar Imperialism', *Journal of British Studies*, vol.34, no.2, April 1995, pp.233–76.
24. P. Thane, 'The British Imperial State and the Construction of National Identity', in B. Melman (ed.), *Borderlines: Genders and Identities in War and Peace, 1870–1930*, London, Routledge, 1997; D. Feldman, *Englishmen and Jews: Social Relations and Political Culture, 1840–1914*, New Haven and London, Yale University Press, 1994, p.272.
25. L. Tabili, 'The Construction of Racial Difference in Twentieth-Century Britain: The Special Restriction (Coloured Alien Seamen) Order, 1925', *Journal of British Studies*, vol.33, no.1, January 1994, pp.54–98.
26. *Parliamentary Debates (Hansard), House of Commons*, vol.453, 7 July 1948, col. 386.
27. Ibid., col. 388.
28. 11 & 12 Geo. 6. Ch. 56. 1 (2), British Nationality Act, 1948.
29. Thane, 'The British Imperial State'.
30. *Report of the Royal Commission on Population*, p.148.
31. Ibid., p.156.
32. Ibid.
33. See P. Thane, 'Towards Equal Opportunities? Women Since 1945', in T. Gourvish and A. O'Day (eds.), *Britain Since 1945*, London, Macmillan, 1991, pp.183–208.
34. University of Sussex, Mass Observation Archive (MO), Topic Collection, Family Planning 1944–9, Box no.2, A.F.30C, Willesden.
35. MO Box no.1, F.25D, Bermondsey.
36. MO Box no.1, F.46C, Bermondsey.
37. MO Box no.2, file A.
38. MO Box no.2, A.F.30C, Willesden.
39. MO Box no.1, F.29D, North Circular Road.
40. MO Box no.1, F.49, Bethnal Green.

41. All interviews from MO Boxes 1 and 2.

7. Disorders of the Mind, Disorders of the Body Social: Peter Wildeblood and the Making of the Modern Homosexual

For their helpful suggestions pertaining to this chapter, I would like to thank: George Chauncey, Simon Edge, Steve Epstein, Regina Kunzel, Peter Mandler, Aron Rodrigue, Sonya Rose, Peter Stansky, James Vernon and Alan Wildblood.

1. For a summary of the trials, see P. Higgins, *Heterosexual Dictatorship: Male Homosexuality in Postwar Britain*, London, Fourth Estate, 1996, chapter 11; S. Jeffery-Poulter, *Peers, Queers, and Commons: The Struggle for Gay Law Reform from 1950 to the Present*, London, Routledge, 1991, pp.16–17, 24–7; J. Weeks, *Coming Out: Homosexual Politics in Britain from the Nineteenth Century to the Present*, second edition, London, Quartet Books, 1990, pp.159–65; P. Wildeblood, *Against the Law*, London, Weidenfeld & Nicolson, 1955.
2. Weeks, *Coming Out*, p.164; Jeffery-Poulter, *Peers, Queers, and Commons*, p.25.
3. S. Edge, 'Peter Wildeblood: Hero Without Applause', *Soundings*, no.3, Summer 1996, p.176. Edge traced Wildeblood to Victoria, British Columbia, where he recently suffered a major stroke. Patrick Higgins has recently challenged this image of Wildeblood, viewing him as a timid conformist, 'a not very attractive individual': *Heterosexual Dictatorship*, pp.247–8.
4. F. Mort, 'Sexuality: Regulation and Contestation', in Gay Left Collective (ed.), *Homosexuality: Power and Politics*, London, Allison and Busby, 1980, p.41.
5. J.T. Rees and H.V. Usill (eds.), *They Stand Apart: A Critical Survey of the Problems of Homosexuality*, London, William Heinemann, 1955, p.188.
6. On the post-war 'homosexual panic', see Higgins, *Heterosexual Dictatorship*; Jeffery-Poulter, *Peers, Queers, and Commons*, chapter 1; T. Newburn, *Permission and Regulation: Law and Morals in Post-War Britain*, London, Routledge, 1992, chap.3; A. Sinfield, *Literature, Politics and Culture in Postwar Britain*, Berkeley, University of California Press, 1989, chapter 5; Weeks, *Coming Out*, chapter 14.
7. R. Croft-Cooke, *The Verdict of You All*, London, Secker and Warburg, 1955, pp.26, 151.
8. M. Abrams, *The Population of Great Britain*, London, George Allen & Unwin, 1945, pp.32–3. See also G.F. McCleary, *Race Suicide?*, London, George Allen & Unwin, 1945, esp. p.60; Birmingham Feminist History Group, 'Feminism and Femininity in the Nineteen-Fifties', *Feminist Review*, no.3, 1979, p.58.
9. *British Medical Journal*, no.4439, 2 February 1946, p.179. See also C. Allen, *The Sexual Perversions and Abnormalities: A Study in the Psychology of Paraphilia*, second edition, London, Oxford University Press, 1949, p.140.
10. *The Times*, 5 November 1953, p.2; *News Chronicle*, 5 November 1953, p.3; *Daily Telegraph*, 5 November 1953, p.1; *Daily Herald*, 5 November 1953, p.1.
11. *Daily Mail*, 7 November 1953, p.1. See also the *Daily Mirror*, 6 November 1953, p.2.
12. *Sunday Pictorial*, 25 May 1952, pp.6, 15; 1 June 1952, p.12; 8 June 1952, p.12. On the *Pictorial*, see H. Cudlipp, *At Your Peril*, London, Weidenfeld & Nicolson, 1962, chapter 30. On the press and homosexuality, see Higgins, *Heterosexual Dictatorship*, chapter 12; F. Pearce, 'How to Be Immoral and Ill, Pathetic and Dangerous, All at the Same Time: Mass Media and the Homosexual', in S. Cohen and J. Young (eds.), *The Manufacture of*

News: Social Problems, Deviance and the Mass Media, London, Constable, 1973, pp.284–301.

13. *Daily Mirror*, 12 November 1953, p.2.

14. *Sunday Express*, 25 October 1953, p.6. See also the editorial, 'Sodom and Gomorrah', *Sunday Chronicle*, 8 November 1953, p.1. For the theme of secrecy and disclosure, see E.K. Sedgwick, *Epistemology of the Closet*, Berkeley, University of California Press, 1990, pp.71–3; N. Bartlett, *Who Was That Man? A Present for Mr Oscar Wilde*, London, Serpent's Tail, 1988, p.128. For a contemporary study of press strategies in the disclosure of homosexuality in the United States see F.A. McHenry, 'A Note on Homosexuality, Crime and the Newspapers', *Journal of Criminal Psychopathology*, vol.2, no.4, April 1941, pp.533–48.

15. E. Chesser, *Sexual Behaviour Normal and Abnormal*, London, Medical Publications Ltd., 1949, p.194. See also 'Sex and Its Problems', *The Practitioner*, vol.172, no.1030, 1954, pp.347, 372.

16. *Parliamentary Debates (Hansard), House of Commons*, vol.523, 18 February 1954, col. 229; see also vol.524, 4 March 1954, col. 1333.

17. The terms are culled from Warth's articles, cited in note 12.

18. *Observer*, 8 November 1953, p.6; 15 November 1953, p.6. See also the *Daily Telegraph*, 7 November 1953, p.6; 9 November 1953, p.6.

19. G. Westwood [Michael Schofield], *Society and the Homosexual*, London, Victor Gollancz, 1952, pp.21, 28, 184.

20. D.J. West, *Homosexuality*, London, Gerald Duckworth and Co., 1955, p.xi.

21. Westwood, *Society and the Homosexual*, p.64; see also pp.26, 36–41; West, *Homosexuality*, esp. p.xiii and chapter 6. On Ellis and Freud in Britain, see J. Marshall, 'Pansies, Perverts and Macho Men: Changing Conceptions of Male Homosexuality', in K. Plummer (ed.), *The Making of the Modern Homosexual*, London, Hutchinson, 1981, pp.133–54; C. Waters, 'Havelock Ellis, Sigmund Freud, and the State: Discourses of Homosexual Identity in Interwar Britain', in L. Bland and L. Doan (eds.), *Sexology in Culture: Labelling Bodies and Desires*, London, Polity Press, 1998, pp.165–79.

22. R. Wood, 'Some Recent Trends in Sexological Literature', *Journal of Sex Education*, vol.4, no.6, 1952, pp.244–5.

23. See J.C. Flügel, *Man, Morals and Society: A Psycho-Analytical Study*, London, Duckworth, 1945, pp.9, 15, 241; J. Bowlby, 'Psychology and Democracy', *Political Quarterly*, vol.17, no.1, January–March 1946, pp.61–76. For psychoanalytic thought in Britain in these years, see E. Glover, *The Roots of Crime: Selected Papers on Psycho-Analysis*, New York, International Universities Press, 1970, pp.60–7.

24. K. Friedlander, *The Psycho-Analytical Approach to Juvenile Delinquency*, London, Kegan Paul, Trench, Trubner and Co., 1947.

25. Allen, *Sexual Perversions*, pp.vii, 120–3, 127, 131. See also his *Homosexuality: Its Nature, Causation and Treatment*, London, Staples Press, 1958.

26. Westwood, *Society and the Homosexual*, p.84. Boothby's words in the Commons were: 'All the laws relating to this subject were enacted before any of the discoveries of modern psychology'. *Parliamentary Debates (Hansard), House of Commons*, vol.526, 28 April 1954, col. 1750. See also vol.521, 3 December 1953, col. 1297; Lord Boothby, *My Yesterday, Your Tomorrow*, London, Hutchinson, 1962, pp.40–4.

27. The Church of England Moral Welfare Council, *The Problem of Homosexuality*, 1954, pp.6–10.

28. K. Soddy, 'Homosexuality', *The Lancet*, vol.267, no.6837, 1954, p.546.

29. *The Criminal Law and Sexual Offenders: A Report from the Joint Committee on Psychiatry and the Law Appointed by the British Medical Association and the Magistrates' Association*, London, British Medical Association, 1949, p.24.
30. C. Binney, *Crime and Abnormality*, London, Oxford University Press, 1949, pp.166–70; *Parliamentary Papers (Hansard), House of Commons*, vol.521, 10 December 1953, cols. 2160–1; vol.525, 16 March 1954, col. 26; W.N. East, *Sexual Offenders*, London, Delisle, 1955, p.87.
31. Wildeblood, *Against the Law*, pp.1–2.
32. Rolf, 'Vor dem Gesetz geächtet', *Der Kreis*, vol.29, no.4, April 1961, p.2.
33. Wildeblood, *Against the Law*, p.178.
34. See E. Cohen, *Talk on the Wilde Side: Toward a Genealogy of a Discourse on Male Sexualities*, London, Routledge, 1993. For late nineteenth-century attempts to map the homosexual as a distinct type of person see M. Foucault, *The History of Sexuality*, volume one, *An Introduction*, New York, Pantheon, 1978.
35. *People*, 24 January 1954, p.1.
36. *Sunday Pictorial*, 24 January 1954, p.3.
37. *Daily Herald*, 20 March 1954, p.2. To make Wildeblood appear effeminate, the *Daily Mirror* published a photograph of him that had been doctored (19 March 1954, p.6). On homosexuality and effeminacy see A. Sinfield, *The Wilde Century: Effeminacy, Oscar Wilde and the Queer Moment*, New York, Columbia University Press, 1994.
38. Wildeblood, *Against the Law*, p.7; also pp.5–6, 24.
39. Westwood, *Society and the Homosexual*, pp.31, 20.
40. Wildeblood, *Against the Law*, p.187.
41. *News of the World*, 21 March 1954, p.2.
42. St. J. Ervine, *Oscar Wilde: A Present Time Appraisal*, London, George Allen & Unwin, 1951, pp.163, 174, 333.
43. G. Gorer, 'The Perils of Hypergamy' (1957), reprinted in Gorer, *The Danger of Equality and Other Essays*, London, Cresset Press, 1966, pp.242–7.
44. Wildeblood, *Against the Law*, p.25.
45. G.T. Kempe, 'The Homosexual in Society', *British Journal of Delinquency*, vol.5, no.1, 1954, p.4.
46. S.C. Lewsen, in the *British Journal of Delinquency*, vol.9, no.1, 1958, p.75.
47. *News of the World*, 21 March 1954, p.2; *Daily Mail*, 23 March 1954, p.5; *Daily Herald*, 23 March 1954, p.5.
48. *Daily Sketch*, 19 March 1954, p.3.
49. Wildeblood, *Against the Law*, pp.2, 11; Wildeblood's statement to the Departmental Committee on Homosexual Offences and Prostitution, p.8, PRO HO 345/8/51 (hereafter 'Statement'); Wildeblood's interview with members of the Departmental Committee on Homosexual Offences and Prostitution, 24 May 1955, p.25, PRO HO345/13/24 (hereafter 'Interview').
50. Wildeblood, *Against the Law*, pp.106–7; 'Statement', p.1; 'Interview', pp.2–4.
51. Wildeblood, *Against the Law*, pp.3–4, 8, 16–17, 91.
52. Ibid., pp.34, 111. His reference to the *Sunday Times* was to an editorial that appeared on 28 March 1954, p.6.
53. *Daily Mail*, 25 March 1954, p.2; *The Times*, 25 March 1954, p.4; 'Interview', p.24.
54. 'Cover Profile: Peter Wildeblood', *Mattachine Review*, vol.5, no.11, November 1959, p.7.
55. P. Wildeblood, 'Letter to an American Mom', *Man and Society*, vol.2, no.2, 1962, p.27.

For Freud's letter, see H. Abelove, 'Freud, Male Homosexuality, and the Americans', in H. Abelove, M.A. Barale and D.M. Halperin (eds.), *The Lesbian and Gay Studies Reader*, New York, Routledge, 1993.

56. 'Interview', p.23. On the 'coming out' story see K. Plummer, *Telling Sexual Stories: Power, Change and Social Worlds*, London, Routledge, 1995, chapter 6. On the links between the press, medical science and narratives of homosexual selfhood see L. Duggan, 'The Trials of Alice Mitchell: Sensationalism, Sexology, and the Lesbian Subject in Turn-of-the-Century America', *Signs*, vol.18, no.4, Summer 1993, pp.791–814.

57. A. Giddens, *The Transformation of Intimacy: Sexuality, Love, and Eroticism in Modern Societies*, Cambridge, Polity Press, 1992, p.29. See also S. Lash and J. Friedman (eds.), *Modernity and Identity*, Oxford, Blackwell, 1992.

58. E.M. Forster, *Maurice*, New York, New American Library, 1971, p.254.

8. The Labour Party: Modernisation and the Politics of Restraint

Some of the themes of this chapter were initially explored in papers presented at Dalhousie University in February 1997 and Stanford University in May 1997. I would like to thank the faculty and students of both institutions for helpful comments. Thanks are also owed to: Stephen Brooke, Sam Goodfellow, Destiny McDonald, Michael Roberts and Peter Stansky.

1. M. Foot, *Aneurin Bevan, vol.2, 1945–1960*, London, Davis-Poynter, 1973, pp.237–44.

2. S. Fielding, P. Thompson and N. Tiratsoo, *'England Arise!' The Labour Party and Popular Politics in 1940s Britain*, Manchester, Manchester University Press, 1995, pp.83–91.

3. G.L. Mosse, *The Image of Man: The Creation of Modern Masculinity*, New York, Oxford University Press, 1996, p.59.

4. For example, Attlee's temperate reply to Churchill's 'Gestapo' scare in the 1945 general election, C.R. Attlee, *Purpose and Policy: Selected Speeches*, London, Hutchinson, 1946, p.3. Or the labelling of Churchill as a 'warmonger' in the 1951 election campaign, *Daily Mirror*, 25 October 1951, p.1.

5. M. Francis, 'Morality, Masculinity and Public Service in Twentieth Century Britain', unpublished paper delivered at Stanford University, 6 May 1997, pp.6–8.

6. P. Mandler and S. Pedersen, 'Introduction: The British Intelligentsia After the Victorians,' in S. Pedersen and P. Mandler (eds.), *After the Victorians: Private Conscience and Public Duty in Modern Britain, Essays in Memory of John Clive*, London and New York, Routledge, 1994, p.24.

7. C.Z. Stearns and P.N. Stearns, *In Anger: The Struggle for Emotional Control in America's History*, Chicago, University of Chicago Press, 1986, pp.163–71.

8. J. Morgan (ed.), *The Backbench Diaries of Richard Crossman*, London, Hamish Hamilton, 1981, p.410; D. Jay, *Change and Fortune: A Political Record*, London, Hutchinson, 1980, p.223.

9. B. Pimlott (ed.), *The Political Diary of Hugh Dalton*, London, Jonathan Cape, 1986, p.539.

10. S. Gubar, '"This Is My Rifle, This Is My Gun": World War Two and the Blitz on Women', in M. Higonnet et al. (eds.), *Behind the Lines: Gender and the Two World Wars*, New Haven, Yale University Press, 1987.

11. See J. Smith, 'Juvenile Delinquency', *Labour Woman*, April 1949, p.76; G. Tomlinson,

'Foreword', Ministry of Education, *Citizens Growing Up*, London, HMSO, 1949, p.7.
12. M. Landy, *British Genres: Cinema and Society, 1930–1960*, Princeton, Princeton University Press, 1991, pp.442–3, 445–7, 465–7, 452–3.
13. J. Bowlby, *Forty-Four Juvenile Thieves: Their Characters and Home Life*, London, Tyndall and Cox, 1946.
14. Reproduced in J. Bonham, *The Middle-Class Vote*, London, Faber, 1954, p.127.
15. N. Tiratsoo and J. Tomlinson, *Industrial Efficiency and State Intervention: Labour, 1939–51*, London, Routledge, 1993, pp.111–30.
16. B. Pimlott, *Harold Wilson*, London, HarperCollins, 1992, pp.217–18.
17. H. Morrison, *The Peaceful Revolution*, London, George Allen & Unwin, 1949, p.77. See also R.S. Cripps, *Democracy Alive*, London, Sidgwick and Jackson, 1946, p.81.
18. Pimlott, *Wilson*, pp.97, 106, 151.
19. C. Mayhew, *Time to Explain: An Autobiography*, London, Hutchinson, 1987, p.88.
20. Ibid., pp.90–1.
21. M. Veldman, *Fantasy, The Bomb and the Greening of Britain: Romantic Protest, 1945–1980*, Cambridge, Cambridge University Press, 1994, pp.156, 201–3.
22. M. Francis, *Ideas and Policies Under Labour, 1945–1951*, Manchester, Manchester University Press, 1997, pp.49–58.
23. Stearns and Stearns, *In Anger*, pp.2, 10–11.
24. A. Light, *Forever England: Femininity, Literature and Conservatism between the Wars*, London, Routledge, 1991.
25. Mosse, *Image of Man*, pp.17–106.
26. I. Mikardo, *Backbencher*, London, Weidenfeld & Nicolson, 1988, p.129.
27. P. Higgins, *Heterosexual Dictatorship: Male Homosexuality in Post-War Britain*, London, Fourth Estate, 1996, p.33.
28. Ibid., pp.285–6.
29. G. Gorer, *Exploring English Character*, New York, Criterion Books, 1955, pp.13–18, 285–90.
30. A. Lant, *Blackout: Reinventing Women for Wartime British Cinema*, Princeton, Princeton University Press, 1991. Although note that Lant fails to consider the Gainsborough costume dramas, which were far from restrained in plot or costume, P. Cook, *Fashioning the Nation: Costume and National Identity in British Cinema*, London, British Film Institute, 1996.
31. H. Morrison, *An Autobiography*, London, Odhams, 1960, p.323.
32. T. Benn, *Years of Hope: Diaries, Papers and Letters, 1940–1962*, London, Hutchinson, 1994, p.145; Jay, *Change and Fortune*, p.206.
33. J. Campbell, *Nye Bevan and the Mirage of British Socialism*, London, Weidenfeld & Nicolson, 1987, p.188.
34. R. Wilkinson, *American Tough: The Tough-Guy Tradition and American Character*, New York, Harper and Row, 1986, p.10.
35. The Earl of Birkenhead, *Halifax*, London, Hamish Hamilton, 1966, pp.479–80.
36. R.M. Fried, *Nightmare in Red: The McCarthy Era in Perspective*, Oxford, Oxford University Press, 1990.
37. Quoted in B. Brivati, *Hugh Gaitskell*, London, Richard Cohen, 1996, p.176.
38. Morrison, *Autobiography*, pp.328, 265.
39. Benn, *Years of Hope*, p.277.
40. Jay, *Change and Fortune*, p.247.

41. H. Gaitskell, *Recent Developments in British Socialist Thinking*, London, Co-operative Union, 1956, p.13.
42. H. Dalton to C.A.R. Crosland, n.d. [1956], British Library of Political and Economic Science, Crosland Papers 13/8.
43. See A. J. Ayer, Preface to *Language, Truth and Logic*, second edition, Harmondsworth, Penguin, 1946.
44. E. Summerskill, *A Woman's World: Her Memoirs*, London, Heinemann, 1967, p.62.
45. P. Brown, *The Body and Society*, New York, Columbia University Press, 1988.
46. Pimlott, *Political Diary*, p.582.
47. Benn, *Years of Hope*, p.149.
48. H. Boardman, *The Glory of Parliament*, London, George Allen & Unwin, 1960, p.133.
49. Benn, *Years of Hope*, p.152.
50. P. Perrot, *Fashioning the Bourgeoisie: A History of Clothing in the Nineteenth Century*, Princeton, Princeton University Press, 1994, p.30.
51. E. Wilson, *Adorned in Dreams: Fashion and Modernity*, London, Virago, 1985, pp.216–18.
52. J. Harvey, *Men In Black*, London, Reaktion Books, 1995.
53. R.P. Rubinstein, *Dress Codes: Meanings and Messages in American Culture*, Boulder, Westview, 1995, pp.57–8.
54. J. Parker, *Father of the House*, London, Routledge, 1982, p.130.
55. A. Horne, *Harold Macmillan, vol.1: 1894–1956*, New York, Macmillan, 1989, p.338.
56. D. Hughes, 'The Spivs', in M. Sissons and P. French (eds.), *The Age of Austerity, 1945–51*, Harmondsworth, Penguin, 1964, pp.87–9.
57. P. Rock and S. Cohen, 'The Teddy Boy', in V. Bogdanor and R. Skidelsky (eds.), *The Age of Affluence, 1951–1964*, Macmillan, 1970, pp.289–91.
58. C. Waters, 'Disorders of the Mind, Disorders of the Body Social: Peter Wildeblood and the Making of the Modern Homosexual', in this volume.
59. F. Mort and P. Thompson, 'Retailing, Commercial Culture and Masculinity in 1950s Britain: The Case of Montague Burton, the "Tailor of Taste"', *History Workshop Journal*, no.38, Autumn 1994, p.121.
60. E. Wilkinson, 'Introduction' to C. Clemens, *The Man From Limehouse: Clement Richard Attlee*, Webster Groves, Mark Twain Society, 1946, p.xiii.
61. Mayhew, *Time To Explain*, p.121.
62. Clemens, *Man From Limehouse*, p.13.
63. J.A. Mangan and J. Walvin (eds.), *Manliness and Morality*, Manchester, Manchester University Press, 1987.
64. Clemens, *Man From Limehouse*, p.137.
65. Ibid., p.133.
66. Pimlott, *Political Diary*, p.623; See also Jay, *Change and Fortune*, p.136.
67. J. Griffiths, *Pages From Memory*, London, Dent, 1969, p.54.
68. Pimlott, *Political Diary*, pp.621, 671.
69. D. Jay, *Socialism in the New Society*, London, Longman, 1962, pp.384–5.
70. Brivati, *Gaitskell*, pp.23, 155–59.
71. S. Crosland, *Tony Crosland*, London, Jonathan Cape, 1982, p.90. See also Benn, *Years of Hope*, p.349.
72. Foot, *Bevan*, p.450.
73. Bevan himself claimed he was not referring to Gaitskell, ibid., p.452.
74. H. Gaitskell, 'Foreword' to E. Durbin, *The Politics of Democratic Socialism*, London,

Routledge, 1957 edition, p.9.

75. P.M. Williams (ed.), *The Diary of Hugh Gaitskell*, London, Jonathan Cape, 1983, p.293.
76. Brivati, *Gaitskell*, pp.273, 285–6.
77. A. O'Shea, 'English Subjects of Modernity', in M. Nava and A. O'Shea (eds.), *Modern Times: Reflections on a Century of English Modernity*, London, Routledge, 1996, pp.22–23, 31–32.
78. W. Susman, 'Personality and the Making of Twentieth-Century Culture', in W. Susman, *Culture as History*, New York, Pantheon, 1984.
79. N. Tiratsoo, *Reconstruction, Affluence and Labour Politics: Coventry, 1945–60*, London, Routledge, 1990, pp.117–20.
80. Brivati, *Gaitskell*, pp.240–1, 245–7, 429.
81. D. de Marly, *Fashion For Men: An Illustrated History*, London, Batsford, 1985, p.133.
82. J. Ramsden, *The Age of Churchill and Eden, 1940–1957*, London, Longman, 1995, p.244. See also Benn, *Years of Hope*, p.291.
83. D. Butler and R. Rose, *The British General Election of 1959*, London, Macmillan, 1960, p.86.
84. E. Shils, 'Britain Awake!', in P. Hall (ed.), *Labour's New Frontiers*, London, André Deutsch, 1964, pp.7,12,15.
85. Pimlott, *Wilson*, pp.266–8.
86. P. Paterson, *Tired and Emotional: The Life of Lord George-Brown*, London, Chatto and Windus, 1993, p.8.
87. Pimlott, *Wilson*, p.268.
88. O'Shea, 'English Subjects', p.19.

9. 'New Conservatism'? *The Industrial Charter*, Modernity and the Reconstruction of British Conservatism after the War

I would like to thank Martin Francis and Ina Zweiniger-Bargielowska for reading and commenting on earlier versions of this chapter.

1. J. Ramsden, *The Age of Churchill and Eden, 1940–1957*, London, Longman, 1995, p.94.
2. Lord Butler, *The Art of the Possible*, London, Hamish Hamilton, 1971, p.126.
3. H. Macmillan, *Tides of Fortune, 1945–1955*, London, Macmillan, 1969, p.289.
4. Ibid., p.292.
5. Earl of Woolton, *The Memoirs of the Rt. Hon. Earl of Woolton*, London, Cassell, 1959, pp.336–7.
6. Ramsden, *The Age of Churchill and Eden*, pp.109–21.
7. Ibid., pp.118–19.
8. *Interim and Final Reports of the Committee on Party Organisation*, London, Conservative Central Office, 1949.
9. Byron Criddle, 'Members of Parliament', in A. Seldon and S. Ball (eds.), *Conservative Century, The Conservative Party Since 1900*, Oxford, Oxford University Press, 1994, pp.160–2. See also D. Butler and M. Pinto-Duschinsky, 'The Conservative Elite 1918–78: Does Unrepresentativeness Matter?' in Z. Layton-Henry (ed.), *Conservative Party Politics*, London, Macmillan, 1980.
10. Oliver Lyttelton, 1st Viscount Chandos (1893–1972) had served as the managing direc-

tor of the British Metal Corporation before the war. He entered politics in 1939, becoming President of the Board of Trade in October 1940. He remained closely identified with City interests, an association which prevented his becoming Chancellor of the Exchequer in 1951.

11. Conservative Party Archives (CPA) CRD2/7/56, 10 February 1946 and 5 November 1946.
12. CPA CRD2/50/11 (1), 17 October 1946.
13. See CPA CRD2/7/30 (1), 5 August 1947, letter from Johannes Vedel of the Danish *Konservative Vaelgerforening*.
14. For example, CPA CRD2/7/2, the *Belgian Worker's Charter*. CRD2/7/4, which contains the papers of the Parliamentary Labour Committee, 1949–64, includes analyses of the industrial relations machinery in other Northern European countries.
15. CPA CRD2/7/56, 10 February 1946.
16. CPA CRD2/7/51, 6 December 1946.
17. Conservative Party, *The Industrial Charter*, London, 1947, pp.3–4, 6, 9–10, 14–16, 28.
18. Ibid., pp.3–6.
19. CPA CRD2/7/57, 27 March 1947, minutes of the IPC.
20. See correspondence in CPA CRD2/7/30 (1).
21. CPA CRD2/7/29, July 1947.
22. The Progress Trust, which still exists, was founded in 1943 with the objective of promoting liberal ideology within the party as a counter to the influence of the Beveridge Report.
23. CPA CRD2/7/31 (2), March 1948, CRD classification of comments on and criticisms of *The Industrial Charter*. The MP Thomas Galbraith signed his name to the Progress Trust memorandum. I believe that he was the present chairman of the Trust.
24. S. Fielding, P. Thompson and N. Tiratsoo, *'England Arise!' The Labour Party and Popular Politics in 1940s Britain*, Manchester, Manchester University Press, 1995.
25. CPA CRD2/7/52, 19 April 1947.
26. CPA CRD2/7/29, 1 September 1947, Mass Observation, *A Report on the Industrial Charter*, pp.1–3.
27. Ibid., p.4.
28. Ibid., p.6.
29. See Fielding, Thompson and Tiratsoo, *'England Arise!'*.
30. CPA CRD2/7/1, 12 January 1948, Fraser memorandum on Mass Observation Report.
31. Ibid.
32. Report, p.9.
33. Ibid., p.12.
34. Ibid.
35. CPA CRD2/7/1, 11 November, 1947, Stelling to Clarke.
36. CPA ACP/1/3, 29 January 1948.
37. CPA CRD2/7/30 (1), 13 June 1947, York to Butler.
38. CPA CRD2/7/42 (2), 23 March 1948, Minutes of Meeting with Aims of Industry.
39. 'Mr Cube' was the cartoon logo used by Aims of Industry from 1949 in its successful campaign against nationalisation of the sugar industry.
40. CPA CCO4/2/88, 29 March 1949, Mark Chapman-Walder to James Hutchison.
41. CPA CRD2/7/7, 13 February 1952, Dear Report on Co-partnership.
42. CPA CRD2/7/7, 1 April 1953, B. Godman Irvine [Wood Green] to the CRD.

43. See CPA CRD2/7/7, correspondence with John Sadd, November/December 1954.
44. CPA CRD2/50/13, 30 March 1949, Clarke to Stephen Pierssene.
45. CPA CRD2/7/6, 4 January 1950, text of speech for Malcolm McCorquodale.
46. See the *Spectator*, 28 April to 19 May 1924.

10. Reveries of Race: The Closing of the Imperial Moment

1. D. Hebdige, *Subculture: The Meaning of Style*, London, Methuen, 1979, p.45 and *Hiding in the Light: On Images and Things*, London, Routledge, 1988.
2. R. Wollheim, 'Babylon, Babylone', *Encounter*, May 1962.
3. E.J. Hobsbawm, *Nations and Nationalism Since 1780: Programme, Myth, Reality*, Cambridge, Cambridge University Press, 1990, p.14; B. Anderson, *Imagined Communities: Reflections on the Origins and Spread of Nationalism*, London, Verso, 1983.
4. See in this context P. Cohen, 'Subcultural Conflict and Working-Class Community', in P. Cohen, *Rethinking the Youth Question: Education, Labour and Cultural Studies*, London, Macmillan, 1997.
5. I have argued this more fully in B. Schwarz, 'The "Re-racialization" of England, 1956–68', *Race and Class*, vol.38, no.1, 1996, pp.65–78.
6. W.K. Hancock, *Smuts: The Sanguine Years, 1870–1919*, Cambridge, Cambridge University Press, 1962, p.215.
7. W.K. Hancock and J. Van Der Poel (eds.), *Selections from the Smuts Papers*, vol.1, June 1886–May 1902, Cambridge, Cambridge University Press, 1966, p.82.
8. J.C. Smuts, *Jan Christian Smuts*, London, Cassell, 1952, p.124.
9. J. Van Der Poel (ed.), *Selections from the Smuts Papers*, vol.5, September 1919–November 1934, Cambridge, Cambridge University Press, 1973, p.436.
10. N. Levi, *Jan Smuts*, London, Longman, 1917, p.293; R. Hyam, *The Failure of South African Expansion, 1908–48*, London, Macmillan, 1972, p.66.
11. The friend was Lady Daphne Moore, wife of the Governor-General and Commander-in-Chief of Kenya, 1943-9. See P. Beukes, *The Holistic Smuts: A Study in Personality*, Cape Town, Human and Rousseau, 1990, p.186.
12. H. Smith, 'Apartheid, Sharpeville and "Impartiality": The Reporting of South Africa on BBC Television, 1948–61', *Historical Journal of Film, Radio and Television*, vol.13, no.3, 1993, p.293.
13. H.C. Armstrong, *Grey Steel (Jan Christian Smuts): A Study in Arrogance*, Harmondsworth, Penguin, 1939.
14. Smuts, *Jan Christian Smuts*, p.423.
15. J. Barnes and D. Nicholson (eds.), *The Empire at Bay: The Leo Amery Diaries, 1929–1945*, London, Hutchinson, pp.839–40, entry for 21 October 1942; R. Rhodes James (ed.), *Chips: The Diaries of Sir Henry Channon*, Harmondsworth, Penguin, 1984, pp.415–16, 418–19, entries for 21 October 1942 and 17 November 1942.
16. G. Orwell, *The War Commentaries*, W.J. West (ed.), New York, Schocken, 1986, p.172.
17. J.C. Smuts, 'Reflections on World Affairs', *The Listener*, 3 October 1946, p.428.
18. P.B. Blanckenberg, *The Thoughts of General Smuts*, Cape Town, Juta, 1951, p.30; Van Der Poel (ed.), *Smuts Papers*, vol.5, p.443.
19. Smuts' comment on Lloyd George is apposite: 'History will show him the biggest Englishman of all', quoted in F.S. Crafford, *Jan Smuts: A Biography*, London, George Allen

& Unwin, 1946, p.14

20. H. Smith, 'Apartheid, Sharpeville and "Impartiality"', p.254.
21. *The Times*, 12 September 1950.
22. *Parliamentary Debates (Hansard), House of Commons*, vol.478, col.1098, 13 September 1950.
23. *Parliamentary Debates (Hansard), House of Commons*, vol.488, cols.1225–6, 7 June 1951.
24. *Parliamentary Debates (Hansard), House of Commons*, vol.503, cols.449–50, 2 July 1952.
25. Ibid., col.451.
26. Ibid., col.452.
27. Ibid., col.453.
28. J. Epstein, *An Autobiography*, London, Art Treasures Book Club, 1963 (first published 1955), p.150.
29. *The Times*, 18 July 1956.
30. Lord Moran, *Winston Churchill: The Struggle for Survival, 1940–1965*, London, Sphere, 1968, p.74.
31. *The Times*, 8 November 1956.
32. J. Street, 'Shock Waves: The Authoritative Response to Popular Music', in D. Strinati and S. Wagg (eds.), *Come On Down? Popular Media Culture in Postwar Britain*, London, Routledge, 1992, p.305 (the reference is from 12 May 1956).
33. M. Perham, *The Colonial Reckoning*, London, Collins, 1962, p.155.
34. *The Times*, 4 September 1956. This phenomenon was not restricted to East London. Three youths in Twickenham were bound over for singing rock and roll songs. 'It was said that people opened their windows and told them to be quiet, but they refused.'
35. During Suez, the connection between decolonisation and immigration did enter the popular imagination. At a pro-war demonstration in Oxford on 4 November placards were seen declaring: 'We want war'; 'Wogs go home'; and 'Shoot the wogs', letter from the indefatigable Nicolas Walter, and others, to the *Manchester Guardian*, 5 November 1956.
36. W.E.B. DuBois, 'The Negro Mind Reaches Out', in Alain Locke (ed.), *The New Negro: An Interpretation*, New York, Johnson, 1968, pp.401–2.
37. Nelson Mandela, *Long Walk to Freedom*, London, Little, Brown, 1994, p.29. In 1985 Zenani Mandela and Oliver Tambo unveiled a bust of Mandela on the South Bank.

11. New Towns for Old: The Fate of the Town Centre

I am more than usually indebted to Andrew Saint for comments on an early draft of this chapter, but he is also more than usually exempted from responsibility for the final version.

1. See J.B. Cullingworth, *New Towns for Old: The Problem of Urban Renewal*, London, Fabian Society, May 1962; W. Burns, *New Towns for Old: The Technique of Urban Renewal*, London, Leonard Hill, 1963.
2. The trailblazers of this diagnosis were D.L. Foley, *Controlling London's Growth: Planning the Great Wen 1940–1960*, Berkeley, University of California Press, 1963; P. Hall, *London 2000*, London, Faber, 1963; and P. Hall et al., *The Containment of Urban England*, two vols., London, George Allen & Unwin, 1973.
3. cf. A. Ravetz, *Remaking Cities*, London, Croom Helm, 1980, and (a highly sophisticated treatment) *The Government of Space: Town Planning in Modern Society*, London, Faber, 1986.

4. See the suggestive comparative comments of D.H. McKay in his own contributions to his edited volume, *Planning and Politics in Western Europe*, London, Macmillan, 1982.

5. J.M. Diefendorf (ed.), *Rebuilding Europe's Bombed Cities*, London, Macmillan, 1990; M. Konukiewitz and H. Wollmann, 'Physical Planning in a Federal System: The Case of West Germany', in McKay (ed.), *Planning and Politics*; J.M. Diefendorf, *In the Wake of War: The Reconstruction of German Cities after World War II*, New York, Oxford University Press, 1993.

6. B. Larsson and O. Thomassen, 'Urban Planning in Denmark', in T. Hall (ed.), *Planning and Urban Growth in the Nordic Countries*, London, E. & F. N. Spon, 1991, pp.30–2; L. Grebler, *Urban Renewal in European Countries: Its Emergence and Potentials*, Philadelphia, University of Pennsylvania Press, 1964, pp.100–3.

7. D. Hardy, *From New Towns to Green Politics: Campaigning for Town and Country Planning, 1946–1990*, London, E. & F.N. Spon, 1991, pp.50–2.

8. Foley, *Controlling London's Growth*, pp.44–5, 57–8; Hall et al., *Containment*, vol.1, p.457, vol.2, pp.366–7; Ravetz, *Remaking Cities*, pp.21–3.

9. See a rare early admission of this point in Ravetz, *Remaking Cities*, pp.46–7.

10. McKay (ed.), *Planning and Politics*, p.172.

11. *Architectural Review*, vol.90, 1941, pp.35–6.

12. Ministry of Town and Country Planning, *Advisory Handbook on the Redevelopment of Central Areas*, London, HMSO, 1947, pp.2–3, 7, 52, 54, 72–3. Gordon Stephenson, co–author of this handbook with W.G. Holford, proposed to extend these recommendations into the idea of the 'special zone' in the historic centre, an idea which was vetoed by cost-sensitive civil servants but which much later resurfaced as the conservation area, see G.E. Cherry and L. Penny, *Holford: A Study in Architecture, Planning and Civic Design*, London, Mansell, 1986, p.277.

13. L. Esher, *A Broken Wave: The Rebuilding of England 1940–1980*, London, Allen Lane, 1981, pp.44–6. In his comments Esher was torn between his own modernist instincts and his horror at what he thought modernism had done to the English town after the mid-1950s.

14. See the range of examples interestingly documented in Diefendorf, *In the Wake of War*, pp.67–107; what Diefendorf evidently considers only a partial victory for preservationism appears, compared to Britain, as a remarkable triumph.

15. T. Hall, 'Concluding Remarks: Is There a Nordic Planning Tradition?', in Hall (ed.), *Planning and Urban Growth*, pp.253–4; Grebler, *Urban Renewal*, pp.38–9.

16. The scale of this U-turn is, naturally, rarely acknowledged by those who pin so much significance on the 1947 system. Thus Foley, *Controlling London's Growth*, p.61, comments lightly that the 1947 Act was 'supplemented by' Acts of 1953, 1954 and 1959.

17. For an excellent survey of these changes, properly acknowledging the broader political (rather than narrowly technical and professional) context see A. Cox, *Adversary Politics and Land: The Conflict over Land and Property Policy in Post-War Britain*, Cambridge, Cambridge University Press, 1984, pp.103–14. For contemporary comments on the 'dismantling' of the planning apparatus, see P. Self, 'Town Planning in Retreat', *Political Quarterly*, vol.27, 1956, pp.209–15, and the views of Robert Matthew in *The Living Town*, London, Royal Institute of British Architects, 1959, pp.14–16.

18. Hoskins at a symposium on 'Perils and Prospects in Town and Country', in the *Journal of the Royal Society of Arts*, vol.105, 1956–7, pp.82–3; others at the same symposium echoed his concerns, as did those at the founding conference of the Civic Trust, July 1957. See also, on comparisons between 'civic pride' in Britain and elsewhere, J.

Holliday, 'British City Centre Planning', in J. Holliday (ed.), *City Centre Redevelopment*, London, Charles Knight, 1973, p.24; McKay (ed.), *Planning and Politics*, pp.173–4.

19. C. Applegate, *A Nation of Provincials: The German Idea of Heimat*, Berkeley, University of California Press, 1990.

20. Hall et al., *Containment*, vol.1, pp.547–8, vol.2, pp.78, 86.

21. The best accounts of these developments are still the near-contemporary ones, despite their polemical nature: C. Booker and C. Lycett Green, *Goodbye London: An Illustrated Guide to Threatened Buildings*, London, Fontana, 1973; S. Jenkins, *A City at Risk: A Contemporary Look at London's Streets*, London, Hutchinson, 1970, and *Landlords to London: The Story of a Capital and its Growth*, London, Constable, 1975; and especially O. Marriott, *The Property Boom*, London, Hamish Hamilton, 1967.

22. Grebler, *Urban Renewal*, pp.116–19.

23. Marriott, *The Property Boom*, p.172. But see John Earl's defence of the Historic Buildings Section's efforts in 'London Government: A Record of Custodianship', in M. Hunter (ed.), *Preserving the Past: The Rise of Heritage in Modern Britain*, Stroud, Alan Sutton, 1996, pp.71–3.

24. On St. Paul's, see Cherry and Penny, *Holford*, pp.160–73; Jenkins, *Landlords to London*, pp.222–6, on the LCC's general inability to control plot ratios.

25. S. Jenkins, *The Selling of Mary Davies and Other Writings*, London, John Murray, 1993, p.74.

26. Planners of all stripes agreed that public interest in planning had gone into sharp decline by the early 1950s. See, for example, the discussion of 'Planning and the Public' at the Town Planning Institute, reported in 'Declining Public Enthusiasm for Planning', *The Builder*, 26 December 1952, pp.948–9.

27. Ravetz, *Government of Space*, pp.87–8; Holliday, 'British City Centre Planning', p.13.

28. As with London, the redevelopment of provincial towns has as yet only been surveyed in polemical works: T. Aldous, *Goodbye, Britain?*, London, Sidgwick and Jackson, 1975; C. Amery and D. Cruickshank, *The Rape of Britain*, London, Paul Elek, 1975; A. Fergusson and T. Mowl, *The Sack of Bath – And After*, Wilton, Michael Russell, 1989. For the counter-example of Norwich see the report of its City Architect, David Percival, in *The Living Town*, pp.8–9.

29. On the shift to 'growthism', which caught most planners by surprise, see Holliday, 'British City Centre Planning', pp.7–13; Ravetz, *Remaking Cities*, pp.98–101.

30. Marriott, *The Property Boom*, p.239.

31. T. Knight, *Let Our Cities Live*, London, Conservative Political Centre for the Bow Group, 1960, pp.6, 8. Similar sentiments can be found in contemporary statements from socialist planners; see also Burns, *New Towns*, pp.9–10.

32. Quotes from W. Burns, *Newcastle: A Study in Replanning at Newcastle Upon Tyne*, London, Leonard Hill, 1967, pp.25–36; Knight, *Let Our Cities Live*, pp.27–30.

33. Critics who have focused on the planners' role may acknowledge the 'democratic' pressure for growth without giving it its due weight: Foley, *Controlling London's Growth*, pp.83–4; Hall et al., *Containment*, vol.2, pp.86–8.

34. Often noted at the time, even by those critical of the schemes' 'clean-sweep' approach, see, for example, *Urban Redevelopment: Report of a Committee Appointed by the Civic Trust*, Civic Trust, 1962, p.19; Cullingworth, *New Towns for Old*, p.7.

35. P. Dunleavy, *The Politics of Mass Housing in Britain, 1945–1975*, Oxford, Clarendon Press, 1981, based in large part on the avalanche of polemical studies defending 'traditional communities' in the 1970s, established the orthodoxy that tower blocks stemmed

from a combination of private greed, public paternalism and arrogant expertise — in other words, democracy had nothing to do with it. This view has now been countered, most impressively, by M. Glendinning and S. Muthesius, *Tower Block: Modern Public Housing in England, Scotland, Wales and Northern Ireland*, New Haven and London, Yale University Press, 1994.

36. L. Brett, 'New Cities for Old', *The Times*, 14 June 1960, p.13.
37. Burns, *New Towns*, p.64.
38. Marriott, *The Property Boom*, pp.239–50.
39. Cherry and Penny, *Holford*, pp.176–92; J.F.Q. Switzer, *Town Centre Redevelopment*, Cambridge University, Department of Land Economy, February 1963; J. Simmie, *Power, Property and Corporatism: The Political Sociology of Planning*, London, Macmillan, 1981, pp.169–88.
40. S. Andreae, 'From Comprehensive Development to Conservation Areas', in Hunter (ed.), *Preserving the Past*, pp.135–55.
41. A. Sutcliffe, *The Autumn of Central Paris: The Defeat of Town Planning 1850–1970*, London, Edward Arnold, 1970 (note the telling sub-title).
42. Most prominently in Germany: L. Holzner, 'The Role of History and Tradition in the Urban Geography of West Germany', *Annals of the Association of American Geographers*, vol.60, 1970, pp.315–39; Diefendorf, *In the Wake of War*, pp.67–107.
43. J.M. Miller (ed.), *New Life for Cities Around the World*, New York, Books International, 1959, pp.58–62.
44. Ravetz, *Government of Space*, p.129.

12. 'Here is the Modern World Itself': The Festival of Britain's Representations of the Future

This chapter is based on research conducted for my Ph.D. thesis which was funded by the Social Science Research Council (New York) and the University of Michigan, Ann Arbor. For their help with this chapter I would like to thank: Laura Lee Downs, Geoff Eley, Peter Mandler, Sonya Rose, Adam Tooze, James Vernon, and Arthur and Peggy Wynn.

* J. Bronowski, 'The Story the Exhibition Tells', Introduction to the guide-catalogue for the Science Exhibition, in M. Banham and B. Hillier (eds.), *A Tonic to the Nation: The Festival of Britain, 1951*, London, Thames & Hudson, with the co-operation of the Victoria and Albert Museum, 1976, p.144.

1. R. Hewison, *Culture and Consensus: England, Art and Politics Since 1940*, London, Methuen, 1995, p.59.
2. I. Cox, 'The Story the Exhibition Tells: F.S. Campania, Festival of Britain 1951', n.d., PRO WORK 25/21, p.4.
3. 'Proposals Regarding the 1951 Exhibition: Draft Memorandum by the Lord President of the Council', June 1947, PRO EL 6/21.
4. I. Ebong, 'The Origins and Significance of the Festival of Britain, 1951', unpublished Ph.D. thesis, University of Edinburgh, 1986, p.50.
5. M. Nicholson, quoted in Ebong, 'The Origins', p.51.
6. Sir H. Casson, quoted by Hillier, 'Introduction', in Banham and Hillier (eds.), *A Tonic*

to the Nation, p.15.

7. Sir P. Wright, in an interview with Ebong, in 'The Origins', p.53.
8. A. Forty, 'Festival Politics', in Banham and Hillier (eds.), *A Tonic to the Nation*, p.37.
9. B. Dorf, 'Alarmingly Like a Private Club', in Banham and Hillier (eds.), *A Tonic to the Nation*, p.186.
10. Sir Hugh Casson, in an interview with Ebong, in 'The Origins', p.55. The same assertion is made by Hillier, 'Introduction', in Banham and Hillier (eds.), *A Tonic to the Nation*, p.14.
11. Hillier, 'Introduction', in ibid.
12. M. Frayn, 'Festival', in M. Sissons and P. French (eds.), *Age of Austerity, 1945–1951*, Harmondsworth, Penguin, 1964, p.331.
13. J. Summerson, *New Statesman*, October, 1951, quoted in R. Hewison, *In Anger: British Culture in the Cold War 1945–60*, New York, Oxford University Press, 1981, p.49.
14. See for example M. Girouard, 'It's Another World', *Architectural Review*, August 1974, reprinted in *Architects' Journal*, vol.179, 27 June 1984, p.108.
15. Report by G. Bowyer and E.W. Swaine on their visit to the Stockholm Exhibitions. Report filed on 16th September, 1949', PRO WORK 25/19.
16. R. Banham, 'The Style: "Flimsy ... Effeminate?"', in Banham and Hillier (eds.), *A Tonic to the Nation*, p.193. See also H. Hopkins, *The New Look: A Social History of the Forties and Fifties in Britain*, London, Readers Union/Secker and Warburg, 1964, p.271.
17. A. Pred, *Recognizing European Modernities: A Montage of the Present*, London and New York, Routledge, 1995, p.100.
18. Ibid., p.101.
19. L. Nordström, 1930, quoted in Pred, *Recognizing European Modernities*, p.134.
20. I. Cox, *Festival of Britain Guide, South Bank*, London, HMSO, 1951, p.4. See also Barry Curtis, 'One Continuous Interwoven Story (The Festival of Britain)', *Block*, 11, 1985–6, pp.48–52.
21. Ibid. See also 'F.O.B./Press/14/49 16th November, 1949, The 1951 Exhibition, South Bank, London', Information Office File, AAD 5/1–1979–5/44–1979, Victoria and Albert Archive of Art and Design, Blythe Road, London.
22. Ibid., p.133.
23. L. Nordström, *Svea Rike*, 1930, quoted in Pred, *Recognizing European Modernities*, pp.133–4.
24. Nordström, 1930 and G. Paulsson, 1937, quoted in Pred, *Recognizing European Modernities*, p.134.
25. Archbishop of Canterbury, quoted in *The Festival of Britain: The Official Book of the Festival of Britain, 1951*, London, HMSO, 1951.
26. Ibid.
27. Ibid., p.106.
28. H. Morrison, quoted in Forty, 'Festival Politics', p.36.
29. Sir H. Casson, quoted in Hewison, *Culture and Consensus*, p.58.
30. Forty, 'Festival Politics', p.37.
31. Labour Party, *Festival*, London, Labour Party, 1951, pp.8–9, in Labour Party Archives, Manchester.
32. H. Morrison, in M. Francis, *Ideas and Policies Under Labour, 1945–1951*, Manchester, Manchester University Press, 1997, pp.56–7.
33. Labour Party, *Labour Believes in Britain*, London, Labour Party, 1949, p.3. See also: Francis, *Ideas and Policies*; S. Fielding, P. Thompson and N. Tiratsoo, *'England Arise!': The*

Labour Party and Popular Politics in 1940s Britain, Manchester, Manchester University Press, 1995.

34. Labour Party, *Labour Believes in Britain*, p.3; Francis, *Ideas and Policies*, p.57.
35. Francis, *Ideas and Policies*, p.57.
36. J. Gloag, 'Furniture Design in Britain', in Council of Industrial Design, *Design in the Festival: Illustrated Review of British Goods*, London, HMSO, 1951, p.14.
37. For discussions of this controversial agenda see: S. MacDonald and J. Porter, 'Mid–Century Modern: The Campaign for Good Design', in *Putting on the Style: Setting up Home in the 1950s*, London, The Geffrye Museum, 1990, n.p.; A. Partington, 'Popular Fashion and Working–Class Affluence', in J. Ash and E. Wilson (eds.), *Chic Thrills*, London, Pandora Press, 1992, pp.145–61; P. Sparke, *As Long As It's Pink: The Sexual Politics of Taste*, London, Pandora Press, 1995, pp.219–21.
38. MacDonald and Porter, 'Mid-Century Modern', n.p.
39. Ibid.
40. Ibid.
41. MacDonald and Porter, 'The Festival Spirit', in *Putting on the Style*, n.p.
42. *Have You A Seeing Eye?* 'Looking at Things' series, BBC Broadcasts to Schools, aired 21 September 1951, quoted in *Brochures from the BBC for the School Broadcasting Council for the United Kingdom*, London, BBC, 1951, p.3.
43. See Sparke, *As Long As It's Pink*, p.215.
44. G. Russell, 'Design in Industry: Today and Tomorrow', in *Design in the Festival*, p.11.
45. P. Garbutt, 'Domestic Appliances', in *Design in the Festival*, p.31.
46. General Lord Ismay and R.S. Edwards, 'Forward', in *Design in the Festival*, p.10.
47. W. Feaver, 'Festival Star', in Banham and Hillier (eds.), *A Tonic to the Nation*, p.54.
48. R. Samuel, *Theatres of Memory, vol.1: Past and Present in Contemporary Culture*, London, Verso, 1994, p.55.
49. B. Donoghue and G.W. Jones, *Herbert Morrison: Portrait of a Politician*, Weidenfeld & Nicolson, 1973, p.492.
50. S. Lambert, *Architects' Journal*, May, 1951, quoted in 'Everything from Townscape', *Architects' Journal*, vol.179, 27 June 1984, p.92.
51. B. Aldiss, 'A Monument to the Future', in Banham and Hillier (eds.), *A Tonic to the Nation*, p.176.
52. 'Festival of Britain, 1951', 1 April, 1948, PRO WORK 25/21, p.2.
53. Labour Party, *Labour and the New Social Order: A Report on Reconstruction*, London, Labour Party, 1918, p 21. See subsequent statements in: *Labour and the Nation* (1928) and *What Socialism Will Really Mean to You* (1935), as cited by J. Minihan, *The Nationalization of Culture: The Development of State Subsidies to the Arts in Great Britain*, New York, New York University Press, 1977, p.185.
54. J. Bronowski, *The Common Sense of Science*, 1951, revised 1960, quoted in W. Eastwood, *A Book of Science Verse: The Poetic Relations of Science and Technology*, London, Macmillan, 1961, p.271. In 1948 Bronowski presented a five-part series with the same title on the BBC Third Programme, see H. Carpenter, *The Envy of the World: Fifty Years of the BBC Third Programme and Radio Three*, London, Weidenfeld & Nicolson, 1996, p.80.
55. P. Reilly, 'The Role of the Design Council: Before, During and After the Festival of Britain', in Banham and Hillier (eds.), *A Tonic to the Nation*, pp.60–1.
56. Ibid., p.61.
57. M. Hartland Thomas, quoted by Reilly, ibid., p.61.

58. Feaver, 'Festival Star', p.51.
59. B. Taylor, quoted by Feaver, ibid.
60. 'Industrial Power at Glasgow', in *The Story of the Festival of Britain, 1951*, London, HMSO, 1952, p.27.
61. Ibid., p.10.
62. 'Exhibition of Industrial Power, Glasgow, Festival of Britain, 1951', in M. Banham and B. Hillier (eds.), *A Tonic to the Nation*, p.152.
63. Ibid., p.152.
64. 'Glasgow's Hall of Power', *Glasgow Herald*, 1 May 1951, p.3. See also: Ebong, 'The Origins', p.425; 'Festival Exhibitions Review', *Architectural Review*, vol.110, August 1951, pp.194–5 and *The Festival of Britain, The Official Book*.
65. 'Industrial Power at Glasgow', p.27.
66. 'Exhibition of Industrial Power', p.154.
67. Ibid.
68. K. Willis, 'The Promotion of Nuclear Power in Britain 1945–1960', unpublished paper presented at the North American Conference on British Studies, Vancouver, October 1994.
69. 'Final Report, The Festival of Britain in Northern Ireland', January 1952, PRO WORK 25/3.
70. Ebong, 'The Origins', p.444.
71. See *1951 Exhibition Ulster Farm and Factory, Belfast Northern Ireland, Festival of Britain Catalogue*, London, HMSO, 1951, in PRO WORK 25/230; 'The Festival of Britain in Northern Ireland', *Architects' Journal*, vol.114, 26 July 1951, p.110; Ebong, 'The Origins', pp.444–7.
72. 'The Festival', *Architects' Journal*, vol.114, 26 July 1951, p.116; *1951 Exhibition Ulster Farm Catalogue*.
73. Samuel, *Theatres of Memory*, p.52.
74. Ibid.
75. See Labour Party, *Festival*, pp.6–7; 'Exhibition of Architecture, Lansbury at Poplar', BBC Radio Broadcast, Summer, 1951, BBC Radio Broadcast 16931, National Sound Archives; *The Festival of Britain, The Official Book*, p.13.
76. *The Festival of Britain, The Official Book*, p.13.
77. Ibid.
78. Ibid.

Index